China
after
WTO

Compiled and Edited by
Laurence J. Brahm

China Intercontinental Press

About the Editor

Laurence J. Brahm, a political economist and lawyer by profession, has been serving as an advisor on economic and financial reform issues and advising Fortune 500 multinationals in China spanning two decades. Author of over 20 books on China including "China's Century" and "Elements of China", he is currently developing media content and television programs on China from his Beijing studio.

Contents

Part III   Financial Management

Part IV   Managing Human Resources

Part V   Telecommunications and Informatizations

Chapter 17

Part VI Finance

Chapter 18

Chapter 19

Chapter 20

Appendices

Appendix I

Appendix II

Appendix III

Preface

WTO Opens An Era Of New Opportunities

Shi Guangsheng

Minister
Ministry of Foreign Trade and Economic Cooperation
People's Republic of China

Since reform and open policy, China's foreign trade has developed rapidly. In 1999, China's total import and export trade value reached US$ 360.7 billion, ranking ninth in the world. The value of exports was US$ 194.9 billion and imports US$165.8 billion. While the scale of foreign trade is constantly expanding, the structure of commodity exports from China has clearly been optimized. Chinese commodities, with their low prices and high quality are generally welcomed by people of all countries in the world. China's trade partners are spread all over the world, reaching the present 227 countries and regions from just a few dozen in 1978.

Absorbing foreign capital was the initial move in opening China to the outside. Upon entering WTO, China cumulatively approved more than 340,000 foreign investment projects and actually used US$ 307.851 billion in foreign capital. China, which is undergoing constant development, has provided a huge market and commercial opportunity for capital and technology coming from all countries of the world. At present, investments in China have originated from more than 180 countries and regions. Among the world's top 500 large multinational corporations, approximately 400 have invested in China. Other large multinational corporations are also preparing to come to China to make investments, especially following China's entry into WTO which creates yet even better conditions.

After entering WTO, China will take a more active stance to further expand its openness to the outside. China will further open its markets in the areas of commodities trading and trade services. China will gradually open further to the outside in the areas of commerce, foreign trade, finance, insurance, securities, telecom, tourism and agency services. The Chinese market has huge potential and broad prospects. Along with the constant deepening of China's open policy and increasing economic strength of China, the relationship between China's economy and the world economy will be increasingly closer. The huge market potential of China will be gradually transferred to actual purchasing power, thereby providing more commercial opportunities for industrial and commercial organizations in countries the world over.

Of course, while on one hand WTO entry brings opportunities to China, on the other hand, development in China is relatively low and the reform of state-owned enterprises has not yet been complete, thus, the international competitiveness of certain professions is not strong. In addition, the legal and regulatory systems needed to adapt to a modern market economy have not yet been completed.

After entering WTO, the economic administrative system of China may not be able to adapt and will need to be further perfected. Certain industries and enterprises may, to some degree, suffer some negative effects from the assault. However, after 20 years of reform and openness, the comprehensive national power of China has been constantly strengthened. China has accumulated experiences that will enable it to cope with the complicated and varied international economic situation. China's international competitiveness and capacity to withstand risk have greatly increased. The deeper reforms and openness are implemented, the stronger our capacity to withstand the risk. Therefore, we are confident and determined to channel this pressure into motivational power through deepening reform and expanding openness, welcoming the challenges brought by WTO and promoting the national economy to constantly achieve new horizons of development.

We deeply trust that China's entry into WTO will certainly push forward the development of Chinese foreign economic trade into a new era and push forward economic trade cooperation between China and the world to a new epoch. This will create new opportunities for the world economy, and for stable prosperity in the new century.

China After WTO

Laurence J. Brahm

CEO

Naga Group Limited

China after WTO will be a China of rapid change and dynamic entrepreneurial spirit. WTO will serve as catalyst for further investment and trade liberalizations which will in turn bring China's complicated investment environment closer in line with international standards and in turn encourage foreign investment on a larger and broader scale than anticipated before.

China's entry into WTO will witness profound structural changes in the investment and trade regime of China, opening up unforeseen opportunities in a range of industries and services. The following highlights key areas where relaxation of former restrictions will effect foreign businessmen creating the most immediate positive impact and opportunities:

☐ restrictions on foreign equity control will be relaxed in all but the most sensitive of sectors;

☐ income tax exemptions and restrictions already afforded to investors in China's coastal regions will be extended to those making new investments in the interior;

☐ foreign participation will be encouraged in previously guarded sectors such as insurance, finance, foreign trade, commerce, securities, telecommunications and tourism in order to promote the service industry;

☐ foreign investment in retail and commercial shopping malls which was previously limited to certain coastal cities and select enterprises will be extended to all regions;

☐ foreign investment approval procedures will be simplified with former approval ceilings on local investment lifted giving local authorities greatly leeway in facilitating inbound foreign investment;

☐ the scope of operations of holding companies established by foreign investors will be expanded giving them greater flexibility in management and operations.

At the same time, one must understand that change will progress at different rates depending on the sector and region involved. The vastness of China as a nation and in turn its business landscape will require patience, conscious due diligence, and in depth understanding of market trends and developments in order for foreign businesses to be successful in trading and investing in China. A realistic approach to the opportunities presented by WTO will be important advice to be heeded by all.

In seeking to provide the most up to date picture of change in "China after WTO", I have invited the leading specialists on the ground in

China to provide straight-forward advice on how to conduct business in this changing environment and to provide insight into how such changes post-WTO entry will effect the way in which one goes about investing and doing business in China.

Efforts have been made to provide the most current information available. However, as China's dynamic business environment is in the course of change as it is still a transitional economy, it is advised to seek professional assistance on specific matters and not rely solely on the contents herein before making critical business decisions.

In this respect, professionals leading their fields have been invited to contribute to this book and greatest of thanks are extended to Minister Shi Guangsheng for writing the preface and lending his support, to Minister Zhao Qizheng for his support and encouragement, Bureau Director Guo Changjian and Madam Wu Wei for their efforts and support, and to all who have contributed to the various chapters within, which have made this book a reality. Through the hard endeavours of all involved, "China After WTO" is now arguably the most current publication introducing foreign investors and businessmen to the regulatory and operational environment in China as it evolves in the post WTO era.

Prologue

China WTO Accession

Michael Furst

Executive Director
American Chamber of Commerce

China's WTO accession is important to foreign companies for two reasons:

Firstly, and most obviously, trade barriers are dropping and will continue to do so, according to the negotiated schedule in China's WTO Accession Protocol. Tariffs and other trade barriers, in a wide range of sectors, are being reduced more or less as agreed, so far. The American Business Community in China is optimistic that China will abide by its commitments. Certainly, at the top of the Government, there is an often re-emphasized commitment (and not a little effort) to rapidly revamp both laws and practice.

Secondly, China's WTO accession is by no means a mere trade arrangement. It is first and foremost a political statement and a commitment on the part of the Chinese leadership that the current policy of reform and opening up will continue and intensify. In fact, the Chinese government sees WTO accession as a monument to its leadership. President Jiang Zemin hopes history will remember him by this major innovation, among others. In addition, reformers within the Chinese government want to use WTO accession as a lever to pry open the resistance to positive change. Currently, China's reform program stands at a crossroads: the huge but inefficient state sector seems virtually incurable; domestic demand in many areas is sluggish; unemployment is rising; corruption is proliferating.

To the reformers in the Chinese system, there is no single remedy that will address all those issues except, perhaps, for the rules-based WTO, which prompts a much greater reliance on rule of law, accountability, transparency of government process, national treatment of foreign businesses, international compliance, and more foreign investment. In short, the WTO provides China with a path to market economics, which will help break local and departmental monopolies that have proven so hard to crack from inside. Reformers can now point to the expectations and requirements of the WTO system as a justification for necessary reforms.

The face factor is also at work. To China, WTO membership affords it long overdue face and dignity. As Vice Minister Long Yongtu of MOFTEC explained once to an audience of SOE managers, China is a member of the United Nations, the World Bank, the International Monetary Fund, the international Olympic movement and countless others; so why can't it join the WTO?

On the diplomatic front, WTO membership has solved China's Normal Trading Relations problem with USA permanently, removing a long-standing obstacle to improved relations between the two countries. This annual ritual, with its outcome always predictable, wastes a tremendous amount of resources from both sides and leaders of both the US and the Chinese governments earnestly have wanted to put it behind them. The American business community could hardly agree more. Business dislikes almost nothing more than uncertainty, even if it is transitory.

Sometimes claiming that the current international order is not fair enough, China hopes to be able to rewrite some of the rules of the game in the international arena; staying outside WTO does little to advance that goal. China's leaders, watching growing globalization gallop along, wants to be a part of the race towards prosperity. China has chosen, probably irrevocably, to be part of the process of the globalization of the world economy.

Culturally, China's WTO accession, if sustained by future events, represents a milestone event in Chinese history – this is China's "coming out party." 2001 was truly a banner year: Capped by WTO accession, last year we saw China's national team make the World Cup's final rounds as well as Beijing being awarded the Olympics – the popular euphoria that resulted from that announcement, many people have said, rivaled the emotional outpouring after the Gang of Four were dumped from office.

The big news is that all of these barriers and obstacles – except the rule requiring minimum 50 percent domestic ownership of vehicle assembly operations – are addressed in the U.S.-China WTO Agreement. The quota for vehicle import licenses will be raised immediately to US$ 6 billion per year and will increase each year until it is eliminated in 2005. Tariffs will drop to 25 percent by mid-2006. Foreign investment enterprises will gradually obtain the right, over a three-year transition period, to import, distribute, sell, and service vehicles. Foreign non-bank financial institutions such as Ford Credit and GMAC will have the right, immediately upon China's accession, to establish companies in China to provide auto financing. Also upon accession, local content, technology transfer, and foreign exchange balancing requirements for vehicle assembly operations will all be eliminated. Obviously, we expect that these rule changes will have a far-reaching impact on both foreign and domestic auto companies.

The potential is there, but our natural optimism needs to be tempered by a sense of reality. Until very recently, most parts of the Chinese government, and certainly the vast Chinese public, have had no idea what had been committed to by Chinaís negotiators. It will take quite a number of years and lots of hard work to bring Rule of Law, Transparency, National treatment, let alone Regional treatment.*

Ultimately, what will make China attractive to foreign investors – and, in fact, for Chinese investors – is a business environment that rewards sound commercial decision making. People and organizations, hopefully, will make buying decisions based on price, quality and suitability in a competitive environment – and NOT base commercial decisions on opaque political factors. This is not only true for China as a whole, but also holds for initiatives like the Central Government's "Go West" campaign.

If the changes that are now transforming China's economy are successfully implemented over the next years, a good bit of the great potential of this country can be realized.

---

* Regional and local protectionism has a very long history in China. The cultural and "procedural" momentum is very well established (over 4,000 years) and will take a long time to change.

China After WTO

Introduction

WTO Shaping China's Future

John C. (Sean) Leonard

Attorney & Counselor At Law Fellow
Asian Institute of International Financial Law, Faculty of Law,
University of Hong Kong

Long March to Geneva

On December 11, 2001, with little fanfare and no discernible celebratory gatherings in either Geneva or Beijing, the People's Republic of China (PRC) quietly acceded to membership in the global trade body, the World Trade Organization (WTO).

China's Long March to Geneva had taken over 15 years since its original application to become a contracting party to the GATT 1947, the multinational trade pact which served as the predecessor treaty to today's GATT 95 and related agreements, whose implementation and enforcement are now overseen by the secretariat of the global trade body called the WTO. As observed by China's Chief Trade Negotiator, Ministry of Foreign Trade and Economic Cooperation (MOFTEC) Vice Minister Long Yongtu, in all of China's long history, not even any war in which the Chinese engaged had lasted more than 8 years!

It was obviously with China's very ponderous WTO accession process in mind, that the WTO's next Director-General, Dr. Supachai Panitchpakdi, in his recent co-authored book, *China and the WTO: Changing China, Changing World Trade*, put forth the view that in the future, the WTO accession process should be more streamlined, an understatement of great subtlety. Dr. Supachai also hinted in his book that on his watch at the WTO, which commences in September 2002, a new category of associate membership will be created to assist under-developed countries to become WTO members by a process involving something akin to an applicant state trade officials receiving on the job training in WTO requirements from its highly professional secretariat during a much-abbreviated accession process. Thus, the lesser developed nations still awaiting WTO membership will become ironic beneficiaries of China's arduous, 15-year struggle for its seat at the conference table in Geneva.

Of course, the accession process was lengthy for China owing to the fact that, in its negotiations with its most significant trading partners (the so-called Quad Powers – Canada, the EU, Japan and the United States) to join the trade body, many issues other than trade came into play over the years. Moreover, during the 15 year accession period, the rules were being altered by the Uruguay Round of plurilateral trade negotiations, resulting in new requirements in the field of intellectual property protection and openings for providers of services, including sectors such as banking, IT, professional services and telecommunications, among others. So as the negotiations stretched out, new rules were being added, or, as Chinese negotiators often maintained: The goal posts were constantly being moved!

At long last the breakthrough came in November 1999 in Beijing, when the then-United States Trade Representative (USTR), Ambassador Charlene Barshefsky, and Minister Shi Guangsheng of the PRC Ministry of Foreign Trade and Economic Cooperation (MOFTEC) signed-off on the US-China bilateral agreement paving the way for China's WTO accession. The deal was virtually identical to that which had been offered to the Americans the previous April by Premier Zhu Rongji during a visit to the States. But President Clinton had rebuffed the offer, feeling that the timing wasn't right. The EU followed suit in April 2000, signing their own separate deal with China. The remaining countries still negotiating with China completed compromise deals over the ensuing months.

But, of course, both the US and the EU followed up their deals with a number of subsequent negotiations to refine their agreements with China. In the case of the US, the level of PRC domestic farm subsidies remained a bone in the throat, but a compromise level of support finally was reached. For the EU, the issue of grandfathered (US) insurance operations in China was the remaining sticking point, but eventually a modality of concession was arrived at with the Chinese.

Ultimately, the terms and conditions of China's agreements with over 35 WTO member countries for its WTO accession were embodied in its Accession Protocol, annexes and schedules, and its WTO membership was approved at the WTO Ministerial Meeting at Doha, Qatar in November 2001. The benefits negotiated between China and those countries, whose representatives served on the WTO Working Party for China's accession, would be made available to all WTO members. Under Chinese law, its WTO accession became effective as of December 11, 2002, pursuant to prior legislation of the National People's Congress (China's legislature) and an executive decree by President Jiang Zemin. General details of China's commitments to its trading partners will be provided later in this chapter, while more specifics of the obligations undertaken by China will be presented by my co-authors in subsequent chapters of this book.

Downstream WTO Culture

The hallmarks of conducting trade among WTO members are: transparency of laws, regulations, etc. relating to trade; national treatment or non-discrimination, that is, according to the products or services of another WTO member treatment (by way of taxation, internal distribution rights, etc.) similar to that accorded to the products or services of domestic producers or providers; and most favoured nation treatment (MFN or NTR), that is, levying duty and other charges on the products or services of **all** WTO members imported into a WTO member's market at the best rates charged to **any** WTO member.

In the near term, China's WTO accession will not prove to be a silver bullet or even a magic pill either for China or its trading partners. Perhaps it is this certainty which accounts for the absence of any celebrations to mark the accession date, unlike the genuinely spontaneous celebrations which erupted in Beijing earlier in the year when it was announced that the capital city would host the 2008 Olympic Games.

Transparency

Transparency will be a threshold difficulty in China. In the first place, there is a cultural tradition of non-transparency throughout the history of the country, dating back to the imperial dynasties. Only the emperor and a coterie of imperial civil servants were aware of legal proscriptions, most of which being criminal in nature. Hapless citizens usually found out when it was much too late. In more recent times, since the initiation of the open door policy in the late 1970s, although much black letter law has been promulgated in China, quite often actual practices of governmental agencies in implementing legislation was hidden in so-called internal regulations (*neibu guiding*) which were only known internally. To comply with WTO standards and China's Accession Protocol, this practice will have to be eliminated throughout PRC government agencies, at least with respect to such internal regulations which relate to trade in goods and services and their treatment within China.

On the other side of the transparency coin, until very recently, it is unfortunately accurate to say that from the corridors of many ministries in Beijing to the most far-flung corners of local government offices throughout the PRC, little detail of the specifics of the deal under which China had entered the WTO was well known, let alone understood. MOFTEC, China's trade ministry, has tried to remedy this situation within the last few months by engaging in mass circulation of both English and Chinese hardcopy versions of China's WTO Accession Protocol and the annexes and schedules which spell out the details of China's obligations. The same information, in both languages, is also now available on MOFTEC's website at: <www.moftec.gov.cn.> MOFTEC's action in this regard is both preemptive – as a means of preparing both governmental agencies and PRC commercial enterprises for what lies ahead, and also to comply with the transparency requirements of China's Accession Protocol.

China's WTO Accession Protocol also requires the publication of an official journal on a regular basis dedicated to the publication of all laws, regulations, and other measures pertaining to or affecting trade in goods, services, TRIPS (basically, intellectual property rights) or the control of foreign exchange? With a few exceptions (national security, law enforcement), a reasonable period for comment is to be afforded **before** the implementation of such laws, regulations and other measures. Moreover, unless such laws, regulations and measures are published and readily available to other WTO members, they are not to be enforced.

As of this writing, the dissemination of such information regarding China's trade-related laws, regulations, and other measures is quite fragmented within China. MOFTEC's own website (above-indicated) has a comprehensive, bilingual (Chinese and English) listing of PRC laws, and so forth, but the indexing and search functions leave much to be desired and the laws, regulations and measures are not published in advance, affording a comment period. Various Chinese universities also maintain similar websites, as does the State Council itself. Most are also bilingual. However, as far as this writer knows, no singular official journal as called for in China's WTO Accession Protocol has yet emerged. It may be that the section of MOFTEC's website containing China's laws, if improved, will eventually be given the title of official journal as envisioned by the Accession Protocol. But that is presuming that other ministries, which also issue regulations and measures which are trade-related, would be willing to yield this authority to MOFTEC in the climate of the downsizing of the Central People's Government (CPG) which is yet in progress. Whatever solution to this dilemma is reached by the CPG, unless it is soon, the absence of such an official journal leaves room for complaint by other WTO members that China is not complying with its transparency obligations under its Accession Protocol and WTO rules.

PRC WTO Compliance Agencies

MOFTEC has recently established a China WTO Notification Enquiry Centre, an entity mandated by China's Accession Protocol. The Centre will handle enquiries from individuals and enterprises, both domestic and foreign-related, as well as from other WTO members, with respect to the effect of specific regulations, measures, etc. which they feel that do not comply with China's WTO obligations in one way or another. After evaluation, the Centre must reply within thirty to 45 days. Such replies from MOFTEC are to be considered the authoritative view of the Chinese government under the Accession Protocol. MOFTEC officials refer to this new process as the abstract track of internal WTO compliance. In a recent conversation with a high level MOFTEC official, this writer was informed that, in the event that the Centre's review of the measure or regulation in question results in a determination that it is WTO non-compliant, it would be either amended or rescinded.

However, it is unclear exactly how the amendment or rescission process will occur after a finding by the Centre of non-compliance with WTO rules, as under present day PRC constitutional law, the Standing Committee of National People's Congress is empowered to annul those administrative rules and regulations, decisions or orders of the State Council (the CPG's highest organ of state administration) that contravene the Constitution or the statutes, whereas the State Council (which controls the various rule-issuing ministries) has the constitutional power to alter or annul inappropriate orders, directives and regulations issued by the ministries or commissions? Therefore, how, and if, the Centre's decisions are implemented by the NPC Standing Committee or the State Council will very much affect whether this new outlet for the rectification of domestic legislation felt to be incompatible with WTO rules actually provides to foreign-connected enterprises substantive rights, as required by the Accession Protocol.

The so-called (by MOFTEC officials) specific track of domestic WTO compliance will be handled by the Administrative Law Division of MOFTEC's Department of Treaties & Law. This Division will handle complaints from enterprises or individuals, whether purely domestic or foreign-related, covering specific PRC governmental decisions or actions which are felt by the complaining party(ies) to have violated China's WTO obligations. It is anticipated that this Division will have a heavy workload in the early years of China's WTO membership, as both governmental agencies and private enterprises progress together through the learning curve of WTO requirements.

However, as with the WTO Notification Enquiry Centre, just how MOFTEC's Administrative Law Division will be able to rectify administrative decisions which are not WTO-compliant, remains to be seen. In this connection, two points must be made: firstly, it is not clear that this MOFTEC Division will have jurisdiction over administrative decisions of other CPG agencies or only over its own. Secondly, China's WTO Accession Protocol requires that such a body be impartial and independent of the agency entrusted with administrative enforcement. The protocol also requires that the decisions of such a body be appealable to a judicial body, with notice of, and a written decision, being provided to the complainant.

If MOFTEC's Administrative Law Division is eventually determined to have jurisdiction over only MOFTEC's administrative decisions, perhaps complaints against other governmental agencies for acts or decisions deemed WTO non-compliant can be handled by resort to the PRC Administrative Litigation Law or Administrative Reconsideration Regulations (or Administrative Review Law). But this begs the question of how MOFTEC's own Division can examine its own internal administrative decisions in view of the threshold independence requirement for such a body under China's WTO Accession Protocol.

Nevertheless, it is to MOFTEC's credit that it has both of these Accession Protocol-mandated agencies up and running, even if they may be found wanting in some respects. However, it will be up to the domestic and foreign-related enterprises to assert their rights before them when deemed necessary. It is envisioned that the efficient and good faith operation of these bodies will function as pressure valves, perhaps in the near term preventing more formal recourse to dispute settlement at the WTO itself against China by other WTO members, on behalf of aggrieved enterprises from their countries. Whether these bodies will continue to exist in their present form, however, in view of their differences with protocol requirements, is at present an unanswerable question, pending review by trade ministry lawyers from China's fellow WTO members.

Enforcement of Law in China

While China's trading partners threw open their markets on an MFN/NTR basis to PRC products and services as the *quid pro quo* for a more predictable and less discriminatory trade and investment regime for them in China, reaching this goal is as yet a work-in-progress. Which is not to say that the CPG is not still now engaged in a good faith, headlong rush to complete amendment, rescission, revision and/or enactment of laws, regulations, measures and guidelines to comply with WTO norms, China's Accession Protocol and its ancillary documents. They clearly are, as I learned from my own first-hand experience as a participant at trade-related law revision/drafting sessions in Beijing within the last few months, which were sponsored by the Asian Development Bank (ADB) to assist the PRC to conform its enormous amount of legislation with WTO requirements.

However, the very size of the country and its own traditions present limitations on the speed with which such work will be completed. The necessity of disseminating the nitty-gritty details of how trade and investment should be conducted under newly-revised or enacted WTO-compliant laws and regulations throughout China to all levels of government and businesses (both private and state-owned) will run into walls erected under – or should one say, despite, the present regime. To name one barrier, there is the notion of local protectionism – local governments and courts taking steps to shelter local companies (usually state-owned) or local partners of foreign-related joint ventures from grievances of foreign-connected parties. Of course, this pervasive practice violates the basic WTO tenet of non-discrimination and it will only end as more and more of the WTO-required, rules-based culture trickles down from the centre in Beijing throughout the provinces, counties, townships and villages, a daunting and perhaps lengthy process.

The CPG, however, is currently promoting numerous WTO training courses for governmental officials, the judiciary, heads of state-owned enterprises (SOEs) and business audiences throughout the country. In fact, if one browses through book shops in China's major cities, it is obvious that a cottage industry in the publishing sector focusing on WTO-related issues has mushroomed. The same can be said of the multiplicity of WTO seminars and conferences being run all over China in recent months by private conference organizers and firms of accountants and lawyers, both domestic and foreign-connected. It has been observed that these firms have become the immediate beneficiaries of China's WTO accession.

A Vice President of the Supreme People's Court (SPC) in Beijing commented at a recent national legal conference that China's WTO commitments would take precedence over domestic law in future trade and investment-related court cases throughout China. This accords with PRC constitutional law. And the SPC officials comments were, to be sure, a very good sign for the foreign businessman or investor looking for a level playing field in China, one of the primary benefits sought from China by her trading partners in the negotiations for WTO membership. Just how any such cases involving China's WTO commitments will arrive on the docket of a People's Court remains unclear to this writer, however, as WTO members obligations are to all of the other WTO members, qua nation-states or customs territories, not to private companies or to individual businessmen. Under the WTO rules-based system, it is up to aggrieved businesses or businessmen to convince their governments to rectify non-compliant practices within other WTO members territories, first by negotiation and, if necessary, by ultimate resort to the WTO's Dispute Settlement Body (WTO DSB).

Putting aside this author's doubts concerning the subject matter jurisdiction of China's courts to adjudicate disputes regarding non-compliance with WTO rules, even when contemplating their use in ordinary commercial or trade-related cases, or to enforce arbitral awards as another example, one must bear in mind that it is unfortunately still the case that China's judiciary has a long way to go in terms of professionalism, not least in terms of actual knowledge of the law on the part of many of its jurists. There is also the lingering issue of the influence exerted upon courts throughout the country by both government and party officials, sometimes in the context of local protectionism, sometimes for political reasons.

In terms of the future, a recent glimmer of hope for court reform and enhanced judicial professionalism has emerged in the form of China's new Judiciary Law which requires actual legal training and practice experience as a pre-qualification for future members of China's judiciary. Unfortunately, only the passage of time will see the departure of the many judges throughout China who have had no formal legal training but were appointed on the basis of past service in either the military or the government. But clearly, with the impetus of implementing China's WTO obligations, judicial and court reform are on the top of the agenda for the CPG.

Anti-dumping, Safeguards, Subsidies and Countervailing Measures

In what some would call a perverse fashion, the PRC has recently put into operation a regime to comply with WTO trade rules under which it was most often a victim prior to its WTO accession. This refers to PRC domestic legislation to protect its own industries from dumping and subsidies of products from its trading partners, as well as safeguard legislation to protect its domestic market from sudden surges of imports.

Although the initial versions of such laws were a bit rough around the edges – leaving out such requirements as permitting interested parties to intervene in such proceedings and present legal briefs of their positions, as well as an appeal procedure, recent sessions in Beijing with ADB-sponsored foreign trade lawyers have gone a long way towards smoothing out this legislation.

A cynic might observe that the recent PRC legislation in these areas was enacted more by way of preemption, rather than to comply with WTO requirements. Some have even implied that theses laws are purely defensive – a means for China to continue protection of key industries, while paying lip service to market opening requirements of WTO rules. And, to be sure, the Chinese officials involved in enforcement of this new legislation have not exactly been shy, judging from the escalating increase in the number of cases filed against foreign export enterprises at MOFTEC's Fair Trade Bureau. But then, as a WTO member, China has as much right to protect its domestic market from genuine predatory practices as any other WTO member.

With the changes recently suggested to MOFTEC by foreign trade lawyers, such proceedings in the future should be more fair, open and subject to appeal. The operation of these laws on anti-dumping, subsidies and countervailing measures is provided by my colleagues in a later chapter of this book in greater detail. Exporters to China and their counsel should be aware of their intricacies.

Good-Bye to the SEZs

Unfortunately for veteran China hands, China's WTO accession will probably result in the end of its current system of special tax treatment (including enterprise income tax abatement and duty waivers on imported equipment) in its numerous special economic zones (SEZs), coastal zones, technology and export zones, and so forth, as such special treatment would be deemed discriminatory in that foreign-related enterprises from other WTO members located outside such zones in China would not enjoy the same benefits. Moreover, many of the laws, regulations and practices governing these special zones would be found to violate the WTO Agreement on Subsidies and Countervailing Measures (WTO SCM Agreement). The *WTO Working Party Report* for China's WTO accession suggests as much, as it calls for China to provide copious details regarding their operation.

These special zones heretofore attracted many, many foreign investors and enterprises, spurring the remarkable, steady growth of China's economy and promoting the transfer of previously unavailable technology, particularly over the last two decades of the 20th Century. However, even though they most likely will be phased out to comply with WTO requirements, it is rumored that the CPG will attempt to replace their benefits in part with a national uniform enterprise income tax rate around the 25% mark, a competitive rate even compared to many highly developed WTO members.

Nevertheless, with the increased certainty brought about by China's (increasing) compliance with WTO requirements, together with the still significantly lower costs of domestic inputs (labour, energy, raw materials, land), doing business in China will remain attractive to foreign investors and enterprises over the near and long term. Moreover, those foreign investors or businessmen who wish a competitive edge can still opt to take advantage of the recent concessions offered by the CPG for investing or establishing enterprises in the central and western provinces of China, as such programs, which are purely regional in nature, are in compliance with WTO rules.

Benefits for Foreign Businesses

There are many, many areas of China's WTO commitments which will be of enormous benefit to the businesses of its WTO trading partners, whether they simply export to China or become more directly involved by establishing factories, offices or businesses within China, either on a joint venture basis or as wholly foreign-owned enterprises (WFOEs). First and foremost on the trade side will be the eventual lowering of import duties to virtual parity with world averages for most goods shipped into China by entities based in other WTO members territories. This will benefit foreign exporters, domestic importers and, ultimately, the Chinese consumer. Although tariff levels will remain initially higher than world averages on many agricultural products, with respect to a number of other protected products a tariff rate quota (TRQ) system will see quantities of such imported products gradually increase over the near term, only to provide a temporary cushion to domestic producers of like products, as permitted by WTO rules. The TRQ system is discussed *infra*.

Although in later chapters of this book my colleagues will go into greater detail regarding many of the changes (and opportunities) wrought by China's WTO accession, a few of the more notable ones will be mentioned here. Within three years, all enterprises within China, local or foreign-funded, will be able to export and import at will, as the state trading companies monopoly in this field will be eliminated.

Another vital change for foreign-connected enterprises will be entry into after sales servicing, as well as into the domestic distribution sectors, the prior prohibitions against which having heretofore seriously hampered operations of foreign-related companies within China in the past. The film industry gains limited improvement of its market access, with the annual number of foreign films being raised to twenty, on a revenue sharing basis with PRC counterpart enterprises.

The future potential of China's vast consumer market for automobiles will benefit both the foreign automakers with manufacturing operations within the PRC, as well as foreign companies specializing in auto finance, the consumer vehicle market obviously having been written off to a large extent by China's leaders. Tariff rates on imported vehicles will also gradually, but dramatically, diminish.

Foreign banks will eventually be able to conduct all foreign and domestic currency business of their PRC counterparts, with domestic and foreign entities and individuals throughout China, within 5 years of WTO accession. They will be able to conduct local currency business with PRC domestic enterprises within two years of accession. Foreign companies will be able to eventually own 49% of certain telecommunications operations within China. IT products will eventually enter China duty-free. The insurance sector will be greatly liberalized and foreign companies in this sector will be able to open multiple offices within 3 years of China's WTO accession.

Even foreign lawyers and accountants will benefit by the lifting of restrictions on the number and locations of their offices in China. While the accountants will be able to establish joint practices with local accounting firms, the law firms will not be permitted to integrate with local PRC practices. However, an arrangement has been provided under China's Accession Protocol whereby they can entrust PRC legal work to domestic law firms. As the Chinese have recently become quite litigious, as rule of man is replaced by rule of law (some would say rule **by** law) to an increasing extent, perhaps this trend will escalate as more and more foreign lawyers flood into the country – clearly an unintended but inevitable result of China's WTO accession.

Moreover, a note of practical caution to executives/managers of foreign-related manufacturing enterprises: a significant number of the proliferating law suits in China involve claims under the Consumer

Protection Law. It would be wise to become familiar with its provisions if the intent is to distribute one's products throughout China.

Pursuant to its WTO accession, China has also agreed to immediately abide by the provisions of the WTO Agreement on Trade-Related Investment Measures (the so-called TRIMs Agreement), whose provisions prohibit the use of various forms of non-tariff barriers to trade, called NTBs or NTMs in WTO parlance. Consequently, a number of practices previously either sanctioned by law, internal regulations or pressure from PRC business approval authorities will have to fall by the wayside. These include local content requirements and export performance requirements, both of which having been frequently employed where, as a component of establishing a business in China, the foreign partner was to transfer technology to the new enterprise.

Although such requirements would now be deemed WTO non-compliant in China under the TRIMs Agreement, it remains to be seen whether PRC approval authorities will be able to resist the temptation to continue to insist upon them. The primary reason for suggesting this possibility is the recent enactment of the PRC Technology Import/Export Regulations, which came into effect on January 1, 2002. The new regulations provide for both an approval and registration process for technology transfer agreements which cover the category of restricted technology, thus putting the authorities in the position of being able to press for concessions from applicants and registrants as a condition of approval and/or registration. It will be interesting to see how the prohibitions of the TRIMs Agreement serve as prophylactic against such impulses on the part of PRC approval authorities in the early years of China's WTO membership.

Prognosis for the Future

The unspoken fear on the part of China's trading partners is that, with its cheaper inputs, China will become the factory of the world and flood all of their markets with anti-competitively low priced goods. However, China's WTO Accession Protocol contains lengthy safeguard measures which will be binding upon China for the first 12 years of its WTO membership, an onerous obligation. Furthermore, most of China's WTO trading partners have domestic legislation to cope with such exigencies. And if in the unlikely event that such market flooding were to actually occur and be extreme and unfair, its trading partners could bring a case against China at the WTO Dispute Settlement Body (DSB) in Geneva, whose jurisdiction is mandatory and whose decisions are binding upon all participating WTO members.

In fact, the ultimate test or barometer of China's living up to its WTO obligations will be at the WTO DSB, to which its trading partners can lodge complaints against China where they see non-compliance with any and all WTO rules, resulting in harm to enterprises from their territories exporting to or conducting operations in China. EU Trade Commissioner Pascal Lamy has indicated that the EU Commission will initially take a laid-back approach to China as a new member of the WTO, implying that negotiation takes precedence over hauling China to the WTO DSB early on in its WTO membership. It is hoped that China's other large WTO trading partners will show such prescience and restraint. To a certain extent, they will have to, as under the WTO's Dispute Settlement Understanding, the agreement which sets forth DSB procedures, negotiation between parties is mandated before formal complaints can be lodged. Moreover, as a developing country, China will be entitled to preferential treatment with respect to certain procedural aspects of such cases.

Of course, legal representation in WTO DSB cases is usually handled either by legal teams from the trade ministries or departments of the most developed WTO members and/or by global law firms with heavy expertise in trade law, usually, although not exclusively, in the case of lesser developed members. The legal fees involved for outside counsel are usually astronomical by anyone's standards. So if, as and when China becomes involved in any cases at the WTO DSB, as a new WTO member with no expertise in such matters, it will most likely be required to retain the services of such global law firms, providing a further unintended and early dividend to the legal profession of its WTO trading partners. This writer has suggested to MOFTEC officials that in initial WTO DSB cases involving China, its staff attorneys should work closely with lawyers from the larger firms who will most likely be representing China, so as to build up their in-house expertise.

China also has another alternative with respect to legal assistance with dispute settlement at the WTO. In a recent discussion with the Executive Director of the newly-opened Advisory Centre on WTO Law in Geneva, it was made clear that China could establish relations with the Centre under its charter. The purpose of the Centre is to provide legal training, support and advice on WTO law and dispute settlement procedures to developing countries. The Centre's staff has expertise in trade law, WTO rules and the functioning of the WTO DSB. The level of legal fees charged for its services is modest compared to the global law firms, as it is subsidized by contributions from participating members. There are some who feel (and fear) that China could become the Centre's best client in the near future.

The real risks in joining the WTO have been taken by China, whose current and immediate-past leadership are betting that living up to WTO requirements will reciprocally reinforce, support and continue the reform and opening up of China, its economy and legal system which was commenced in the late 1970s. Clearly, the challenges to domestic enterprises from the proliferation of more efficient foreign competitors within China in the early years of its WTO membership will lead to much hardship and the danger of an increasing army of the unemployed and dispossessed from rural areas and the SOEs pouring into the cities seeking non-existent jobs, a situation with the potential for civil unrest. The oft-touted argument put forth by many, to the effect that that the foreign enterprises operating in China will take on this burden, is somewhat disingenuous. One need only consider the massive layoffs in all sectors of business world-wide, in the wake of the September 11 attacks in the United States, to come to this conclusion.

One can not predict with great precision what the future will hold for China and its trading partners as its participation in the WTO unfolds. But it is safe to point out a few areas which an astute observer should track. On the trade policy level, look for China to become a champion of the under-developed member countries of the WTO, as well as its attempt to stamp on the current plurilateral trade negotiating round, concern for issues which such countries consider vital. On a more practical level, it would be wise to study the results of enquiries/complaints brought by foreign-related businesses to MOFTEC's two agencies, the China WTO Notification Enquiry Centre, and the Administrative Law Division of its Department of Treaties & Laws, as the number of cases handled by each of these agencies, as well as the fairness, quality and transparency of decisions made, will be an immediate and early barometer of China's compliance of the commitments it has undertaken to become a WTO member.

China's WTO accession has enormous positive potential and could become a win-win situation both for global trade, as well as for global relations. Fair treatment of China by its trading partners in the early, rough years that lie ahead – as its officials and businessmen learn to cope with WTO requirements, could lead to a new era of cooperation and warmer relations on all levels between China and other WTO members. This, in turn, could lead to a softening of respective policies and mutual understanding – if not outright agreement, on issues as diverse as non-proliferation of biological weapons, weapons of mass destruction and their delivery systems; cooperation on sustainable, environmentally-friendly development; cooperation on anti-terrorism; cooperation on anti-narcotrafficking; cooperation on halting the spread of deadly viral-based diseases and a host of other areas deemed vital to our collective survival, now and into the increasingly uncertain future.

Years ago, on the stolid old IBM office building at the corner of 57th Street and Madison Avenue in New York – which has since been replaced by a typical steel and glass tower, there was a very simple, largely-lettered sign dozens of stories above the dense traffic. It read, quite eloquently: World Peace Through World Trade. There were only five words on the sign. But they spoke volumes. They still do. It's a pity that they took down the sign.

PART I

THE CHINA MARKET

Is the "China market" of 1.3 billion people an illusion or reality? In fact it may be many markets of various segments and niches. The question is how to penetrate and to do so effectively with the resources at hand? The answers are not simple, but involve intensive research in understanding the behavioral patterns of the market, coupled with balanced coordination between well-placed advertising, strategic public relations and careful, step-by-step long-term relationship building.

Chapter 1

Cracking The China Market

By Scott Kronick, Managing Director, Ogilvy PR/China
with Lily Pu, Regional Planning Director, Ogilvy & Mather

Tougher Competition

On December 11, 2001, after 15 years of negotiations, the world's most populous country finally joined the world's most important trade body. Yet China's accession to WTO, although hailed by some as signaling "a seismic shift in global marketing", should nudge perceptive observers to look beyond the rhetoric and focus on the actions that will be needed to prosper in China's complex market. Those who fail to do so will likely experience more pain than profit.

Far from being a signal that foreign companies can sweep into China and establish market dominance, WTO accession marks the first milestone in what promises to be a long and potentially grueling contest between foreign and local brands. For the past 20 years, foreign companies have enjoyed a clear advantage in brand marketing and product quality. Foreign products were perceived to be inherently more desirable than local ones, even if they were less affordable. But a growing brand savvy among Chinese enterprises is rapidly eroding this perception, making it harder for foreign companies to establish and maintain leadership in China.

Foreign companies will also have to adjust to the realities of being guests in a country undergoing profound social and economic stress. For the first time, Chinese enterprises will face full-blown international competition and closer regulatory scrutiny from entities located outside their own borders. The huge tasks of restructuring state-owned enterprises and jettisoning the social welfare system of the past half century are certain to make the next 5 to 10 years difficult for many Chinese, no matter how adeptly the government manages the transition. In the final section of this chapter, we offer a few recommendations on how to develop effective communications appropriate to a large, complex society in a state of social and economic flux.

China represents a potential goldmine for the ambitious marketer. In addition to having a large and growing number of middle-class consumers, it has shown a singular knack for weathering the financial and economic storms that have buffeted other countries in Asia and throughout the industrialized world. Many foreign companies are thriving here. Starbucks, Kentucky Fried Chicken, and McDonald's dot the maps of China's major cities, while technology companies such as IBM, Nokia, and Motorola are among the most successful brands in their categories. The growth extends into the financial and professional services sectors as well.

Yet foreign brands face a serious challenge in China, and for those who care to read them, the warning signs are already visible: strong local brands, Chinese nationalism, and the readiness of local firms to compete according to the new rules of the game.

Over the past two years, Chinese companies in industries from banking to pharmaceuticals have recognized the need to build their brands quickly before the tide of foreign competition becomes a flood. This awakening brand consciousness can be seen in a 47 percent jump in ad spending in China from 2000 to 2001. It rose from RMB 6.6 billion (US$ 795 million) to RMB 9.7 billion (US$ 1.17 billion); all of the top 10 spenders were Chinese brands.

"Local companies increasingly are coming to major international agencies for help in building their brands," said Sandeep Vasudevan, Strategic Planning Director at Ogilvy & Mather in Shanghai. "In the past, brand identity was not important; local companies were focused purely on driving sales. Today, it is more critical for them to build a brand for long-term viability."

Increased ad spending is already creating brand recognition for Chinese products. The 2000 Gallup research report found that of the country's 10 most widely recognized brands, seven were Chinese. In addition to advertising, local companies are turning to PR firms for advice on brand building. The Beijing municipal government (itself a brand) is perhaps the most salient example, having retained two international PR agencies to provide counsel on external communications in the city's bid to host the 2008 Olympic Games.

Some argue that short bursts of heavy spending do not build brand equity over the long term, but research conducted in China by Ogilvy's parent company WPP suggests otherwise. A comprehensive year 2000 survey shows Chinese brands not only achieve better brand recognition than their foreign competitors, but generate greater brand loyalty as well. The Brand Z survey, an attempt to measure brand loyalty in markets worldwide, shows the five brands in China with the highest loyalty ratings were all local, beating such high-profile international competitors as McDonald's (7th place), Coca-Cola (9th place), and KFC (10th place). The leading Chinese brands included China Telecom, Mudan credit cards, and the Industrial and Commercial Bank of China. Significantly, these are brands in the telecommunications, finance and banking sectors – all of which will open their respective fields wider to foreign competition as a result of WTO.

Why are these local companies succeeding in edging out more established international brands? The answer lies in a combination of three factors.

☐ ***Increased attention to brand building***. As noted above, local companies have intensified their brand communications substantially in recent years. They are communicating more because they have more to say about themselves. Manufacturing is no longer the domain of inefficient state-run enterprises, local product quality has improved greatly, and local companies are eager to spread the word.

☐ ***Chinese nationalism***. Patriotism tends to make local brands more popular. In the 2000 Gallup poll, 80 percent of consumers said they preferred to buy Chinese branded goods or products made in China regardless of the brand. Nearly 70 percent said the phrase "Made in China" indicated good product quality, suggesting patriotism is no longer equated with sacrifice. Many new brands tout their local origins as badges of honor: The slogan for one Chinese soft drink reads, "Chinese Cola for Chinese people." Even a Hong Kong brand, Shanghai Tang, states proudly that it is "Made by Chinese."

☐ ***Growing brand literacy***. It's not just Chinese companies that are becoming increasingly brand savvy; consumers are, too. They face an abundance of choices compared with 10 years ago, and brands make it easier for them to decide what to buy. That is especially true of the country's burgeoning middle class, defined here as consumers with disposable incomes up to US$ 8,000 a year. This group is projected to swell to 500 million by 2010. For them, shopping has become a national pastime, one reason China has seen such an explosion of department stores and luxury goods.

As China's quality standards rise, global markets will witness the emergence of China as an exporter of branded products rather than mere commodities. Qingdao-based Haier Corporation, for example, has already become the world's six-largest appliance maker, with more than US$ 7 billion in global sales in 2001. Clearly, foreign brands have a serious contest ahead of them, both within China and elsewhere in the world.

Economic and Social Stresses

WTO agreements that require more open trade will increase pressure on Chinese companies steeped in ancient customs of business practice and outlook, forcing them to adjust to new and more western standards and methods of doing business. Local industries vulnerable to challenges by foreign competitors include agriculture, insurance, banking, and automobiles, are a few such areas about to undergo momentous change. Major factors affecting China's ability to compete include legal reforms made necessary by WTO rules; changes in the political administration; and the impact of the world economy on China's markets.

The most profound structural change facing China in the immediate future is the reform of its money-losing state-owned enterprises (SOEs). An article posted on the web site of the *People's Daily*, a newspaper that serves as the Chinese Communist Party's official mouthpiece, read in part: "SOE reform is an extensive and profound revolution, an arduous and prolonged task. Reforming SOEs will remain a crucial part of the entire systematic economic reform in the period to come."

The challenge of adapting to the new realities of WTO was summed up nicely by Chinese Premier Zhu Rongji, the driving force behind China's campaign to enter WTO for the past few years. Addressing a gathering of business executives following successful WTO negotiations in Geneva, he said, "Friends, you clap, but even I don't yet know how big the competition is that we'll face after we enter the WTO. My heart is not yet very settled."

The Way Forward

Both foreign and local companies will be working harder in the coming years, as WTO re-shapes the economic playing field. Against that backdrop, what is Ogilvy telling its clients about delivering effective brand communications in post-WTO China?

We offer three basic recommendations, all aimed at addressing the tougher competition, increased brand awareness, periodic surges of nationalism, and social dislocations from restructuring outlined earlier in this chapter. These recommendations are aimed at creating deeper understanding of target consumers and remembering always to be a sensitive guest in a country undergoing profound structural change.

Recommendation #1: Invest in the Necessary Research

Successful brands in China, whether local or international, must invest in research to understand their markets. Research provides a foundation for every advertising campaign, and increasingly PR firms are using qualitative and quantitative research as a way of providing their clients with benchmarks against which success can be measured.

This may seem obvious, but many of the horror stories coming out of China in the past decade stem from a failure to conduct adequate research. Ogilvy has always told clients there is no substitute for primary research, and in post-WTO China, this is doubly true. Companies will need to know their consumers inside out: who they are, what they want or need, and what would make them abandon their current brand to try a new one. Fortunately, WTO will lead to changes in China's regulations governing market research, enabling companies to conduct surveys with greater flexibility and confidence.

Recommendation #2: Be Mindful of China's Sub-markets

Although nearly everyone uses the term "the China market", there really is no such thing. Rather, there exist within China a handful of sub-markets, each with its own tastes, customs, and dialects. Mandarin is the official language of China, for example, but many hinterland provinces have their own dialects, as different from Mandarin as German is from Arabic. Several provinces have more than a dozen dialects, some of which are mutually unintelligible to speakers from villages a few kilometers apart from each other.

Unilever, the Anglo-Dutch corporation, is one of the leading international consumer goods companies operating in China. It makes an extra effort to understand regional variations among Chinese consumers, customizing everything from product formulations to marketing strategies and going to great lengths to understand the cultural and geographic differences of China's many consumer groups. In fact, Unilever has gone so far as to site a dedicated research center in Shanghai with the aim of developing products especially tailored to the tastes of Chinese consumers. That kind of commitment to understanding consumers goes a long way toward enabling the company to serve

China's various sub-markets.

Recommendation #3: Focus on Corporate Citizenship and Issues Management

Regardless of how many years (or decades) foreign companies have operated in China, they are likely always to be regarded as guests. As such, they must remain on their best behavior more or less permanently, and must be sure to focus on social responsibility, internal communications, and issues management. Historically, these were "nice to have" options for a brand communications program; in a post-WTO environment they are a necessity.

☐ *Corporate social responsibility.* The values a company stands for – beyond the simple products or services it provides – are becoming more important in building long-term brand equity in China. This growing emphasis on corporate values has created a need for communications that feature the company's social conscience as an integral part of the brand. Again, Unilever provides an exemplary illustration. In 2000, the company worked with local communities to plant more than 2 million trees throughout China to help fight desertification. It was just one part of a comprehensive corporate branding program linking Unilever with the concept of "home" in China.

☐ *Internal communications.* Increasingly, foreign companies want to make their own internal corporate cultures a point of competitive differentiation, using them as a selling point to attract and retain the best employees in China's fluid labor pool. This trend shifts internal communications perceptibly closer to center stage, as pressure grows to communicate effectively with larger local staffs.

☐ *Issues management and crisis management.* Business and

social issues will take on new meaning as China wrestles with the challenges it has signed up for by joining WTO. Corporate crises, traditionally solved with a few phone calls, will soon reflect the sophisticated crisis management practices employed in the developed world.

After 15 long years, the WTO era has finally dawned in the world's most economically promising country. For anyone seeking to market goods and services there, the potential for both pain and gain will be available in equal measure. Experienced China hands and newcomers alike will find that by doing the necessary research, keeping focused on the variations of China's sub-markets, and being prepared to manage issues and crises, they can maximize their gains while keeping the pain to a minimum.

Chapter 2

Branding For China

By Scott Kronick, Managing Director
Ogilvy Public Relations/China

Public Relations Build Brands in China

Brand building is not only the domain of advertising agencies. In China, where government influences all business and industry, public relations (PR) is often the communications discipline of choice for companies engaged in early brand building efforts. PR is equally critical for companies with established business in China as a tool for negotiating the minefields of governmental regulations and communicating with important constituent groups.

What does PR really mean? While there is some debate about where PR's exact boundaries lie, Ogilvy Public Relations Worldwide offers the following definition of the field: "Communications that build a brand and provide bottom-line results by explaining, motivating, selling, and protecting a product or idea by direct interactions or through the news media." It has been said that advertising is what a company says about itself, while PR is what others say about a company. PR thrives where influence matters, and influence matters immensely in China.

China's highly centralized power structure means key influencers and opinion leaders are concentrated within a more defined range of institutions than elsewhere in the world, which sometimes (although not always) can make them easier to identify and approach. In any event, communicating with individuals who have a disproportionate influence on a company and its brands is the primary objective of public relations in the PRC.

As anywhere else in the world, public relations in China are composed of four basic functions: education, media relations, government relations, and crisis or issues management. Implementing each of these functions in the Chinese market requires a strong understanding of the country's social conditions, culture, consumer preferences, and changing business environment. This chapter will address each of PR's functions for the China market in detail.

Education and Information Campaigns

Prior to China's opening to the outside world in 1978, popular awareness of major foreign companies and their brands was limited to a select few Chinese who were able to travel abroad. The re-entry of international products over the past 20 years and the rapid growth of local brands has made Chinese increasingly receptive to commercial messages, and today China presents companies with tremendous opportunities for brand building.

Education and information form the foundation of many PR campaigns worldwide, but PR's educational function is ideally suited to developing countries such as China, where information is less readily available than in the developed world. Once China viewed information as a potential threat to social stability and has generally restricted its flow. But that situation has changed considerably, and today there are dozens of informational campaigns underway aimed at delivering educational and commercial messages to specific audience groups. In the automotive industry there are campaigns aimed at brand building for new cars. In the healthcare industry there are doctor and patient education campaigns, and in the technology field there are targeted communications efforts directed at IT strategists and implementers.

A good example from the auto industry is BMW. Throughout the 1980s, BMW conducted no advertising or public relations in China. Few Chinese owned BMWs, and understanding of the BMW brand – "the Ultimate Driving Machine" – was limited to a small handful of auto enthusiasts. In 1994, BMW established a representative office in China and began committing the resources necessary to build its brand in a country where few people owed cars, much less expensive imported models. BMW's first move was to establish a representative office in Beijing, where it centralized its communications and government relations activities. From there, BMW communicated with the government, managed its dealer network, and recruited new partners. It also began an intensive effort to build brand understanding among wealthy consumers. A public relations team was assigned to provide market intelligence and communicate with the news media.

To celebrate the opening of its representative office, BMW appointed Ogilvy Public Relations Worldwide to introduce the BMW brand to the market through a press conference. The event was hosted by senior executives from Munich, and more than 50 journalists attended. The conference began a dialogue between BMW and journalists throughout China, and today BMW operates a news bureau that provides education and information to more than 200 journalists aimed at deepening understanding of the BMW brand among upwardly mobile Chinese. The news bureau promotes this dialogue through special events such as road shows, corporate sponsorships, driving tests, and new model introductions. BMW's communications program has worked splendidly: Year-on-year sales have grown, and today the company is among the leading luxury automobiles in the China market.

Cellular phone maker Nokia is another company that pays great attention to providing information and education to targeted audience groups in China. Whether Nokia messages center on fashion, technology-driven mobile phones for young consumers, network systems for operators, or investment decisions for central and municipal governments, the company has established a communications infrastructure within its organization that educates stakeholders about the Nokia brand in China.

Media Relations in the PRC

Media relations play a key role in any public relations campaign aimed at communicating messages about a company or its brands. In China, this is especially true, for a number of reasons explained below.

As elsewhere in the world, news media in China have a great impact on public opinion, and press coverage (both positive and negative) plays a critical part in shaping brand perceptions here. Major regional publications and broadcast outlets are affiliated with the government, making it easy for China's leadership to disseminate controlled messages to the public. Leading newspapers such as *People's Daily* are the voice of the Chinese Communist Party, while *Economic Daily* serves as the voice of the State Council, China's highest executive body. These publications remain mandatory reading for senior government officials, and other publications follow their lead in defining what is acceptable editorial content.

Chinese journalists operate differently than their Western counterparts, but their attitudes and behavior are changing rapidly to align more closely with those of the foreign press. Ten years ago, for example, local journalists were docile and willing to be fed information. They might show up at a press conference without knowing clearly why they were there, and without any background knowledge of the company that had invited them. That situation is far less likely to occur today, especially if the company holding the press briefing is well known. Nevertheless, there remain key differences between the foreign and the local press.

Many foreign executives, for example, believe Chinese journalists are easily controlled. While it is true that Chinese reporters are inclined to produce positive stories (having been trained to convey good news as part of their government propaganda function), it is dangerous to conclude that they will always be supportive. China's media remain government-controlled, but they are being given more freedom to function as watchdogs, especially where the foreign companies are concerned. Although coverage is generally fair, most local media are still sufficiently nationalistic that they want to know what makes a brand relevant to China's development. If a foreign company appears somehow to be acting counter to the national interest (dumping hazardous waste, for example, or shuttering a joint venture factory and laying off workers), local journalists can become aggressive and partisan very quickly.

Economic reform has led to great interest in business stories among the media, and advertising space has grown dramatically since the 1980s, creating a bigger news hole to fill. Some publications will accept pre-written articles (foreign news publications seldom do, with the exception of opinion pieces), but most of the influential presses hesitate to show strong support for a company or product, especially if it is foreign.

One of the key points to remember about doing PR in China is the importance of providing a comprehensive press kit. Journalists here often want extensive product information and company background, as they are less familiar with foreign companies than a foreign reporter would be.

Another point to bear in mind is the importance of giving "face." At press briefings, journalists derive face from having access to senior executives. When government or other officials are in attendance, gatherings must be carefully arranged to ensure that officials of the same level participate, are seated with others of the same rank, and exchange gifts of roughly equal value and size.

Social interaction is highly valued in Chinese society. Stay in touch with local journalists, even when no specific media events are planned. Invite the media to lunch occasionally, even when you don't need them for anything in particular. Such gestures are appreciated in China and will pay dividends in the long run.

Public Affairs

Foreign companies bewitched by the prospect of selling to China's 1.3 billion consumers sometimes fail to realize there is a powerful force that pervades the world of Chinese business. Like gravity, it is invisible but exerts a strong pull. This force is the Chinese government.

Public Affairs, also called Government Relations, is perhaps more important in China than in any other country in the world, and is therefore a critical component of a company's corporate strategy and PR efforts. Most Chinese industry is owned or controlled by the government, giving senior officials the power to alter the course of multi-billion dollar industries with a single decision. The thumbnail estimate at the time of this writing is that two-thirds of all Chinese industry is state-owned, while only one-third is privately owned; key industries are tightly controlled by the government. In the energy sector, the State Development Planning Commission sets production quotas and import/export targets for oil and natural gas. The Ministry of Information Industry sets prices for fixed-line and mobile phone calls, and selects top management at China's telecom carriers. In the pharmaceutical industry, the State Drug Administration creates a special list of drugs for which patients will receive reimbursement from China's social security administration; whether foreign companies can sell their products in the Chinese market is effectively determined by whether or not they manage to get on that list.

At the root of public affairs in China is "*guanxi*", the Chinese word for "relations." Among foreign executives, it has long been an article of faith that *guanxi*, almost to the exclusion of all other factors, determines a foreign company's success in China. Many foreign companies have chosen to deal with the central government's power by appointing government liaison experts to develop *guanxi* with key government ministries.

While *guanxi* is certainly important, it has its limitations. Internal power struggles can wipe out the value of one's contacts overnight, and the changing political and regulatory landscape in China means no arrangement is guaranteed to last forever. While international standards are still far off, transparency and rule of law are working their way into the system as foreign multinationals bring their management systems to bear on China. More important than simple *guanxi* are the twin expedients of aligning business objectives with government interests, and cultivating government contacts at multiple levels.

A strategy of aligning corporate and state goals is basically an attempt to find win-win situations for dealing with the government. In its drive to modernize, the Chinese government faces real problems, which it needs real help in addressing; foreign companies are in a good position to provide some of that help. Those that provide substantive assistance where it is needed, while showing a genuine commitment to the market, will be much better positioned than those that rely on an empty strategy of courting favor with selected officials.

Cultivating multiple level contacts, a sound public affairs strategy anywhere in the world, is especially critical in China because of the government's bureaucratic structure and propensity for consensus-based decision making. For example, Chinese ministries employ a system of cross-checking called *hui qian*, or "meeting and signing off." Under the *hui qian* system, for example, a decision about a company's business issue may be made by Ministry X. But Ministry X cannot operate in a vacuum; it must give other interested ministries a chance to review the decision, even if they do not have a direct say in the final outcome. A memorandum outlining the pending decision will circulate among all primary and secondary decision-makers, and eventually an official document will be issued. Only then is the final decision made. Clearly, this type of multi-level decision making necessitates the cultivation of contacts at various levels of government.

While it is no longer true that guanxi is the sole determinant of a foreign company's success, neither is it true that China's membership in WTO will relegate the government to a secondary role in business dealings. The government will remain a key player in all large-scale business projects. Nevertheless, in post-WTO China, business success will hinge less on *guanxi* and more on knowledge and diplomacy. Although WTO obliges China to adhere to certain international rules, those rules still must be interpreted. More important than personal connections will be the ability to identify and help meet the government's critical needs so as to ensure its support; and to find ways of working within the new rules of trade so as to resolve the disagreements that will inevitably arise from conflicting interpretations of those rules.

Crisis Communications/Issues Management

Crisis communications and issues management are really two sides of the same coin: If a company manages its issues correctly, they may never become crises. It is often pointed out that the Chinese character for crisis is a combination of two sub-characters: danger and opportunity. While the danger component is clear enough, it may be less obvious why a crisis should represent an opportunity.

The reason is simple: A company will never have the undivided attention of its stakeholders as surely as it does during a crisis. And under no other circumstances will the company's behavior speak more loudly than during such a time.

Foreign and local companies in China have faced almost every form of crisis imaginable, ranging from staff and operational issues to product quality and JV partner disagreements. All of this makes crisis communications a popular topic amongst the business community here.

While crises can generate negative publicity and disrupt business operations anywhere in the world, the risk of a small event spiraling out of control is particularly acute in China. One reason for this is a basic desire by the media to protect local industries, sometimes at the expense of foreign ones. Journalists may respond in a defensive or nationalistic way to the competitive threat foreign companies pose to domestic industries. But local companies are not immune to crises either, often finding themselves the object of unwanted attention stemming from consumer complaints or regulatory intervention by the government related to poor product quality.

Issues management, the reverse side of crisis management, is the practice of identifying social issues with which a company is most closely linked and leveraging them in a way that strengthens the enterprise and its brands. Companies worldwide have an interest in building goodwill among government regulators and in the communities where they operate. But because of the comparatively nationalistic character of China's media and government, extra effort is needed if foreign companies are to win the hearts and minds of Chinese consumers.

Most companies can easily identify a few major issues relevant to their brands. A maker of detergents, for example, will want to stay on top of environmental issues because its product is continually washed into rivers and lakes. In addition to issues related to a company's business, certain basic issues exist that are specific to China. While these may have nothing to do with a company's core business, they must be anticipated nevertheless. Smart companies will always prepare answers for unexpected questions about political situations or governmental announcements.

In its drive to become a developed country, China faces a host of problems. Environmental protection, housing, labor, health, education, and foreign investment all represent potential areas of both vulnerability and opportunity for multinational companies in China. The central government is retreating from its traditional role of providing cradle-to-grave care for its citizens, and now "appears to be recasting itself as a facilitator, rather than as a direct provider, of social services," according to Nick Young, editor of *China Development Brief*. Young points out that the government is passing the baton to "social forces an unspecified blend of private and non-profit service providers." Government appeals to these vague forces are common, and have even appeared in laws enacted by the National People's Congress, the country's highest legislative body.

Many foreign companies in China have demonstrated good corporate citizenship by donating money to charity. Motorola has given US$ 2 million to Project Hope, a foundation that puts disadvantaged Chinese children through school. IBM has invested millions of dollars in technology centers at Chinese universities, while providing training for teachers and setting up scholarship programs.

Accepting the largesse of big multinationals was the first step in opening the door to foreign influence in the area of social issues. But now the central government is cautiously endorsing efforts by selected groups to promote environmental protection, women's rights, and the rights of China's migrant workers. At this stage, it is unrealistic to expect Chinese companies to play a leading role in this area, for only recently have they been allowed to jettison the welfare functions they have performed for the past half century and get down to the business of making money. This acceptance of non-governmental organizations therefore gives foreign companies a significant opportunity to make a contribution.

"The most visionary proponents of the concept of corporate social responsibility see it not merely as a charitable retrofit, somewhere between community relations and brand promotion, but as a redefinition of the role of the company in society," according to *China Development Brief*'s Nick Young. Regardless of the industry in which one operates, preparing for crises and managing issues are necessities in China.

People who work in public relations today say China may be the best place in the world to practice PR. The rapid growth of the economy, the optimism of the people, and the host of issues confronting the citizenry and its leaders provide a dynamic backdrop against which to influence, inform, and educate key audiences. WTO and the 2008 Beijing Olympics only add to this mix of economic development and social change. Companies here have a unique opportunity to shape the perceptions of their brand amongst a large and increasingly affluent consumer base, and to make a contribution to the development and prosperity of the world's oldest, largest civilization.

Eight Questions to Ask When Using PR in China to Build a Brand:

1) What are the social trends in China that could increase/decrease demand for the brand in the future?

2) Are there any issues external to the brand in China that could nevertheless affect it, either positively or negatively? Can any be created?

3) Who has a big influence on this brand in China, or on the decision-making power of its consumers in China?

4) How favorable is the media coverage this brand receives? What do Chinese consumers know about the brand?

5) How do professional experts in China feel about recommending this brand?

6) Does the brand live up to its promises in China in a way that is (or could be) visible to the public?

7) Is the brand a good citizen of the community in China? Is this widely known?

8) How do the brand's own employees in China feel about their association with the brand? Is their behavior aligned with the CEO's vision?

Chapter 3

Advertising In Post-WTO China

By T.B. Song, Chairman, Ogilvy & Mather China

A Look At Advertising's Past

For the ambitious marketer, China has long been regarded as a kind of El Dorado, a faraway land full of consumers to whom vast quantities of goods could be sold if only one could reach them.

An early proponent of this view was Carl Crowe, an American who founded one of the first foreign advertising agencies in China. His 1937 book *Four Hundred Million Customers* contains some questionable observations (that Chinese dogs always bark at foreigners, for example), but its main point still holds true: China represents the world's largest potential market for goods and services.

For centuries, foreign entrepreneurs have been seduced by China's size, reasoning that making money here would be easy once they found a way to make the scale work in their favor. Nineteenth-century English textile merchants calculated the profits they could make by getting every man in China to lengthen his shirt-tail by one inch. For many businesses, such schemes remained commercial fantasy. But others were able to profit – among them Carl Crowe, who became quite successful advertising foreign cold cream to China's beauty-conscious women.

While trade between China and the West goes back at least to the seventeenth century, its foreign media can be traced to the mid-1800s, when missionaries introduced the first modern newspapers as a way of spreading Christianity. These publications were soon transformed into vehicles for commercial messages, and foreign businesses began to advertise regularly through newspapers, magazines, and outdoor billboards. One of the largest advertisers was British American Tobacco. Bat's ad campaigns were so far-reaching that one Chinese journalist commented, "Many Chinese don't know who Sun Yat-sen is, but very few places don't know Ruby Queen (a leading BAT cigarette brand)."

China's first foreign ad agency was founded in 1915 by an Italian named Bruno Perne. Based in Shanghai, it specialized in billboard advertisements. By 1937, there were about 30 agencies on the mainland, five of them foreign. Most were in Shanghai, with a few smaller agencies in Beijing and Guangzhou. When the Sino-Japanese War broke out in 1937, foreign ad agencies left China and did not return for half a century.

The founding of the People's Republic in 1949 created an environment in which advertising had little chance of survival, as the Chinese Communist Party emphasized industrialization, discouraged consumption, and rationed food supplies. Nevertheless, Communist leaders recognized advertising's propaganda potential, declaring in 1959 that "socialist advertising" should combine commercial communication with political propaganda. Naturally, all ads had to reflect Communist ideology.

During the Cultural Revolution (1966-1976), the number of Chinese media outlets fell sharply. In 1965 the country had 343 newspapers and 790 magazines; five years later only 42 newspapers and 21 magazines remained. Outdoor advertising was eliminated and billboards were replaced with "big character" signs bearing Party slogans. The Shanghai Advertising Corporation was renamed the Shanghai Fine Arts Company and charged with designing propaganda posters. Despite the political turmoil of the period, however, advertising never stopped completely. Newspapers continued to run ads for industrial products and raw materials throughout the decade.

The 1980s Onward

After China's economic reforms got underway in the 1980s, the number of media exploded. Today, there are more than 1,100 TV channels and nearly 300 radio stations, each of which operates one or more channels. In the print media, China has more than 2,000 newspapers and nearly 8,000 magazine and 8,000 titles.

At first, the central government operated the news media, freeing newspapers and magazines from financial pressures and making advertising irrelevant. The situation changed after economic reforms began to gather momentum and the news media were instructed to become profitable; suddenly, they needed to sell ad space. The government's unwillingness to support money-losing media created an environment that encouraged the growth of advertising, and today China is the fourth-largest ad market in the world and the second largest in Asia. Recognizing the vast potential of this market, Ogilvy & Mather was among the first international advertising agencies to set up offices here.

The Growth of Brands in China

Ogilvy & Mather defines brands as "The way a consumer feels about a product or service, or the company or institution behind it." According to that definition, China had few (if any) brands from 1949 until the late 1970s, when advertising aimed at building brands slowly began to re-emerge. During the decades following 1949, it was ideologically unacceptable to advertise specific brands. Moreover, basic commodities were scarce, so creating a brand identity for a product was far less important than simply ensuring there was enough supply to meet demand. Under those circumstances, most Chinese had no strong feelings about particular products or the factories that made them.

As economic reforms took effect and products became more widely available, Chinese brands of a sort began to emerge. Each city or province had one or two major manufacturers – Shanghai Cosmetics Factory Number 2, for example – and because the quality of goods varied from one factory to another, consumers began to form associations with particular manufacturers. These associations marked the first glimmerings of a brand consciousness that would evolve rapidly over the next 25 years.

Today, China's consumers categorize brands into three distinct types:

☐ **Global**. Imported products or goods made locally by wholly foreign-owned enterprises. They are viewed as expensive, high-quality products that employ the latest technology.

☐ **Joint venture (JV)**. These locally made goods are produced for the China market by partnerships between Chinese and foreign companies. They are less expensive than imported goods, but their quality is still perceived to be good (although not as good as imports).

☐ **Local**. In the past, Chinese brands were perceived as being of poor quality. While many locally made goods are still viewed this way, others have made rapid strides in quality control and are rightly seen as well made. Examples include Haier white goods, Legend computers and Li Ning sports apparel.

China's size and diversity tempt some companies to generalize about the country as a way of simplifying complex issues. One such bromide holds that Chinese "buy face" when times are good and fall back on price when times are bad, a guideline of doubtful utility, since to a large extent it is equally true of every other market in the world.

Another misconception still prevalent today is that Chinese consumers are literal-minded in their interpretation of advertising. This is simply untrue, according to Ogilvy & Mather Worldwide CEO Shelly Lazarus: "There is a prevailing view amongst some western commentators that the idea of brand in China is somehow less developed, less rich, that communication has to be much more grounded in the rational than in the emotional, and that brands are seen as 'authority symbols' and not as things which actively engage consumers. Nothing could be further from the truth. Chinese are as advertising-sophisticated as any of their Asian counterparts. In fact, we find they are sometimes quicker to pick up on symbolism than in the West, which indicates that there is a cultural depth to viewing advertising in China that will in the long term be highly sympathetic to brand building."

As Chinese become more able to appreciate brand messages of greater subtlety, local companies will develop their own brands to compete with foreign products. While it is tempting to think that foreign marketers possess an advantage in the area of brand communications, rising quality standards and heavy ad spending by local companies have created a handful of powerful Chinese brands such as Haier, Qingdao, and Little Swan, among others.

The Building Blocks of Advertising in the PRC

This section addresses the basic elements of an advertising campaign: research that provides insight into the target audience group, and the right channel for communicating one's message. It also discusses China's Advertising Law, which defines, to some extent, the content of advertising messages in the PRC.

Given the sharp variations in tastes, habits, and even language among China's different regions, good advertising in China is preceded by market research to identify a campaign's target consumer and define its appropriate messages. The key is finding the unique insight that helps build a brand in a target consumer's mind. One large multinational maker of food products found through research that Chinese typically drank Western bag tea at restaurants and on special social occasions, but rarely drank it at home. This insight into local consumer behavior helped the company formulate a creative response: creating street-side tea stands aimed at driving consumption of bag tea outside the home.

In China, qualitative and quantitative research are conducted by specialized market research firms. Most international firms have offices in China; there is a local research industry here as well, which tends to perform more qualitative research. In addition to helping companies develop message strategies for their advertising, research can illuminate opportunities a marketer might otherwise have missed. For example, many companies aim their entire marketing effort at Beijing, Shanghai, and Guangzhou, when second-tier cities such as Chengdu and Dalian may have many consumers who can afford their brands. One company in China conducted research that revealed the existence of a thriving market for secondhand cell phones in Chengdu, where many consumers regarded cell phones as a fashion accessory and traded in their old models after only a few months. The plethora of comparatively new, traded-in phones created a booming market for used handsets.

In addition to using research for specific client campaigns, Ogilvy and Mather conducts a major survey every few years to evaluate consumer attitudes within a particular demographic group, or to assess sentiment about a product category. The most recent study, centering on attitudes toward food, showed that work-related time pressures accompanying China's economic growth had turned eating and buying food into stressful experiences for many Chinese. One insight the research uncovered: Survey respondents said the large number of commercial food brands had made them skeptical about manufacturers' health claims, but that they still relied on nutritional information printed on food product labels. This information gave food companies new ways of speaking to consumers about a timeless topic (eating), and also showed them a clear opportunity to build more trust with customers.

Research in China's regionally fragmented market is so important that some companies set up permanent R&D facilities here to ensure their

China's Fragmented Market

China is a huge country with great diversity whose people have widely differing tastes, customs, and political views. Many of these differences are geographically based. Southern Chinese, for example, are strongly influenced by Hong Kong media and culture, while those in the northeastern city of Dalian look to Japan as an arbiter of taste and fashion. These differences are compounded by a widening income gap between the 450 million people living in the country's economically thriving coastal zones and the 900 million inhabitants of its backward inland provinces.

In such an economically polarized environment, advertising can be effective in building a national brand, but below-the-line activities such as direct marketing are needed to address regional differences. Some examples of this approach are outlined below.

Yili, a popular Chinese brand of milk, had a strong customer base in Guangzhou, while two competing brands, Sanyuan and Guangming, were strong in Beijing and Shanghai. Yili chose to focus on developing a core of priority customers where it already had a solid base. It set up "milk stations" – combination stores/information centers – to deepen customers' experience of the Yili brand. Customers could buy Yili products and get company brochures and other informational material. The stations also served as processing centers when promotional campaigns required a central hub for customers to return milk carton labels or responses to marketing questionnaires. The stations were effective in establishing Yili as the dominant player in its priority market.

Sina.com provides another example of the need to address regional variations in taste and perception. Sina is one of China's most widely accessed Internet portals, but its Beijing location and connections with official news media had given it a reputation as being staid, conservative, and semi-official – not the choice of China's hip, upwardly mobile professional class. Two competing portals had established loyal user bases in particular geographic areas – Sohu.com in Shanghai and Netease.com in the southern province of Guangdong – cutting Sina.com out of those potentially lucrative markets.

To address this competitive threat, Sina.com launched a Shanghai site, which the company had promoted with outdoor advertising written in Shanghai dialect. "We were trying to play with the Shanghai market, to make people feel, 'This is a site that speaks my language,'"said Billboard Kwok, business director at Ogilvy & Mather Advertising in Beijing. Later a Guangzhou web site was launched, with a separate advertising campaign created to position Sina as irreverent, countercultural, and fun.

brands meet local needs. Such companies include IBM, Microsoft, Motorola, and Unilever. These R&D centers create products to meet local consumer needs, from Chinese voice-recognition software to beauty creams that match local skin types. Companies that display this degree of commitment to understanding China have a much better chance of succeeding in this market.

The Advertising Law

In China, what a company may say in its advertising is limited by the country's Advertising Law, developed by the State Administration of Industry and Commerce (SAIC) and introduced in February 1995. The text of the Law actually makes no provisions for a central censorship authority; lawmakers apparently assumed advertisers and the media that ran their ads could be relied on to censor themselves. "The advertisers, the ad agency, and the media should go through study groups to strengthen their concept of social responsibility and public morals," according to the law.

The Advertising Law is vague in places (it inveighs against commercials with "hidden implications that play around with the viewer's mind"), and more than a little outdated, reflecting an official mindset focused on telling consumers what is good for them. It cites as unacceptable a commercial "showing parents and children walking and eating at the same time," an activity described as "unhealthy."

Because it is difficult to interpret the law, responsibility for vetting ads and commercials has been shifted to the China Advertising Association, a body directly beneath the SAIC. The Advertising Association farms out the actual censorship to various "consultants" who, for a fee paid by the advertisers, review the concept and execution of all ads and issue an official certificate stating that the ads fall with the law. TV stations and print media may ask to see the certificate if they believe a commercial is potentially sensitive.

Among other things, the law provides for "truth in advertising," making manifestly false or vague claims illegal. Ads that have been rejected because they violated the Advertising Law have included those attempting to promote:

☐ a toothpaste to fight senility
☐ a facial soap that claimed to wash away wrinkles
☐ a pill designed to cure hepatitis within minutes

Other ads have been rejected for making what were felt to be excessively strong claims about their products. These include an ad promoting a beer with the slogan, "Probably the Best Beer in the World," and a commercial demonstrating the long life of an international battery brand.

Public safety is always a concern when deciding whether an ad should be approved. For example, a particular brand of cellular phone allowed users to record sounds to be used as ring tones. A proposed ad showed a man standing close to a runway recording a jet's takeoff, and standing close to a railroad track recording the sound of the locomotive. The ad was banned on the grounds that it encouraged dangerous behavior. Other problem areas include nudity, ads showing children disobeying adults, and ads that show superstitious practices.

Although the Advertising Law was passed in response to a spate of deceptive product claims by local advertisers, foreign advertisers must be careful to stay within the Law's guidelines lest they provoke a backlash against multinationals. Updating the Advertising Law is discussed periodically, but as of this writing the original version of the law remains in effect.

Channels and Media Buying

Once research is conducted and a creative campaign is devised, media buyers decide whether TV, radio, print, billboard, Internet advertising, or a combination of these will best serve the client's needs.

When it comes to buying ad space, China historically has been a seller's market. Despite the large number of media nationwide, demand has outstripped supply, thereby reducing the bargaining power of ad buyers; and because advertising-related revenues have become an important source of income for the government, publishers and broadcast outlets usually take a tough stance on price, trying to extract maximum revenue from each ad placed. While it is less expensive to advertise in China than in the developed world, inflation has driven advertising costs up sharply since the early 1990s, especially for TV commercials.

By the time this book is published, some of the information that follows will probably have changed. Nevertheless, here is a quick breakdown of the major media channels in China.

Newspapers historically have been the least flexible media, adopting a "take it or leave it" attitude toward media buyers that leaves little room for negotiation. High prices have not been offset by good service: Reproduction quality is often poor, and sellers show little concern about problems that may emerge when an ad is run. "Historically they haven't been business oriented," said Chris Walton, CEO of MindShare China, China's largest full-service media buying and planning agency. "They didn't care if they made a profit or not. You'd find your ad being placed next to a competitor's ad, the reproduction quality was terrible, and you had to book 6-8 weeks in advance (a long timeline for a daily newspaper)."

Walton says service and reproduction quality have improved significantly in recent years, a change he attributes to the launch of many new titles. But there's still a long way to go. "Newspapers are in a localized market, and there's usually one title that has a stranglehold," he said. "In Shanghai, it's *Xinmin Wanbao* (*Evening News*), a daily paper with 70 percent coverage of the city's readership. With that degree of coverage, they have buyers queued up to place ads, so the media owner is in a very strong negotiating position."

Outdoor advertising has been fragmented in the past but is rationalizing quickly. This category has developed faster than any other advertising medium in the last five years. Quality standards are much higher now, especially in Shanghai or Beijing, and advertisers can buy into a network of outdoor sites (for example, one bus company will control the bus shelters in 25 markets, so ads can be run on shelters in cities across China).

Television. China did not begin to experiment with TV until 1956, but the medium exploded in the 1980s, and today there are more than 1,100 TV channels nationwide. Every Chinese city has two terrestrial stations and one cable station, and those in Beijing, Shanghai, and Guangzhou have penetration rates of up to 95 percent. Inflation has pushed prices up sharply over the past five years. In 1996, for example, rate card inflation at Shanghai Television reached 170 percent. The price spiral was caused in part by the large influx of advertisers into China, all of whom wanted to advertise in a limited number of first- and second-tier cities. As the market matured, TV stations began competing with each other for business, putting a cap on ad rates. Inflation leveled off to between 7-8 percent in 2001, and the first glimmerings of a buyer's market were "visible" until the central government announced a consolidation of the television industry. (See "Creating Chinese Media Powerhouses" below.)

Radio, first introduced to China by an American journalist in 1923, was considered a key tool for reaching rural areas during the first decades of the PRC. Like TV, it boomed in the 1980s: China had 38 radio stations in 1980, while today there are nearly 300 radio stations, each of which broadcasts one or more channels. Radio has been the most flexible ad medium because it usually makes up a smaller fraction of advertising spending and therefore has less bargaining power. Stations are going through a tough period right now as they compete with TV for advertising money. "The further you get from the main urban centers, the stronger TV becomes," says Chris Walton. "You would think that in poorer areas there would be more radios and fewer televisions, but it's not true." TV penetration rates are around 90 percent. It is forecast that in the near future, radio will undergo significant development, which should aid its fight for a large portion of advertising spend.

Magazines. China has 8,000 titles. This sounds like a lot, but compare that number with the 25,000 titles available in the United States. Quality varies widely. High-end publications such as *Elle* and *Cosmopolitan* are world class; other titles have glossy covers but are newsprint on the inside.

Cinema, like outdoor advertising, less companies buy into a network of movie houses across China. However, buyers have little control over when their ad appears. When the movie *Titanic* opened, for example, many companies paid to run cinema ads before a film that was sure to be a blockbuster. Since movie trailers can last up to 10 minutes, some advertisers paid a premium to be one of the last ads shown before the film started. "Because so many advertisers wanted those slots, the cinema managers actually began selling ad space themselves," recalls Chris Walton. "So the ad for which somebody paid top dollar was getting bumped by commercials for local hot-pot restaurants." So far, no reliable method exists for monitoring ad placement, beyond the agencies actually visiting the cinemas themselves.

The Internet and so-called New Media still represent marginal channels in China, but their influence has great potential for growth. With an estimated 33.7 million Internet users, China's penetration rates are still relatively low. Only about 15-20 percent of the comparatively affluent, well-educated users living in Beijing, Shanghai, and Guangzhou have Internet access. When the field is broadened to encompass China's 18 largest cities, penetration drops to just six percent. That compares with penetration of about 50 percent in the United States, and more than 30 percent in Hong Kong and Taiwan.

The demographic composition of China's user base is evolving rapidly. Although the Internet in China is still dominated by men, the number of female users is climbing, with the user base at the time of this writing skewing about 60 percent male, 40 percent female. Moreover, while 37 percent of the country's Internet users are between 18-24 years old, the over-30 age cohort is growing quickly. "For a long time, the Internet was perceived to be kid stuff, but that perception is changing as the market matures," according to Sarah Chen, director of m-digital China, the online media division under MindShare.

IT and telecom companies are the main online advertisers; most consumer products advertisers allocated less than one percent of their marketing budgets to online advertising. But with higher PC penetration and a growing online population, the Internet is expected to play an increasingly important role in companies, overall marketing communications plans. "The Internet is not just an online medium," said Chen. "It's a one-to-one direct marketing platform where advertisers will be able to have interactive communication with the target."

"The traditional media are getting very crowded now," said Sandeep Vasudevan, Strategic Planning Director at Ogilvy & Mather in Shanghai. "People are moving from putting car ads on TV to bringing the car to the consumer. Audi is a good example of this. Through its web site, the company creates an online experience, complemented by workshops for the sales force, weekend test-drive outings for potential buyers, interactive information kiosks at airports, and other tactics. There is a host of other ways in which the brand can impact daily life, and increasingly these will be used to maximum effect as competition becomes sharper. It will no longer be enough simply to put an ad for your product in the newspaper."

Overall, media buyers in China should bear in mind the following guidelines:

☐ *Focus on advertising quality, not just quantity.* "People are too focused on the cost of buying ad space, rather than on the quality of the space," said Chris Walton. "One of our clients told us their competitor was getting an 80 percent discount on the cost of TV advertising, and asked why we couldn't negotiate a similar discount. When we checked it out, we found the competitor was getting the cheap rate by buying all unsold ad space, regardless of the time or channel. So their ad was running 10 times in one hour, or airing between 4:00 and 5:00 a.m. It was probably totally ineffective. But it was cheap. Value calculations should be based on the numbers of eyeballs reached by the advertising, rather than the absolute monetary amount paid."

☐ *Advertising does not drive distribution.* "People often think that if they advertise their product, more retail outlets will want to stock it, but in the vast majority of cases, that has not been our experience," says Chris Walton. "Advertising doesn't seem to influence shop owners the way it might persuade consumers, so if your brand isn't already well known, people won't pick up on it. Set up your distribution network first. Get your products into the shop before you start telling people about it."

Creating Chinese Media Powerhouses

More competition among TV stations had pushed down the rates stations could charge for advertising space. But moves by the central government to consolidate the media are intended to reverse that trend and create local powerhouses (in effect, local monopolies) that can charge premium rates. Shanghai Media and Entertainment Group, for instance, formed in July 2001, combines the sales operations of Shanghai TV, Oriental TV, and Shanghai Cable TV. Together, these account for 90-95% of all TV viewers in Shanghai.

The highest-profile example of consolidation is the **China Radio, Film and Television Group**. Formed in December 2001, it unites the largest entities in China's broadcasting pantheon: national broadcaster China Central Television; a national network of cable-television stations; China Film Group Corporation, the largest film producer and monopoly importer of films; and both China National Radio and China Radio International, the national and international radio stations. According to the State Administration of Radio, Film and Television, the combined Group has revenues of US$ 1.3 billion and more than 20,000 employees.

Experts predict that eventually China will have several regional broadcasting powerhouses, including some in Beijing and others in Shanghai and Guangdong Province. So while the number of Chinese TV channels may continue to increase, the number of owners will drop. The creation of large domestic media groups could spawn China-based global media brands' miniature AOL/TimeWarners or News Corporations that will form a media network spanning different markets and different media.

"With WTO a reality now, local media realize there are huge opportunities that exist within China, plus significant threats if they don't start acting like News Corp," said Chris Walton of MindShare. "They don't want to lose ad revenue to foreign media groups, such as Star TV, or to other domestic media groups, perhaps a Beijing-based group with a strong presence in Shanghai."

Chapter 4

Distribution

By Douglas Gerber, Vice-President, Pepsi Co.

Seven Axioms of Going to Market in China

The China market is the last frontier for many consumer companies. With 1.3 billion potential customers, growing incomes and much room left for development, organizations are allocating increasingly greater resources to this land of great promise. Yet, there is no easy or quick formula; success is achieved on city by city, market by market basis.

So when approaching the China market, what is the paramount consideration – production, marketing, or distribution? The answer to the question depends on the company and industry. Yet ask any consumer organization, and invariably, the answer is that **availability** is the critical and most challenging aspect of going to market. Setting out on the right track is an imperative to a successful long-term business. These pointers, if carefully observed, will avoid costly mistakes, and put the Company on the road to success.

First, Be Clear about Your Model

Geographic Focus

In going to market in China, many organizations take the obvious and easy route to market: locate the industry distributors, approach them, then negotiate territories, margins, coverage; presto you are in business! This is in fact a fairly short-term way to achieve some degree of presence and, superficially, at least one can say, "we have 80% of the market covered," or "the eastern seaboard is all wrapped up." On deeper analysis, however, market penetration in China doesn't happen so quickly, and this type of rapid coverage is a recipe for loss of control. Most importantly, one risks being held hostage by distributors.

The key, therefore, is to understand and be clear about the staging of geographic and retail coverage. Market penetration **phasing** is essential to maintaining control. Don't compromise your model for the promise of rapid geographic expansion. Focus your resources, control distribution, and phase in implementation of the strategy.

Channel Clarity

The next area of critical importance is achieving clarity on the targeted channels. All too often, companies take a shotgun approach, trying to hit all channels in their industry at once. For example, does the Company focus on traditional groceries, supermarkets, or hypermarkets? This determination will affect everything including distribution, selling, advertising and pricing. As with the geographic approach, it is better to execute well in one channel, than trying to hit all of them.

Using Third Parties

What aspects of the distribution does one want to control? The entire supply chain can in fact be contracted out, and understanding the key control levers is a prerequisite for market success. Yet, some organizations try to do it all, thereby retaining control, at the expense of increasing costs and complexity. Other firms may **contract selling and distribution** to third parties, thereby lowering costs, with the risk of loss of control. Understanding the Organization's strengths and weaknesses, culture, industry dynamics and leverage points must take place prior to executing the strategy.

Second, Create Market Beachheads

This point cannot be overemphasized. A leading multinational decided that achieving market leadership in Shanghai was critical for success, and also believed that it was within reach. They concentrated management and distribution resources in Shanghai, and invested in marketing, and developing the supply chain. Within two years, they moved from a distant number two, to the market leader. This was achieved through focus and concentration of resources.

Unlike some other more developed countries, the regions and provinces of China can differ greatly in terms of brand leadership in any given industry. In fact among consumer industries, one finds significant share disparities from market to market. A number of factors are behind this. National advertising and brand building, outside of the national TV media (CCTV), is still underdeveloped, although municipal and provincial media are developing very rapidly. Another factor is limited national travel. While travel across provincial boundaries is rapidly growing, the frequency of cross-market exposure opportunities is still very limited for the vast majority of consumers. Given China's geographic scope, organizations have had no choice but to concentrate resources. The implication is that developing a **provincial and regional** approach is paramount to achieving progress in China.

Taking the beachhead approach allows for the development of capable human resources, which can then be leveraged to create success in new targeted areas. It might look something like this:

☐ **Phase I** – determine which is the optimal market to target leadership; focus resources on setting up sales, marketing and distribution infrastructure in that market. Determine target share, distribution, and other key performance objectives, with the aim of achieving market leadership. Concurrently set up small manageable offices in Phase II markets, to attain some degree of market contact and familiarity.

☐ **Phase II** – after targeted market share or outlet coverage is achieved in the beachhead market, it's time to move to Phase II markets. Here again, the key is not to be too ambitious, picking two to three markets for this phase. Move some of your Phase I human resources, who understand and know how to achieve market leadership, to the Phase II market.

At this stage, one may also start developing provincial markets outside of the main beachhead market. For example, if Shanghai is the Phase I market, it may be time to start developing Jiangsu and/ or Zhejiang provinces.

☐ **Phase III** – by this time, the Company has achieved strong positions in 3-4 important markets. Phase III means developing a regional approach; at this stage, for example, one might sub-divide China into regions, e.g. Northeast, North, Central, South, Southwest, etc.... and target several regions. Realistically, 5-10 years effort may be required before moving to phase III.

Remember that the beachhead approach **continuously targets, focuses and develops**. While targeting new geographies, continue to develop primary territories to drive volume; there is still much growth to be realized in markets which appear developed by relative standards. For example, if the Company has 60% penetration of distribution outlets, it should drive to 80%.

But that's not all; it is also the time to expand **sales per outlet**. Companies often assume that their job is finished after achieving high levels of distribution – undiscovered treasures can be realized through increasing sales per outlet. This can be achieved through expanding the number of packages or SKUs, which are carried by the retailer. Ensuring that outlets are well merchandised will create the perception of market leadership to both consumers and retailers, and allow for greater off-take.

Third, Nurture the Direct Relationship with the Customer

A common mistake made in developing distribution in China is abdication of customer contact to third parties. This happens all too often, and is a recipe for business decline.

Distributors and third parities have developed an impressive array of relationships and distribution coverage with retail outlets. Superficially, the numbers are boggling... "our distribution network covers 30,000 outlets," or, "we have leverage with all the major retailers." Indeed, distributors often paint a rosy and convincing picture. Yet behind the surface, one often finds a passive distribution system, with minimal efforts to create real presence at the retail level.

Just as foreign enterprises hold out positive prospects for China, local distributors ambitiously strive to be the kings of distribution in their respective industries. Distributors want to amass greater territory, carry more brands and SKUs, and are willing to give up margin, extend credit, and invest in warehouses and vehicles to achieve their desired aims. Yet in this free for all, the real distribution work of active selling, on time delivery, achieving shelf space, and effective merchandising, is often poorly executed in a high percentage of outlets. The understanding of the levers, which create retail execution success, is lacking, and often glossed over; just what are those levers?

- ☐ Account planning
- ☐ Effective well planned out sales calls
- ☐ Shelf space
- ☐ Store presence and merchandising
- ☐ Monitoring
- ☐ Price harmony

What has been shown time and again is that these are the areas, which are critical to control and own by the Company. Thus the following principle can be followed in most cases:

> *Sales, pricing, and merchandising belongs to the Company, and the distributor executes logistics.*

Control is paramount. Monitoring programs and distributor emphasis at the *outlet level* creates the right focus. The Company wants to be in a position to dictate sales routes, pricing, and executional principles. Where possible the distributor should be exclusive. If not feasible, a separate sales room just for the Company should be set up, to create the right focus and control.

Fourthly, Organize by Channel

The old and perhaps traditional way of going to market is to organize around a sales manager or director, handling all customers and market units. This tends to be the sales warlord, managing his territory, customers and sales force with an iron grip. While workable in the less sophisticated China of the 20th century, it is certainly outmoded in today's environment. The market has complexified and demands greater specialization. Sales resources are best organized around channels. In the consumer markets, the channels are usually classified as 1) Modern or organized trade, 2) On Premise consumption, 3) Traditional trade, and 4) Specialty channels.

Channel development has indeed mushroomed in the last decade, and some degree of specialization is creeping up. The implications on how to go to market are fundamental. Using the traditional sales manager concept for all channels neglects the specific needs of the channel. Ultimately, the sales manager spends valuable time bogged down in negotiating terms with modern trade customers, and neglecting the traditional channels, which may in fact provide higher a sales and profit mix.

The solution becomes obvious. Sales and distribution efforts need to be organized by channel, in order to capture and lead the initiatives with the customer. This installing means **channel managers**, who are responsible for profitability at the customer level, and have decision making ability around trade marketing, distribution, margin, pricing, packaging, terms etc... for his or her respective channel. In fact, sub-channel managers, and even key account managers, are becoming a necessity in many consumer companies.

Unlike European or American markets, where organized trade dominates the business environment, China still retains a healthy channel balance. Intelligent companies are therefore able to balance pricing, promotion and packaging programs across channels. In this way, one channel is not given an unfair advantage in development over another.

In fact, a degree of balance is essential to the rational development of the channel, and consumer companies need to keep this in mind as they develop customers.

Fifthly, Focus on Execution

If a well-conceived distribution strategy is an imperative to success in China, execution is the key to bringing home the results. Execution is where the best of intentions fall through the cracks. Why? It's a day to day, account by account, city by city struggle. Unfortunately, it is the toughest battle of all.

The first key to execution is focus on the customer; not on the distributor, nor on the wholesaler, but on the outlet which comes face to face with the consumer... the customer. This implies that programs need to be targeted primarily to customers, as opposed to distributors.

Here **trade or customer marketing** is a core imperative. Many organizations question the value or need of trade marketing. In the past, it was a luxury; today it is a necessity. Trade marketing creates the customer, promotion and merchandising programs, which will provide presence and sell through of the product. Trade marketing shepherds the standards by which products are displayed and priced.

Trade marketing not only becomes critical in organized trade, where secondary display and merchandising drive sales; it is also a bonus for traditional trade in creating the competitive advantage and market leadership.

Given the challenge to achieve superior, or even decent execution, customer programs, which focus on the right priorities, are essential. Communication is the first task. Sales force and customers need to understand how products are to be displayed, priced and promoted. Sales communication vehicles such as selling sheets, merchandising guidelines, and promotion mechanics, communicate **the right way** to execute to both the channel, and the sales force. Frequent Sales force briefings and training on execution of programs are essential to making it happen. An effective solution is to set up a trade room in the sales office, with model store displays, highlighting the right way to market.

Merchandising contests and loyalty programs are also a successful way to ensure effective execution of distribution objectives. Give the trade and front line sales organization simple display contests, and watch them compete for excellence. These programs really work, and encourage greater customer goodwill along the way.

What gets measured gets done. Therefore, the next leg in the execution journey is to create an efficient way to **track and monitor** results. The following examples illustrate this need:

□ The old-line sales manager corrals his sales people every morning, imploring them to greater results. "Sell, Sell Sell! Go out to the market, and I don't want to see you back here until you have made your numbers! Use whatever it takes, give them a discount, better credit, load them; just get the order!"

□ Conversely, the data driven channel manager meets on specified days, reviews results with sales people around key dimensions, brainstorms with his reps on how to exceed targets, and provides very clear parameters on the use of credit, price, promotion etc.... Furthermore he goes out with his sales people on scheduled calls, engaging on the job coaching.

The data driven channel manager's key advantage is data. The sales force is required to input simple but essential results, so that everyone knows sales vs. targets. It is posted in the sales offices for all to see.

The sales force is organized by routes and customers. Quality, speed and success are all clearly measured and reported. Tracking and monitoring is part and parcel of superior execution. They are the mundane, yet core weapons to surpass the competitor.

Sixthly, Focus on Pricing

Using price as a tool will facilitate long-term market share gains in China. Conversely, the misuse of price can destroy a market, and wreak havoc on profitability.

Much can be written about this much-misunderstood topic; here the focus is on the channel, or customer piece. Once you have found the optimal price point in the market, the key is to stick to a price strategy. In that way channel programs can be created which are not sabotaged by irrational price activity. In other words, pricing across channels needs to be carefully balanced.

This is no easy task given the different terms and conditions across channels. Organized or Modern trade, particularly hypermarkets, uses price promotion as a draw for customers; sometimes in the form of "everyday low price"; other times as periodic promotional offers. That is fine to attract consumers and reap large sales, as long as it doesn't impact other channels. The problem occurs when the promotion price of the hypermarket dives below the wholesales price level. **Transshipment**, or shipment across territories, sets in, and very rapidly, the hypermarket or club store becomes the wholesaler! In fact, in Europe and US, this phenomenon translates to an inordinate percentage of sales through club stores and value marts, driving profit down to the lower level. In China, fortunately there is still hope... as long as manufacturers keep the pricing discipline. The basic rule of thumb is that the price to organized trade, including all discounts and trading terms, should not drop below your wholesale price.

Enforcing pricing discipline is no easy task. The sales force always needs to push sales. Price is the easiest mechanism to make that happen, yet the most detrimental to profit and an orderly marketplace. A few obvious, but executionally challenging principles are paramount:

- ☐ No month end loading of product.
- ☐ Keep cash discounts modest.
- ☐ Manage credit terms tightly.
- ☐ Keep year-end rebates small.
- ☐ Price promotions and discounts should be within a tight range, and short in duration.
- ☐ Organized trade price should not drop below wholesale price.

Finally, using price incentives is the worst way to motivate wholesalers and distributors. Rather, distributors should be motivated through the development of new and existing customers in their assigned territory and rewarded commensurately. Keeping the price equal and consistent among distributors will ensure supply continuity, market harmony, and discourage transshipment across territories.

Seventhly, Charge up the Sales Team!

The ability to motivate and energize sales teams in China is one of the more satisfying aspects of working in this dynamic market. It's easy to charge up and energize sales teams, and move them along the march to share gains. The other side of the coin is also true. A poor motivation and compensation program is a recipe for employee turnover, and dissention amongst the ranks. A few concepts really work to create the desired energy and focus:

- ☐ Create **friendly competition** across teams – sales teams have a strong pride in their unit, and want to win. Creating friendly competition energizes them to success.

- ☐ **Reward individuals and groups** – as strong as the team spirit might be, the individual desire for success and recognition is also present. There should be ample programs and recognition for individual excellence, which are aspirational in nature.

☐ **Everyone can be a winner!** – Modest rewards for hitting targets is a good way to galvanize all individuals, who know they aren't the best, but are good enough to be recognized.

☐ **The "big" winner** – Prizes, such as overseas trips, are effective aspirational tools to drive the team and individuals.

☐ **Communicate successes widely** – Giving great face is an essential motivator, sometimes even more than cash.

The power of effective recognition and motivational programs cannot be underestimated. Unlike other more developed countries, sales teams in China are not yet jaded by flat performance and saturated markets.

It is essential to break up sales recognition programs into various programs:

☐ **Annual programs** are effective for overall winners of teams, market units and individuals.

☐ Sales incentives work to create focus on the agenda at hand, when launching new products or promotions. **Seasonal programs** such as rewards in the peak sales period are an excellent way to focus on boosting volume at critical times of the year.

Finally, a major stumbling block for many organizations is the dilemma of "percentage of pay at risk." In other words, what should be the fixed and incentive component in sales force pay? There is no standard solution; rather, the approach should be designed around the market, industry and objective. The rule of thumb here is that the fixed pay should be competitive in the industry and allow the sales person to cover his basic living expenses.

Fifty percent of pay at risk is the upper limit in consumer companies; on the other hand, going below twenty percent leaves little room for the employee to score big. Whatever the case, targets need to be administered fairly, and commensurate with market conditions. Making the sales force pay for poor pricing decisions or transshipment issues is surefire way to create turnover in the organization.

Putting It All Together

There are many "go to market" models in China. Clarity around your model, and sticking with it, is paramount. Focus on the right geographic markets and channels to create the roadmap for success. And speaking of success, one needs beachheads, which provide market power, a breeding ground for new ideas, the nurturing of human resource excellence, and a springboard to new markets. Phase in the distribution strategy with discipline.

"The customer is king" is nowhere more true than in China. Therefore, developing direct relationships with customers is essential to the strategy. Third party distribution should be used more for logistic purposes, than for selling. Remember that the direct selling relationship is what the Company should own. Furthermore, customers vary across channels, so vary the organization and approach according to the channel. Similarly, pricing discipline across channels is an imperative to orderly market development. Finally, the sales team is the major controllable asset. Use it wisely and motivate it to fit organizational objectives.

Distribution is the strategic priority to achieving effective market development in China. Make your products available in a focused, orderly and intelligent manner, and you are sure to enjoy success.

PART II

INVESTMENTS AND PROTECTIONS

Investing in China involves selecting the appropriate structure which will fulfill investment horizons and serve operational functions suitable to the business one is engaging in. Finding the right structure however, is only the first stage as an elaborate and often complicated approval process is involved, requiring investors to learn the intricacies of China's government administrative structure. In addition requisite protections for intellectual property and technology transfer have assumed greater importance as China's investment atmosphere undergoes a clear shift toward brand images and high technology production. Preparing for disputes before they happen is also advised with the correct contract language to assure protections in the event that problems arise.

Chapter 5

Making An Investment

By Sara Yang Bosco, Partner, Perkins Coie LLP - Hong Kong
and Paul McKenzie, Partner, Perkins Coie LLP - Hong Kong

Joining the Trading Club

China's entry to the WTO represents a fundamental shift in Chinese policy, a qualitative change of a magnitude not seen since China first decided to open its doors to foreign direct investment in the late 1970s. By joining the "international trading club" as it is often called, China agreed to eliminate long-standing dual pricing practices and to provide the same treatment to foreign companies and foreign-funded enterprises in China that it accords domestic firms.

Accession to the WTO by any nation is premised upon two basic principles: non-discrimination and national treatment. These principles are reflected in three core agreements:

☐ the General Agreement on Tariffs and Trade (GATT), covering goods;

- [ ] the General Agreement on Trade in Services (GATS); and
- [ ] the Trade-Related Aspects of Intellectual Property Rights (TRIPS).

A plethora of new legislation is emerging as China attempts to meet its bold, new commitments. Revisions to the laws and regulations related to trade, technology transfer, banking, insurance, securities, intellectual property, telecommunications and professional services have been promulgated as of this printing, with more new and revised legislation expected in the near to medium term.

Choosing a Corporate Form

While China's accession to the WTO has opened up some business sectors previously off limits to foreigners (*see box*), the choice of business structures available to foreign investors under Chinese law remains largely unchanged.

Representative Offices

Setting up a representative office is often the first step in establishing a presence in China. A representative office is essentially a liaison office without the status of an independent legal person. It may not conduct business in its own name; instead, the offshore parent must sign all contracts. Nevertheless, a representative office may introduce and promote products, conduct market research and engage in technical exchanges. Local employees must be hired through an authorized employment agency, while senior foreign representatives are permitted for an initial stay of three years.

Representative offices are relatively inexpensive and easy to open or

Services Sector Opened

Various industries within the services sector will be opened to foreign investment, though phase-in periods, equity limitations and geographic restrictions may apply.

Foreign suppliers of basic and value-added telecommunications services may invest in equity joint ventures. Permitted foreign ownership increases to 49% for basic services and 50% for value-added services and geographic restrictions are eliminated in phases over the first six years after accession. Nevertheless, entry barriers in the form of registered capital requirements are steep for basic services and the approval process may be lengthy.

Foreign banks may provide local currency services after two years. Within five years of accession, foreign banks may offer a full range of services to all Chinese customers.

Likewise, insurance providers are allowed to operate in China, first in joint ventures and then as wholly foreign-owned subsidiaries. Equity limitations on non-life insurers are removed after two years, while life insurers must wait until five years after accession. Capital requirements are high and licensing requirements involve a three-step process that could be drawn out in excess of eight months.

close. The most common sites for the establishment of representative offices are Beijing, given its proximity to both the central government and the head offices of the major state-owned enterprises, and Shanghai, as the emerging commercial center of Greater China.

Equity Joint Ventures

An equity joint venture is an independent legal person with limited liability established for a fixed term (usually 15-50 years). Prior to China's WTO accession, an equity joint venture was permitted to sell only the products it had manufactured itself. This will change as the distribution sector gradually opens to foreign investment over the next few years (*see box*).

Distribution and Trading Rights Extended

One year after accession, minority foreign-owned joint ventures are permitted to distribute most types of locally manufactured and imported products. Within three years, joint ventures and wholly foreign-owned enterprises may engage in retailing, wholesaling, franchising, warehousing, packaging and leasing activities in China with respect to nearly all products, although the phase-in periods are longer for certain products.

Most existing foreign invested enterprises (FIEs) in China will need to amend their scope of business to include these new rights, a process that requires government approval. Hence, China may still exercise a certain amount of control over which foreign companies are permitted to take full advantage of the new rules.

Both investor liability and equity ratios are based strictly on the value of the contributions made by the foreign and Chinese partners. Contributions may include cash, equipment, land use rights and technology or trademark licenses. The foreign partner must provide no less than 25% of the registered capital of the venture.

The operation of an equity joint venture is based on a two-tiered management system comprised at the highest level by the board of directors. Board representation also strictly reflects the value of the capital contributions of each partner. The management team, responsible for the day-to-day operation of the venture, normally includes a general manager, a deputy general manager, a financial controller, and production and sales managers. Senior foreign employees are permitted entry for an initial stay of three years.

As Chinese currency, the *Renminbi,* is neither fully convertible nor remittable outside of China, foreign exchange is required to purchase imported supplies and equipment, remunerate expatriate employees and remit profits. Necessary foreign currency may be obtained through export receipts, loans and other infusions of additional capital. In addition, as local currency is partially convertible for current account items, foreign currency may be acquired in China to pay for imported goods, profit remittances to foreign investors and royalties.

Accounting for equity joint ventures is based on the accrual method. Official records must be maintained in Chinese and audited by registered accountants. Tax incentives and holidays may be available for favored investments in preferred locations, though it is expected that most tax preferences for foreign-funded enterprises will eventually be eliminated in post-WTO China (*see box*).

Tax Preferences for FIEs

Foreign-funded companies in China have traditionally enjoyed preferential tax treatment. For example, while the income of domestic firms is subject to a 33% tax rate, many FIEs pay at a 15% or 24% rate and are eligible for tax holidays.

There has been a good deal of debate within the Chinese government concerning the elimination of tax preferences for FIEs in the wake of WTO accession. The most recent indications are that China will largely maintain the existing system for a period of years.

At some point, however, China is expected to institute a unified tax regime, applicable to both domestic and foreign businesses. One proposal is to replace the current national and local income taxes with a single income tax levied at a 25% rate.

The advantages of choosing an equity joint venture are often thought to lie primarily with the local partner's "*guanxi*", for instance, its ability to promote distribution and sales through a web of personal contacts or to obtain favorable treatment through personal contacts with government agencies. The disadvantages of this form may appear in the conflicting management styles and, in some cases, the business goals of the parties. There has been a marked shift from joint ventures to wholly foreign-owned subsidiaries over the past five years.

Cooperative Joint Ventures

Two types of cooperative joint ventures are available to foreign investors, both of which offer more flexibility than the equity joint venture form. In the first, a new legal person is established with limited liability. In the second, a new legal entity is not created and each partner remains independently responsible for accounts and liable to third parties. In either case, shareholding ratios, profit distributions and liabilities for the business are determined by contract. The foreign partner still may not contribute less than 25% of the investment, but may recover its investment at an accelerated pace with the agreement of the partners. Likewise, board representation and management structures are determined by contract.

Otherwise, cooperative joint ventures operate under rules similar to those that apply to equity joint ventures. In addition to greater flexibility in structuring the relationship between the partners, the primary advantage in choosing a cooperative joint venture lies in the early recovery of capital invested by the foreign partner. Hence, this corporate structure is often used for large, fixed asset projects involving the development of real estate or infrastructure.

Wholly Foreign-Owned Enterprises

A wholly foreign-owned enterprise (WFOE) is a 100% foreign invested legal entity, normally with limited liability and a fixed term of 10 to 30 years. While the legal rules and requirements for WFOEs are broadly similar to those for joint ventures, operation and management, foreign exchange, accounting and tax are more effectively under the control of the foreign owner. In post-WTO China, the right to establish a WFOE is no longer conditioned upon a demonstrable benefit to China's development and WFOEs no longer have to engage in production or export the majority of their products. Furthermore, the industrial sectors in which WFOEs are permitted will increase considerably over the next few years. Thus, the WTO reforms should promote the existing trend away from joint ventures.

Holding Companies

A holding company, literally an investment company, may be established as either an equity joint venture or a WFOE. Intended as a vehicle for major foreign multinationals to increase investment, consolidate holdings in China, and achieve management efficiencies, the minimum thresholds for capitalization and total assets are steep. The foreign parent must either have assets in excess of US$ 400 million, as well as three or more investments in China with a total of US $10 million in registered capital, or have ten or more investments in China with an aggregate registered capital of US $30 million. The registered capital requirement for holding companies is US $30 million, not including the equity value of pre-existing investments. Though not subject to double taxation on subsidiary income and dividends, holding companies are also not eligible for tax incentives and holidays.

Choice of Business Structure

With the expansion of trading and distribution rights, certain business forms, though still available as investment vehicles, may become less attractive to foreign investors. Representative offices, in particular, may become redundant, as an FIE with trading rights may achieve more of the goals of a foreign company selling into the Chinese market.

Likewise, bonded zone enterprises may lose their present appeal as distribution vehicles for sales inside China. An entity with trading rights established in China proper is almost certainly more useful than an entity operating outside of Chinese customs territory. Bonded zones still may be useful in providing offshore storage to defer the payment of customs duties, as well as for export processing and entrepot trading.

Additional Operating Vehicles

Processing and Assembly Operations

In a processing or assembly operation the foreign company ships raw materials or semi-processed goods to a Chinese factory for production or assembly and re-export. Agreements for processing and assembly usually include the provision of equipment and/or technology and detail ports and means of shipment, as well as permissible wastage rates. Incentives include tax holidays and waiver of import licensing requirements, taxes and customs clearance. Customs registration is required within 30 days of establishment.

Bonded Zone Enterprises

Bonded zones are established in most major port cities to facilitate import and export trade. Services permitted within the zones include marketing and exhibition, trading, warehousing, trade financing, packaging, transportation, and processing and assembly operations. Technical services and research and development may be provided to affiliates outside of the zone. Customs clearance and duties do not apply within the zones.

Foreign Invested Joint Stock Limited Companies

A foreign invested joint stock limited company (FISC) is a limited liability investment vehicle that resembles Western notions of a share-issuing corporation and enables a foreign investor in China to purchase shares rather than assets. Foreign purchasers must pay in cash for shares of listed joint stock companies, while shares of an unlisted joint stock company may be acquired by contributing equipment, proprietary technology, or land-use rights at an appraised value.

An existing FIE may be reorganized as a FISC after three years of profitability. A domestic joint stock company may be reorganized as a FISC after five years, and three consecutive profitable years, if the shares held by the foreign investor represent at least 25% of the registered capital of the company. The reorganization may be accomplished either by the private placement of shares or by listing special *Renminbi*-denominated shares (B shares) on an appropriate Chinese exchange. MOFTEC approval is required for the establishment of a new FISC, the reorganization of an existing FIE into a FISC, and the listing of A or B shares by a FISC.

Chapter 6

Investment Approvals

By Sara Yang Bosco, Partner, Perkins Coie LLP - Hong Kong
and Paul McKenzie, Partner, Perkins Coie LLP - Hong Kong

Documents and Procedures
for Approval

Once a decision is reached on the appropriate legal form for a business in China, foreign investors face what can be a rather lengthy approval process. Obtaining approvals in China often depends to a great extent on personal relations. "*Guanxi*", or one's network of personal contacts, is an important part of Chinese culture and almost certainly will remain a crucial aspect of doing business in China, irrespective of the legislative changes mandated by PRC accession to the WTO.

The details of the approval process vary depending on the type of entity, but the process generally involves two major steps: approval by one or more government agencies that may include the industry regulator and the foreign investment authority, and registration of the entity with the administration for industry and commerce.

Representative Offices

Various documents are submitted, via a local sponsor, to the local government foreign investment department, including an application signed by the head of the foreign entity, the certification of incorporation or similar legal document certifying the existence of the foreign entity in its home country, proof of credit worthiness issued by a foreign bank, and the credentials of the main representatives. The approval authority will issue an approval certificate that normally is valid for three years, and may be renewed.

Following approval, the representative office is registered with the State Administration for Industry and Commerce (SAIC) at the local level. The SAIC issues a registration certificate, which must be renewed annually. The representative office also has to register with the public security bureau (PSB) and the tax authorities, customs authorities, foreign exchange authorities and several other government agencies, as well as open a bank account.

Foreign Invested Enterprises (FIEs)

The documentation and approval processes required of equity joint ventures, cooperative joint ventures and WFOEs are largely similar. The legal documents include the letter of intent, project proposal, feasibility study, joint venture contract and articles of association. In general, the approval authorities include the State Economic and Trade Commission (SETC) and the State Development Planning Commission (SDPC), which are responsible for approving the project proposal and feasibility study; and the Ministry of Foreign Trade and Economic

MOFTEC Connected

MOFTEC set up three departments related to China's accession to the WTO that interested parties may contact for further information:

☐ **Department of WTO Affairs (86-10-6519-7340)**
☐ **China-WTO Notification Inquiry Center (86-10-6519-7340)**
☐ **Fair Trade Bureau for Import and Export (86-10-6519-8170)**

Information is also available on MOFTEC's web site at HYPERLINK <http://www.moftec.gov.cn>.

Cooperation (MOFTEC), which is responsible for approving the joint venture contract and articles of association. The SAIC handles the enterprise registration of FIEs.

In some cases, approval may be required directly from these central government agencies, while in many cases approval from the subordinate local or provincial departments of each is sufficient. The approval level is determined mainly by the amount of the investment: local up to US$ 10 million; provincial between US$ 10 million and US$ 30 million; and central between US$ 30 million and US$ 100 million. Projects in excess of US$ 100 million require approval by the State Council. While these are the basic rules, a number of other factors may affect the required level of approval, such as the industrial sector, the geographic location or the identity of the Chinese partner.

Neither the letter of intent nor the project proposal is a legally binding agreement, but as both documents tend to set the framework for future negotiations, foreign investors should not view them as unimportant. The Chinese partner (or an authorized agent, on behalf of a WFOE) is required to submit both documents for preliminary approval of the project.

The feasibility study is prepared and submitted jointly by the parties (or by the foreign investor alone on behalf of a WFOE). It sets forth the basic economic and technical assumptions of the proposed business and, where state-owned assets form part of the investment, includes an asset evaluation conducted by an approved accounting firm and certified by a local branch of the State Asset Evaluation Bureau.

The joint venture contract and the articles of association are negotiated and signed by the parties and then submitted to MOFTEC (or its subordinate local department as applicable). Accompanying documents include proof of the legal status of the foreign entity, a list of directors on the board, the resumes of the directors and the general manager, letters recommending and appointing the chairman of the board and the general manager, proof of credit worthiness, a list of equipment to be imported and any subsidiary contracts requiring approval, such as a technology licensing agreement. Upon approval by MOFTEC or its subordinate, an approval certificate is issued.

The final step in establishing the joint venture or WFOE is to apply for enterprise registration with the SAIC at the appropriate level and obtain a business license. After establishment, an FIE must register with the PSB, tax authorities, customs authorities, foreign exchange authorities and other government agencies, open bank accounts and conclude labor contracts with its employees.

Chapter 7

Protecting Interests

By Jon Eichelberger, Partner, Perkins Coie LLP - Beijing
and Lim Mei Yin, Of Counsel, Perkins Coie LLP - Hong Kong

International Rules

In the years to come, one concrete measure of China's adherence to its commitments under the WTO will be found in its willingness to protect the interests of foreign investors. In the past, China has tended to favor local business through its reluctance to enforce the intellectual property rights (IPR) of foreign firms or to resolve disputes and implement rulings against the interests of local companies. Over time, however, the combined impact of two new and emerging factors may level the playing field in China.

First, China must now accept the primacy of WTO rules and incorporate those rules into domestic legislation and policies. By joining the WTO, China acknowledged that the core principles of non-discrimination and national treatment apply not only to its regulatory framework for foreign investment, but also to the protection of foreign investors in areas such as IPR, technology transfer and dispute resolution. Like all WTO members, China must respect the rules of the multilateral system if it intends to reap the advantages of membership, even if that entails protecting foreign property rights or enforcing actions against domestic companies.

Second, and more significantly, the pressure exerted by local business to develop a transparent, uniform and impartial legal system to protect its own interests may prove the most compelling means of bringing about the changes mandated by the WTO. As local firms demand concrete improvements in the responsiveness of administrative authorities, courts and arbitration tribunals to enforce their own property rights, China should develop a rules-based legal environment of benefit to both domestic and foreign investors.

WTO Dispute Resolution Mechanism

The WTO system for resolving disputes among member countries represents a significant advance over the uncertain and fragmented GATT system. The old system required a consensus to establish a panel or adopt a decision, allowed one party to block remedial action and effectively operated under several different sets of rules.

The new system empowers a single authority, the Dispute Settlement Body (DSB), to establish a panel and adopt decisions. DSB panel rulings must be implemented within a reasonable time, absent a consensus to the contrary. In addition, the Appellate Body, a quasi-permanent tribunal broadly representative of WTO membership, has the authority to uphold, reverse or modify panel decisions.

Despite the increased certainty provided by the WTO system, however, it must be remembered that no private right of action exists. An offended entity must lobby its own member government to take action in the WTO forum on its behalf.

Chinese Judicial System

The Chinese court system now handles over 5 million cases each year. The legal profession, resurrected after the Cultural Revolution, claims upwards of 120,000 practitioners. The Supreme People's Court, which sits atop three tiers of lower courts, the lower level, intermediate level and higher level People's Courts, is educating the lower courts on the consequences of China's WTO membership, and its leaders acknowledge the primacy of WTO rules over domestic legislation.

Corruption, however, remains a serious issue in China. Judges are appointed, promoted, compensated and removed by the local party and government elites and local protectionism remains strong. Foreign parties to a dispute cannot completely escape these deficiencies in the PRC court system by adopting arbitration, because enforcement of arbitration awards requires the assistance of the local court where the defendant or the available assets are located.

The lower level People's Court generally has jurisdiction to hear civil cases in the first instance. However, most cases involving foreigners are heard by the Intermediate People's Court as the court of first instance.

Arbitration

Traditionally, public conflict, such as litigation, was culturally taboo in China, but the situation is changing gradually with economic development and wider availability courts. Nonetheless, arbitration is often a preferred form of dispute resolution in the business world and is the standard for disputes involving foreign businesses. Arbitration clauses normally require the parties to attempt an amicable settlement before moving to formal arbitration.

If an amicable settlement is not achieved, forums available to hear arbitration claims include CIETAC, domestic arbitration bodies set up in China's major cities and, if there are foreign-related elements in the dispute, international arbitration (most often institutional rather than ad hoc). The parties are free to negotiate the scope of issues to be decided by arbitration, including the forum designated to hear the dispute, the appointment of arbitrators, the issues to be heard and the public or private nature of the hearings.

Arbitration panels under CIETAC are comprised of three arbitrators, unless the parties agree on only one. Where there are three arbitrators, each party nominates a single arbitrator and the two arbitrators then jointly select the third member of the panel, or the third member may be selected by CIETAC. Arbitrators with a personal or familial interest in the case or who meet privately with or accept gifts from a party or lawyer involved the case may be disqualified. Foreign lawyers are permitted to appear on behalf of clients in Chinese arbitrations.

An arbitration panel may gather and examine its own evidence and evidence may be preserved upon application to the People's Courts. Failure to file an available defense or counter-claim does not constitute a waiver of the right or claim. Arbitration awards are final and binding, but actions to enforce an award must be filed in the People's Courts.

Chapter 8

Intellectual Property Protection

By Jon Eichelberger, Partner, Perkins Coie LLP - Beijing
and Lim Mei Yin, Of Counsel, Perkins Coie LLP - Hong Kong

Trademarks

The PRC first established a regulatory framework covering trademarks in the mid-1980s. It also joined the Paris Convention, pledging to grant to foreign nationals of other convention member countries the same rights and protections against trademark infringement accorded to Chinese nationals. While some revisions were made in the 1990s, it was only in late 2001 that China revised the Trademark Law to bring it more closely in line with the Trade-Related Aspects of International Property Rights (TRIPS), the core WTO agreement regarding IPR.

The administrative authority responsible for the regulation and control of trademarks is the Trademark Office (TMO), under the supervision of the State Administration of Industry and Commerce (SAIC). The local bureaus for the administration of industry and commerce (AICs) are empowered to halt infringement and deal with day-to-day issues. The *Trademark Review* and Adjudication Board handles most appeals concerning registration matters, while the People's Courts hear appeals involving infringement issues decided by local AIC officials.

To qualify for registration, a trademark must possess qualities sufficiently distinctive to render it easily distinguishable from other marks. Trademarks may contain combinations of words, numerals, devices, colors and, in a new addition, three-dimensional images, but may not use government names or symbols. Categories of trademarks include marks for goods, service marks, collective marks and certification marks. Well-known trademarks of registrants from other WTO member countries may also be eligible for protection in China, given sufficient public recognition and a demonstrable record of protection by the registrant.

The exclusive right to use a trademark commences upon registration of a formal application with the TMO and public notice in the *China Trademark Gazette*. Oppositions must be filed within three months of the public notice. Registered trademarks are valid for a renewable term of ten years. However, the registration of one form of mark does not protect other forms. Moreover, the form of the mark that is used must be identical to the form of the mark that is registered. Hence, a prudent defense involves registering the mark in roman, pinyin, simplified and traditional characters, as well as in each of the relevant stylized or combination forms.

Trademarks may be licensed by contract and the license contract must be submitted to the TMO for recordal. Recordal also should be carried out with the relevant AIC(s) in both the licensors and the licensees locality. Applications to assign a trademark must be submitted to the TMO by both parties, though the formalities tend to be carried out by the assignee. Simultaneous assignment is required of all identical or similar marks covering all identical or similar goods. An individual application is required for the assignment of each mark. An assignment may be rejected if the assignment causes mistaken recognition or confusion in the marketplace.

Infringing acts include the use of identical or similar trademarks on identical or similar goods, counterfeiting, making or selling representations of a registered mark, selling or distributing goods known to bear an infringing mark, or intentionally facilitating infringement. In line with TRIPS, a trademark owner now has the right to apply to the People's Courts for preliminary orders when its rights are infringed, such as injunctions to cease unlawful activity.

In developing a Chinese character trademark, a foreign investor must be conscious of both marketing and translation issues. The mark must effectively convey its meaning across the many dialects and regions of Greater China. Homonyms are common in Chinese and this easily leads to confusion or to unintended and unflattering meanings. It can be extremely costly to change a market identity or nickname once it has taken hold among the public, so great care should be taken when initially selecting a Chinese mark. The preferred method is to recreate the basic sounds and/or the meaning of the original mark with Chinese characters, then crosscheck the new mark with native speakers of the major dialects.

Copyright

The first law on copyright in China originated in the imperial days of the Qing Dynasty. The PRC abolished this law soon after the Revolution, but only enacted new copyright legislation in the early 1990s, but revisions to the existing implementing regulations have not been promulgated as of this printing. China amended the current Copyright Law to

conform to the TRIPS agreement in 2001. The administrative authority in charge of copyright matters is the National Copyright Administration (NCA), under the State Press and Publications Bureau.

Under the Copyright Law, ownership of both published and unpub-
lished work generally belongs to the author, i.e., the person who created the work. Exceptions occur where ownership by the author is pro-
scribed by law or where the work is created in the course of one's
employment, in which case the employer is deemed to be the author.

There are also separate regulations that specifically address the protection of copyright in computer software. The new computer software
regulations were promulgated in December 2001 ("Software
Regulations") and replaced existing regulations on the same subject.
Under the new Software Regulations, registration of software copyright is now voluntary. In addition, the term of protection for software
is now fifty years after the death of the author (if the author is a natural
person) or fifty years from development (where the author is a legal
person).

Copyright may be assigned by a written agreement that identifies the
rights to be assigned and the territory and term of the assignment, as
well as the amount, time and method of remuneration. Copyright may
be licensed pursuant to a contract containing similar terms, which also
specifies whether the license is exclusive or non-exclusive. Moral rights,
often referred to as authors rights, may not be assigned or licensed.

Copyright authorities may order cessation of an infringing act, confiscate illegal income, seize and destroy infringing copies, and impose
fines where the infringement harms the public interest. If the conditions are deemed serious, the authorities also may seize the materials
and tools used to commit an infringing act.

Those who publish, produce or rent infringing software works are liable to the copyright owner unless they can prove their acts were innocent. Holders of infringing software are prohibited from continuing to use pirated copies without permission from the copyright owner, but they need not pay compensation if they were unaware of the infringement.

In addition to traditional remedies such as damages, judicial remedies in the post-WTO era include preliminary orders to cease infringement, preserve evidence and confiscate goods. When actual damages are difficult to prove, statutory damages are capped at RMB 500,000.

Patents

Patent rights were not recognized in China until the Patent Law was promulgated in 1985 to protect inventions and creations, i.e., utility models and designs. The Patent Law was revised in 1993. China is also a member of the Paris Convention and the Patent Cooperation Treaty. The latter agreement provides a multilateral filing system for member countries and requires China to process applications filed by applicants from member states.

Administrative authority rests with the Patent Office, under the State Intellectual Property Office (SIPO). Patent rights are not enforceable in China unless registered and approved by the Patent Office. Individual applications are required for each patent.

Assignment of patent rights to foreigners requires approval from the Patent Office. In addition, the regulatory procedures for technology exports need to be observed. Hence, approval of the assignment by the Ministry of Foreign Trade and Economic Cooperation (MOFTEC) is required if export of the patented technology is restricted. Assignment to a domestic assignee, however, including assignment to a foreign invested enterprise (FIE) in China, is not considered a technology export and approval is not required.

Domain Names

China's first laws governing the administration of domain names on the Internet, as well as the implementing rules, were issued in 1997. The China Internet Network Information Center (CNNIC), under the Ministry of Information Industry (MII), is the sole recognized authority in China for registering Chinese language domain names.

CNNIC registers both domain names in the Latin alphabet with the .cn suffix, denoting China, and domain names in Chinese characters with *zhongguo* (China), *gongsi* (company) or *wangluo* (network). No distinction is made at CNNIC between simplified and traditional characters in domain names.

Potential conflict with the international community exists because the Internet Corporation for Assigned Names and Numbers (ICANN) is recognized as the international authority for the registration of domain names. ICANN has authorized various registrars to handle domain name registrations, including Chinese language domain names. For example, one accredited registrar, Network Solutions Inc. (NSI) registers Chinese character domain names with the .com and .net suffixes and maintains separate lists for simplified and traditional Chinese characters.

Remedies against cyber-squatting and bad faith registrations include civil actions for damages in the People's Courts. Applications also may be submitted for arbitration by the China International Economic and Trade Commission (CIETAC), China's chief international arbitral institution. In 2001, CNNIC promulgated rules governing the resolution of disputes involving Chinese language domain names and conferred authority on CIETAC to hear such disputes.

Technology Transfer

All imports and exports of technology are subject to regulation by MOFTEC based on a new, post-WTO regulatory framework that took effect on January 1, 2002. The regulation applies to all cross-border technology transfers, including the assignment of patent rights and patent application rights, the licensing of patents and technical secrets (which are defined in China to include not only unpatented technology such as know-how, but also computer software), and the provision of technical services.

Technology imports are classified as prohibited, restricted or unrestricted. Imports of restricted technologies are subject to a licensing system, while unrestricted technologies are subject to a contract registration system. A parallel system applies to technology exports. The government has published catalogues for the various categories of technology imports and exports, also effective on January 1, 2002.

A technology transfer must be based on a written contract. Licensors of imported technology may not require PRC licensees to buy unnecessary materials, equipment or services or to pay royalties after the expiration of a patent; may not restrict a PRC licensee from making improvements, using technology from other suppliers, or purchasing materials, parts and equipment from other suppliers; and may not limit a PRC licensees production volume, pricing or export channels.

Income taxes on royalties paid to foreign licensors are withheld and paid by the licensee at a base rate of 20%. In most cases, however, the actual tax rate is 10% due to tax treaties or special rules for transfers involving encouraged technologies or geographic regions.

PART III

FINANCIAL MANAGEMENT

Undertaking financial due diligence before making an investment in China is a laborious and delicate task to assure that assets are in order and liabilities are not beyond one's wildest expectations. That finished, investors often discover that after approving a project and establishing a new entity in China, the hard work is not over, it has only begun. In fact, managing a business in China is often more difficult than making the investment. Careful consideration of an imbroglio of corporate and individual taxation issues involve complex considerations which can test the accounting skills of even the best financial controller. Customs procedures and duties often carry a host of surprises as well. Strong preparation and knowledge of the rules is a prerequisite.

Chapter 9

Corporate Taxation

By Dawn Foo, Partner, Price Waterhouse Coopers

An Even Playing Field Post-WTO

In the past, the income tax laws that foreign investment enterprises have been subject to in China were different from those applied to domestic enterprises. On balance, the set of laws applicable to foreign investment enterprises has been more favourable (to the foreign taxpayer) as it contains a greater number of incentives including a lower rate.

These incentives stem from the aim of the government to attract foreign investment into the country. However, with the accession of the country into the World Trade Organization as well as increasing pressure from domestic enterprises to be accorded equal treatment, a decision has been made to unify the two sets of laws.

Drafting of the new law was completed in 2001. This draft law is subject to the approval of the National People's Congress, which should take place this year. As implementation of the new code is not expected till 2003, the discussion that follows is based on current laws.

Income Tax Law

The Income Tax Law of the People's Republic of China for Enterprises with Foreign Investment and Foreign Enterprises (the Income Tax Law) came into effect on July 1, 1991 and applies to foreign investment enterprises (i.e., equity joint ventures, contractual joint ventures, and wholly foreign-owned enterprises) and foreign companies. In the absence of special circumstances, these two categories of companies are taxed at a flat rate of 33% (30% national and 3% local).

For foreign investment enterprises, tax is based on worldwide income. While the branch of a foreign enterprise is not taxed based on worldwide income, the basis of its computation of taxable income is the same as that for foreign enterprises.

Income Determination

Taxable income is defined as "net income in a tax year after deduction of costs, expenses, and losses in that year." The accrual method of accounting should be used.

Inventory Valuation

Inventory is valued at cost. Under the tax regulations, inventory can be valued in accordance with one of the following methods: the FIFO, shifting-average, LIFO, or weighted-average method. Approval from the local tax authorities must be obtained before changes can be made in the method of valuing inventory.

Capital Gains

There is no separate tax regime for capital gains. They are taxed in the same manner as all income derived from business activities in China.

Intercompany Dividends

If a foreign investment enterprise invests in another enterprise in China, the dividends obtained from that enterprise may be excluded from the investing enterprise's taxable income. Any expenses and losses incurred in the investment are not deductible.

Foreign Income

The worldwide income of a foreign investment enterprise and its branches both within and outside China is taxable. Tax credits are allowed for foreign income taxes paid on income sourced from outside China.

Depreciation

Fixed assets with useful lives of two years or less and items that cost RMB 2,000 or less can be expensed. Other fixed assets must be capitalized and its cost after providing for a residual value of 10%, be depreciated evenly over its useful life. The minimum useful lives are as follows:

Fixed Assets	Years
Houses and buildings	20
Trains, ships, machines, equipment, and other facilities used in	10
Electronic equipment, means of transportation other than ships	5

Under certain circumstances, an application may be made to the tax authorities to use accelerated methods of depreciation.

Amortization of Intangible Assets

A deduction is allowed for amortization of intangible assets, such as patents, proprietary technology, trademarks, copyrights, the right to the use of sites, and other intangibles. Intangible assets that are contributed as investment by a foreign enterprise with a provision for time limit of use should be amortized according to the time limit. Those not subject to such provisions are to be amortized over a period of not less than 10 years. Organization expenses incurred during the preparation period can be amortized over a period of not less than five years. Offshore oil projects can amortize exploration expenses over a period of not less than one year after commencement of commercial production.

Net Operating Losses

Operating losses can be carried forward for a period of no longer than five years for offsetting against future profits.

Payments to Foreign Affiliates

Royalties and interest charges paid by a foreign investment enterprise to foreign affiliates are deductible if the amounts are charged at armslength. General management fees paid to a foreign affiliate are usually not deductible.

Taxes

Income taxes paid are not deductible. Other taxes, such as irrecoverable value added tax, business tax, consumption/excise tax and real estate tax, are deductible.

Head Office Expenses

A deduction can be claimed by a foreign enterprise with an establishment or a place of business for reasonable overhead expenses that are relevant to production and business operation, provided the following documents are submitted with its tax return:

- ☐ A report documenting the total amount, categories of expenses, and allocation basis.
- ☐ An audited statement of head office expenses.

Group Taxation

Consolidated filing on a group basis is not permitted. However, a combination of profits and losses for different projects/activities of a single legal entity is permitted in a single tax return.

Tax Incentives

Inward Investment

Foreign investment enterprises of a production nature that expect to operate in China for more than 10 years can apply for an exemption from income tax for two years, beginning from the first profit-making year, and a 50% tax reduction in the following three years. A range of other reductions and exemptions is available, subject to certain criteria.

A reduced income tax rate of 15% may be possible for productive foreign investment enterprises in the Economic and Technological Development Zones and for enterprises engaged in production or business operations in the Special Economic Zones. A tax rate of 24% may apply to productive foreign investment enterprises located in certain zones in coastal cities.

Capital Investment

Where a foreign investor of a foreign investment enterprise reinvests its share of profit in China, it may obtain a tax rebate of the income tax paid by the enterprise and attributable to the foreign investor if the profit is reinvested for a period of at least five years. The reinvestment must be either in the original venture by increasing its registered capital or in another foreign investment enterprise. The rebate is 100% if the foreign investor reinvests its profits in an export-oriented or technologically advanced enterprise and 40% for other reinvestments.

Withholding Taxes

There is a temporary exemption on withholding tax levied on business profits remitted overseas as dividends to foreign investors by foreign investment enterprises.

Corporations Resident in Nontreaty Countries

Subject to the exception noted above for dividends from foreign investment enterprises, foreign enterprises without establishments in China will be subject to a withholding tax of 10% on gross income from interest, lease of property, royalties, and other non-business income sourced from China, with the following exceptions.

☐ Withholding tax on proprietary technology usage fees may be exempt if approval has been obtained.
☐ Withholding tax on dividends and gains from disposal of domestic companies listed on local exchanges by foreign investors are temporarily exempt.

Tax Administration

Returns

The tax year commences on January 1 and ends on December 31. Enterprises are required to file their income tax returns and audited financial statements within four months after the end of the tax year.

Payment of Tax

Enterprises are required to pay provisional taxes on a quarterly basis within 15 days after the end of each quarter. Three options are available to the taxpayer in computing the provisional tax:

- ☐ actual quarterly profits,
- ☐ one-quarter of the taxable income of the preceding year, or
- ☐ other formulas approved by the local tax authorities.

The final settlement must be made within five months after the end of each tax year.

Other Taxes

Turnover Taxes

On January 1, 1994, China introduced a new turnover tax system consisting of three taxes: VAT, business tax, and consumption/excise tax.

Value Added Tax

The sale or importation of goods and the provision of repairs, replacement, and processing services are subject to VAT. VAT is levied based on the value added at each stage of a production cycle. At each stage, the seller collects VAT on sales (output VAT) from the purchaser on behalf of the tax authorities. The seller can generally deduct the VAT incurred on the purchase of raw materials and certain overheads that are used for taxable sales (input VAT), and account for the balance to the tax authorities. VAT is typically a recoverable tax, except for VAT incurred on acquisition of fixed assets. It is treated as part of the cost of the fixed assets and depreciated.

VAT is generally charged at a standard rate of 17%. The sale of certain necessity goods and the importation of certain special equipment could be exempt from VAT or be subject to VAT at a reduced rate of 13%, as specified in the VAT regulations. With effect from January 1, 2001, exports of all foreign investment enterprises are zero rated. However, "zero rated" does not mean that all input VAT will be refunded; this depends on the type of product. Nevertheless, after several revisions of VAT refund rates, most products are now entitled to 100% refund. Sales of self-developed software are subject to an effective VAT burden of 3%.

Business Tax

Business tax is an indirect tax imposed on the provision of services (other than replacement and repair and processing services which are subject to VAT instead), the transfer of intangible assets, and the sale of immovable properties. Immovable properties include buildings, any attachments to the underlying land and the land use rights if they were transferred together with the building.

Intangible properties include land use rights (if transferred alone), trademarks, trade names, exclusive rights of technology, non-exclusive rights of technology and copyrights. Business tax is payable by the provider of the services or the transferor of the intangible or immovable properties. Unlike VAT, business tax is not a creditable tax, that is input tax cannot be recovered by the taxpayer. Business tax is levied on the full selling price, including the business tax. The tax rates range from 3% to 20%.

Consumption Tax

Consumption tax is levied on the production, processing and importation of specific categories of consumable goods that are deemed to be luxurious in nature.

Land Appreciation Tax (LAT)

LAT applies to gains derived by enterprises and individuals from the transfer of real estate, including land use rights, buildings and attached structures. The tax is computed by applying the applicable tax rate to the gain, which is the transfer price less allowable deductions.

The progressive tax rates range from 30% to 60% depending on the size of the gain compared with the sum of deductible items. The LAT is levied on the transfer of real estate in addition to any applicable income tax.

Real Estate Tax

A real estate tax is assessed on land and buildings according to the standard value on the basis of a general market evaluation.

Chapter 10

Individual Income Tax

By May Huang, Partner, Price Waterhouse Coopers

Defining a "Resident"

Individuals who have a "place of abode" in China are subject to individual income tax on their worldwide income.

Individuals who have a "place of abode" in China are individuals who are deemed to maintain a place of residence in China by virtue of their legal residence status, family, or economic ties.

For the individual who does not have a "place of abode" in China, taxes are based on the length of the individual's residency in China:

☐ Non-residents or resident foreigners who reside in China for less than one year will be taxed only on their China-sourced income.

☐ Foreigners who reside in China for more than one year but not more than five years will be subject to tax on both their China-sourced income and their foreign-sourced income. However, approval may be obtained from the tax authorities to limit taxation to China-sourced income only.

☐ Foreigners who reside in China for more than five consecutive years will be subject to tax on their worldwide income from the sixth year onward.

☐ Foreigners who travel to China and derive income from an overseas employer with no permanent establishment in China will be tax exempt if they do not physically stay in China, consecutively or cumulatively, for more than 90 days in a calendar year. The 90-day test is extended to 183 days if the individual is a tax resident of a country that has executed a taxation treaty or arrangement with China.

Gross Income

Employee Gross Income

Salaries or wages of an individual include basic salary, bonus, foreign service premium, area allowance, cost-of-living allowance, housing allowance in excess of actual rental, local tax reimbursement, insurance and pension contributions, and stock benefits.

Other Individual Income

Taxable income also includes compensation for personal services, income from the publication of articles, royalties, interest, dividends, incidental income, and rentals.

Capital Gains

Capital gains are treated as "other income" (see above) and are subject to tax in the same manner.

Real Property Gains Tax

In addition to income tax, taxpayers are subject to a land appreciation tax levied on gains from the transfer of real property. The rate of this tax ranges from 30% to 60%, depending on the size of the gain. This tax is in addition to any applicable income tax on such transfers.

Deductions

Business Deductions and Nonbusiness Expenses

In calculating taxable income for wages and salaries, there are no allowances for actual business expenses. Specific deductions are given for income from compensation for personal services, that is, income of independent contractors, from the publication of articles, from royalties, or from the lease of property.

If the amount received in a single payment is less than RMB 4,000, a standard deduction of RMB 800 is given.

If the amount received from a single economic transaction exceeds RMB 4,000, a deduction equal to 20% of the payment is allowed.

Interest and dividends are taxed on the gross amounts received without deductions. For sales of property, the original value of the property and reasonable expenses incurred are deducted from the sales proceeds to arrive at the taxable income.

Personal Allowances

All individuals are allowed a standard deduction of RMB 800 per month from wages and salaries. The standard deduction for local Chinese individuals may be increased up to RMB 1,600, depending on their place of work and returns filed. Foreigners including those from Hong Kong, Macao, and Taiwan residents, are given an additional allowance of RMB 3,200 per month. Accordingly, the monthly deduction from wages and salaries available to such a foreigner is RMB 4,000.

Tax Credits

Income tax paid to foreign countries for income earned abroad is allowed as a credit against China tax liability. The credit is limited to the amount of China tax on the foreign income. Documentary evidence of the tax payment to substantiate claims for foreign tax credits is required by the Chinese tax authorities.

Other Taxes

Social Security Taxes

Social contributions to retirement funds, housing funds, and so on, which are mandatory for local employees, are usually not applicable to expatriates.

Local Taxes on Income

The local governments do not impose any tax on individual income.

Tax Administration

Returns

Individuals are required to submit individual income tax returns to the Chinese tax authorities on a monthly basis and to make tax payments within seven days after the end of each month.

Payment of Tax

The tax liability is assessed on income computed in *Renminbi* (RMB). Foreign currencies are converted to *Renminbi* according to the exchange rate quoted by the People's Bank of China.

Tax returns must be filed on a timely basis. A surcharge of 0.05% per day will be imposed on all taxes that are not made promptly.

Withholding

When paying taxable income to an individual, the employer, unit, or person making the payment is required, as the withholding agent, to withhold the individual income tax due and remit the tax withheld to the tax authorities.

Tax Rates

Wages and Salaries

Where an individual's income tax liability is borne by the employer, the tax liability is calculated on an infinite gross-up basis (i.e., tax on tax). Examples follow:

Monthly taxable income		Tax rate %	Quick deduction RMB
Not grossed up RMB	Grossed up RMB		
0-500	0-475	5	0
501-2,000	476-1,825	10	25
2,001-5,000	1,826-4,375	15	25
5,000-20,000	4,376-16,375	20	375
20,001-40,000	16,376-31,375	25	1,375
40,001-60,000	31,376-45,375	30	3,375
60,001-80,000	45,376-58,375	35	6,375
80,001-100,000	58,376-70,375	40	10,375
Over 100,000	Over 70,375	45	15,375

Other Income Categories

A flat rate of 20% is applied on all other categories of income other than remuneration income. For independent contractors, if the income received for services performed is deemed to be too high, an additional tax will be assessed. In summary, 30% will be assessed on income portion from RMB 20,000 to RMB 50,000 and 40% will be assessed on that portion exceeding RMB 50,000.

Chapter 11

Customs, Tariffs And Trade

By John Robinson, Price Waterhouse Coopers

Import/Export Rights

China finally acceded to the World Trade Organization (WTO) on December 11, 2001. The impact in terms of customs and trade laws, regulations and practices in China is unprecedented in modern times. China has committed to progressively liberalize the availability and scope of the right to trade so that within 3 years after accession – all enterprises would have the right to import and export goods (except for some specified goods).

Foreign-invested enterprises would be granted new or additional trading rights based on the following schedule:

☐ 1 year after accession joint venture enterprises with minority share foreign investment would be granted full rights.

☐ 2 years after accession majority share foreign-invested joint ventures would be granted full rights

☐ Within 3 years after accession all enterprises would be granted the right to trade.

Tariff Reductions

No tariff reductions were introduced on the date of accession i.e. December 11, 2001, as originally committed by China. China adopted the Harmonized Commodity Description and Coding System (HS) with effect from January 1, 1992. Instead a "double drop" takes place on January 1, 2002. Tariff rates are then scheduled to be reduced over time based upon an agreed timetable and scale. Although the reductions are generally material and across the board, nevertheless there are significant exceptions. One important commitment by China is to largely eliminate duty and other charges on goods covered by the Information Technology Agreement (ITA) on January 1, 2002. Any residual items which have not been reduced to zero on that date will see duty eliminated by 2003 (see separate section on ITA).

Customs Valuation

Upon accession China has applied fully the WTO customs valuation agreement including the customs valuation methodologies set forth in Articles 1 through 8. China also affirmed that it would not reintroduce minimum or reference prices as a means to determine Customs value.

In addition China is to apply the provisions of the decision on the treatment of interest charges for customs valuation purposes and the decision on the valuation of Carrier Media Bearing Software for Data Processing Equipment (G/VAL/5) as soon as practicable, but in any event within two years.

It is unlikely that in practice China Customs will be able to fully implement the WTO Customs Valuation Agreement on the day of accession. Therefore, for some time to come there will be uncertainty and inconsistency in this vitally important area to importers.

China accepts the final transaction value for entry into China as the basis for dutiable value. Hence, China will not accept values based on a "first sale" principle.

Tariff Exemptions

Goods covered by these measures include such things as low value items, samples, temporary imports etc. China confirmed that upon accession it would adopt and apply tariff reductions and exemptions so as to ensure Most Favoured Nation (MFN) treatment for such imported goods.

Simplification and Harmonization of Customs Procedures (SHCP)

China joined the SHCP International Convention in 1988 and was a signatory (June 2000) to the draft protocol on the amendment to the SHCP international convention.

Pre-shipment Inspection

China agreed to comply with the agreement on preshipment inspection. Furthermore China confirmed that it would ensure that upon accession, any laws and regulations relating to preshipment inspection by any inspection agency, including private entities, would be consistent with relevant WTO agreements, in particular, the Agreement on Preshipment

Inspection and the Customs Valuation Agreement. Moreover, any fees charged in connection with such preshipment inspection would be commensurate with the service provided, in conformity with Article VIII of the GATT 1994.

Anti-dumping, Countervailing Duties

China's current investigations were judged to be inconsistent with the GATT 1994 Anti-Dumping Agreement. China had therefore committed to revising its current regulations and procedures prior to its accession in order to fully implement China's obligations under the Anti-Dumping and SCM Agreements. A new Countervailing Regulation was announced in December 2001. It will come into effect from January 1, 2001.

In turn, China complained that it had not received open and transparent treatment from the WTO members in the past (China was categorized as a non-market economy) and so the WTO members agreed to comply with a range of measures designed to rectify this in future investigations against China businesses. These measures included, inter alia, the right for Chinese producers and exporters to a full opportunity for the defence of their interests and also to be provided with a sufficiently detailed reasoning of a WTO member's preliminary and final determinations in a particular case.

The four Chinese government bodies responsible for anti-dumping and countervailing duty investigations are as follows:

☐ Ministry of Foreign Trade and Economic Cooperation (MOFTEC) – responsible for receiving petitions, conducting investigations and issuing preliminary determinations and decisions etc. It was also responsible for negotiating "price undertakings" if necessary and providing proposals on the imposition of definitive anti-dumping or countervailing duty.

☐ State Economic and Trade Commission (SETC) – responsible for the investigation of injury.

☐ General Customs Administration (Customs) – responsible for coordinating investigation with MOFTEC, enforcement (collecting duties) and monitoring implementation.

☐ Tariff Commission of the State Council – make the final decision on whether or not to levy anti-dumping or countervailing duties in cooperation with MOFTEC.

Exports, Customs Tariffs, Fees and Charges and the Application of Internal Taxes

There are currently 84 items subject to export duties based on the FOB prices for those goods. No commitment was made by China to remove these or phase them out. The following provides a thumbnail sketch of the key issues to be aware of.

Export Licensing

There has been a steady reduction in the number of products subject to export licensing in China. China confirmed that it would abide by WTO rules in respect of non-automatic export licensing and export restrictions. The Foreign Trade Law will also be brought into conformity with GATT requirements.

Taxes and Charges Levied on Imports and Exports

Upon accession China is to ensure that its laws and regulations relating to all fees, charges or taxes levied on imports or exports would be in full conformity with its WTO obligations. This commitment was given to assuage concerns about the application of VAT and additional charges levied by sub-national governments on imports. Non-discriminatory application of VAT and the other internal taxes was deemed essential.

Rules of Origin

Currently in China the criteria for making the determination of substantial transformation was:

☐ change in tariff classification of a four-digit tariff line in the Customs Tariff; or
☐ the value-added component was 30% or more in the total value of a new product.

When an imported product was processed and manufactured in several countries, the country of origin of the product was determined to be the last country in which the product underwent substantial transformation.

These rules were used to determine non-preferential origin. Once the international harmonization of non-preferential rules of origin was concluded, China would fully adopt those rules. Furthermore, China will ensure that its laws and regulations etc. relating to rules of origin would be in full conformity with the WTO agreement.

Information and Technology Agreement

According to the Report of the Working Party on the Accession of China, China confirmed that, upon accession, China would participate in the Information Technology Agreement (ITA) and would eliminate tariffs on all information technology products as set out in China's schedules. Furthermore, upon accession, China would eliminate all other duties and charges for ITA products.

The Ministerial Declaration on Trade in Information Technology Products (ITA) was concluded at the Singapore Ministerial Conference in December 1996. At that time 29 countries or separate customs territories signed the declaration

The ITA is solely a tariff cutting mechanism. There are three basic principles that one must abide by to become an ITA participant:

☐ all products listed in the Declaration must be covered,
☐ all must be reduced to a zero tariff level (by January 1, 2000), and
☐ all other duties and charges must be bound at zero.

There are no exceptions to product coverage, however for sensitive items, it is possible to have an extended implementation period. The commitments undertaken under the ITA in the WTO are on an MFN basis, and therefore benefits accrue to all other WTO Members.

Under ITA, all participants (China included in this case), would be obliged to reduce customs duties and other taxes on a prescribed list of products predominately classified in Chapter 84, 85 and 90.

Tariff Quota Rates

China has been widely criticized for its use and administration of its tariff rate quotas (TRQ) regime.

In response China has committed to the following:

☐ Upon accession TRQs on a number of products have been eliminated e.g. barley, rapeseed, peanut oil and quantitative import restrictions would be lifted on others e.g. sugar and cotton.

☐ Upon accession China will ensure that TRQs are administered on a transparent, predictable, uniform, fair and non-discriminatory basis using clearly specified timeframes, administrative procedures and requirements that provide effective import opportunities. China will apply TRQs fully in accordance with WTO rules and principles.

☐ For certain other goods the granting of trading rights to non-state trading companies to import TRQ allocations set aside only for state trading entities.

☐ To administer a consistent national allocation policy for TRQ's through a single, central authority.

Quantitative Import Restrictions (Including Prohibitions and Quotas)

On non-tariff measures China committed not to introduce, re-introduce or apply non-tariff measures other than those listed in Annex 3 of the draft protocol when justified under the WTO agreement. Measures specified in Annex 3 will be phased out over time to an agreed schedule and timetable. With regard to administration of quotas allocation and the timing of import licenses China confirmed that this would be carried out in conformity with the WTO agreement, the process would be simple and transparent. Further commitments and reassurances were given by China over the speed and transparency of the processes involved in applying for and obtaining import licences with firm commitments being given concerning document processing and turnaround times.

China intends to allocate quota in accordance with the following criteria:

☐ Basic principles.
☐ If the relevant quota quantity exceeded total requests for quota allocations, all requests would be approved.

In other cases, the criteria for allocation would be as follows:

☐ Historical performance of applicants where relevant;

☐ Production or processing capacity, in the case of intermediate products and raw materials;

☐ Experience and ability in producing, importing, marketing, or servicing in international markets, in the case of finished products or products destined for wholesale or retail distribution.

In cases in which average imports over the 3-year period immediately prior to the year of China's accession, for which data was available, exceeded 75 percent of the relevant quota, applicants that had not previously been allocated quota would be allocated 10 percent of the total quota in the first year and the majority of any quota growth in any subsequent year. In other cases the following may apply:

☐ In the first year, 25 percent of the total quota would be allocated to applicants that had not previously been allocated quota; however, an applicant that had imported under a quota on the relevant products in the year prior to China's accession would not receive a decrease in the absolute amount of its quota allocation;

☐ In the second year, for the amount of the quota growth as well as an amount equivalent to the amount of any quota that had not been filled in the previous year, China would give priority consideration to requests from enterprises with foreign ownership equal to or less than 50 percent;

☐ In the third and fourth year, if relevant, for the amount of the quota growth as well as an amount equivalent to the amount of any quota that had not been filled in the previous year, China would give priority consideration to requests from enterprises with foreign ownership greater than 50 percent.

In all cases, a quota-holder receiving an initial allocation that had fully utilized or contracted for its quota allocation would, upon application, receive an allocation in the following year for a quantity no less than the quantity imported in the previous year. A quota-holder that did not import its full allocation would receive a proportional reduction in its quota allocation in the subsequent year unless the quantity was returned for reallocation by September 1.

PART IV

MANAGING
HUMAN RESOURCES

Investing in a business in China means more than just structuring the deal and obtaining the approvals and licenses. When all this is over the tough work really begins with management. Managing human resources in China involves sourcing the best talent, training programs to inculcate corporate culture and develop teamwork systems, and the management of a host of complex problems ranging from social welfare arrangements, labor issues, and benefits for long-term employees. While these issues are familiar to human resource managers throughout the world, in China they often carry the twist of cultural factors hard to recognize requiring on the ground insight and experience to cope with human resource concerns and maximize management efficiency.

Chapter 12

Sourcing Labor And Recruitment

By Bonnie Furst, BIMBA Executive MBA Program
Professor, Beijing University

China's Labor Situation Post-WTO

The labor situation in China post-WTO is a function of the status of the labor market at this point in time in general as well as developments associated with WTO in particular. Generally speaking, labor supply is plentiful although recruiting skilled and managerial staff is still problematic especially in areas outside the large key first tier cities, and the situation will get worse in the next seven years as over a million new jobs are created. To make matters worse, it could take another five to ten years for young Chinese midlevel management staff to become seasoned and capable enough to handle the top positions which are currently staffed by more costly expatriates, foreign local hires and repatriated overseas Chinese.

Moreover, with the exception of unskilled labor that remains plentiful and affordable especially in the areas outside the major cities, labor costs in this new millennium are no longer the bargain they were when China opened up to the outside world in the early 1980s. While it is true that service companies starting up in China tend to find that labor costs for their unskilled service delivery staff are lower than in the west and manufacturing companies are not having difficulties recruiting finding workers, nevertheless, the costs for recruiting and retaining skilled technical and professional staff are generally higher than other southeast Asian countries such as the Philippines, Thailand and Indonesia. More importantly, there is growing competition for staff with computer skills especially in the area of information technology management. In recent years, salaries for people with IT skills have increased at rates double and triple the average rate for other positions.

In addition, the Chinese government is facing a pension-funding deficit that it cannot satisfy using its own resources. As a result, companies and employees are being required to contribute more and more to meet the retirement needs of employees and the unemployed at large. In recent years this has had the effect of almost doubling benefit costs, raising them to as much as 50% of total payroll in recent years. This trend of shifting the burden for social welfare away from government onto employers and the working public will likely continue for the foreseeable future.

In addition, the government continues to exert more influence on the daily affairs of corporate life than in western companies. In Sino-foreign joint ventures, for example, the CCP organ continues to play visible and formal roles in company management, and all types of foreign enterprises are expected to report periodically to Party and/or local labor authorities on the status of various business and labor matters, including staff pregnancies, religious affiliation, etc. In some cases foreign investors find they must deal with several political groups, including local CCP representatives, local labor bureaus and union management. This makes doing business in China even more challenging than in the west. Many companies employ Chinese professionals who specialize in the areas of government relations, public relations and Chinese labor law to help them monitor and manage these numerous and critical relationships.

WTO will impact the labor situation in subtle and not so subtle ways. While WTO will improve the ethics of business practices generally and the transparency of management practices and decisions specifically in foreign and domestic companies in China, the most immediate and obvious effects will be:

☐ the need to step up training efforts to improve management and computer-related skills and the quality of electronics and machinery products, and

☐ increasing competition for scarce talent as the levels of investment of foreign firms in China increases.

No Longer the Wild East

China is no longer the wild east. It is no longer the case that anything goes. WTO will likely trigger higher turnover and wage inflation for managerial and technical positions, especially in the areas of information technology, and companies will be challenged to find more effective ways to motivate and retain skilled staff. In the past it was often enough to just offer Chinese people a position in a foreign firm, but now talented staff have more options and higher expectations of how these firms are managed and how they are treated as employees working for them. Foreign firms will also be at greater risk of losing the key staff that has knowledge and skills of their proprietary technology.

Finding ways to create and sustain company cultures that are based on ethical business practices and attractive enough to retain critical staff will be a top priority. Both multinational and domestic firms need to improve their management methods and their company cultures to hold onto their best talent. China is no longer the wild east. As recent lawsuits by female employees and injured staff attest, it is no longer the case that anything goes.

Finally, as the eyes of the world turn to China, all companies will have to make greater efforts to demonstrate how they are good corporate citizens in terms of protecting the health and safety of their workers and providing a fair wage not only for full time staff but also for part-time and contract workers as well. Meeting these expectations will require increased labor-related expenditures and improvements in the areas of compensation, training and development as well as improvements to factories, facilities and technologies used to protect the environment. The days of being able to use and in some cases abuse rural migrant labor to mass-produce cheap goods are coming to an end. The smart firms are now rethinking the types of expatriate staff they send to work in China and budgeting for improvements in a number of areas related to labor-wages, management training and development, safety, to sharpen their competitive edge post-WTO.

Recruiting the Right People

Finding job applicants is not a problem in China. As the government downsizes state owned enterprises to make them more competitive and shuts down firms that cannot be competitive, large amounts of unskilled and semi-skilled workers are released into the labor pool. A small reverses brain drain has also begun, with experienced Chinese returning to China looking for work and better opportunities.

The challenge is to find the best people to fill the key management and technical positions in each firm. This is easier said than done in China,

The Reverse Brain Drain to Silk Valley

The reverse brain-drain has begun, and with WTO prospects and the recent award of the 2008 Olympics to Beijing, we can expect it to accelerate. Hi-tech business investment in China is on the rise, pulling overseas Chinese, and expatriates, from Silicon Valley to new Silk Valleys in special development areas in the major cities like Beijing and Shanghai and less developed areas such as Hangzhou and Xi'an.

One example is a small Silicon Valley start-up in Santa Clara, California-Newave Semiconductor, which opened a semiconductor design firm in Shanghai in 1999, with the help of a local Shanghai-based investor group, Shanghai Huahong Group, which gave Newave US$ 1.5 million in seed money to return to the mainland. One of Newaves founders, Howard Yang, is typical of the reverse brain-drain: he was born in China, he and his co-founders hold PhDs from US universities and design experience with major US companies.

They felt that compared to Silicon Valley, Shanghai has cheaper land and labor, and the Chinese government offered a chance to participate in a large semiconductor development programme providing a ready-made market for its services, products, and expertise.

Business China, March 1, 1999

and the recruiting situation is different for the different types of people needed. Finding the right managers is difficult. Finding technical staff is a little easier, while it is still a buyer's market for administrative staff. Foreign investors must hire people with different cultural and linguistic backgrounds to fill positions that involve a great deal of fiduciary and operational responsibility. This is a difficult enough task in their home countries, and that much more difficult in a foreign environment. Following are strategies used in China to recruit the different types of people required to start up and run most operations in China.

Finding Managers

Ramping up an operation usually begins with finding the right managers. The hottest competition is for managers with good planning, financial control, quality management, business development and people management skills. They can be found, but command bigger compensation and benefits packages than other types of managers.

Foreign firms either compete aggressively for people who are able to assume top-level management positions, or make significant investments in training and development to grow their own. It is also much easier to fill these jobs in the large cities. Filling them in the second- and third-tier cities can take longer and involve incurring the additional labor costs associated with expatriate or inpatriate (i.e., relocated PRC managers) packages.

Companies that recruit from outside tend to find managers from online/website advertisements, word of mouth, head hunters, newspaper advertisement, joint venture partners, and even government enterprises or the ranks of the laid off and unemployed, which are growing. These can provide large pools of possibly experienced, if not highly motivated managerial candidates. Most westerners are surprised to learn that in several places in China, the civil service has begun its own reform to adopt modern management practices such as performance based pay, profit sharing and elimination of the seniority system.

Therefore, it is getting easier to find people able to fit into a western working environment from state owned enterprises. Moreover, as of 1995, state workers have the right to resign at will with 30 days notice, but employers should be aware that state enterprises can charge fees to let people go in the name of file transfer fees which can run as high as RMB 10,000.

Managerial candidates can also be found in the pools of graduates of management programs, but they often lack relevant experience, with the exception of the few top international and domestic MBA programs, which can require up to 10 years prior work experience.

Over 50,000 people now graduate each year with post-graduate degrees, mostly in technical and scientific fields, but the number of degree holders with business credentials is still relatively small. Only about 30,000 people have received MBAs in China over the last ten years. However, the number of sanctioned domestic and international MBA programs has increased to about 60 and 40, respectively, so the supply of MBAs is expected to increase in the foreseeable future.

The easiest route to find suitable managers and top-level executives is still to hire a recruiter to poach or lure experienced managers away from competitors or from overseas.

Finding Technical Staff

Ramping up to fill technical positions is a little easier in China. While competition for technical staff is less stiff than for top managers, the competition for experienced technical staff is still tight and will remain so in strategic and high tech industries. As citizens migrate from the countryside to urban areas, the numbers of low-level staff with technical qualifications available to work in the cities will increase, but the migration will not make much of an impact on the size of the qualified managerial labor pool.

Recent government initiatives to improve education in areas outside the large cities, particularly the western region, will yield a larger pool of qualified workers, but not for some time. Given the large numbers of job seekers throughout China, technical staff can be found in both the large cities and outlying areas. Retaining them, however, is still easier in the large cities, especially for people with IT background.

While job-hopping has slowed down in the last two years as the size of salary increases decreased across the board, technical people still move around freely, as urban areas provide more attractive opportunities with respect to salaries, development, and quality of life for the most qualified people.

Finding Administrative Staff

It is still a buyer's market for qualified administrative staff that can be easily found by word of mouth, advertisements in local newspapers, at job fairs and via the Internet.

Almost every type of recruiting method used in the western world is now used in China. In the past, firms were limited in their choices of recruiting methods depending on the nature of their legal entity. Representative offices were only allowed to hire through their government labor agency, for example. However, firms may now hire whomever they wish provided they follow the required formalities to formalize the employment relationship, which can range from submitting documentation to terminate employment with a prior employer to entering into new individual labor contracts with the employee and/or their

---

Officials Lure It Experts Back to China

In Shanghai, Suzhou, Hefei, Xi'an, Hangzhou, and even Beijing, the government and universities are trying to offer conditions to attract overseas graduates and business people in high-tech areas to return home. Special tax incentives, compensation and benefit enhancements, business parks and special development zones, streamlined entry and exit procedures, promises of good jobs with good local pay, and opportunities to invest in start-up businesses are some examples of typical inducements. The recent recession in Silicon Valley has also had a positive impact on decisions to return to the mainland.

respective labor agency, depending on the situation. At this point in time, representative offices must still hire employees through the auspices of an approved labor agency. Joint ventures and wholly owned foreign enterprises may hire directly.

The following chart presents the pros and cons of the most typically used recruiting methods in China in 2002:

Recruiting Approaches That Work in China

Method	Pros	Cons
Use the internet, e.g., <www.51job.com>, <www.zhaopin.com>	This is the newest and one of the least expensive methods of finding computer-literate, young people. Ads can cost as little as RMB 1,000 per month. Ads need not be approved in some situations provided the employer can produce a business license.	Results in large numbers of emails to be sorted and resumes which are not suitable for the posted position.
Use local newspapers	This is still the preferred method to find administrative and some entry-level staff. It is cost-effective and millions of people check the papers daily looking for work.	Results in large numbers of resumes to be screened. Ads often have to be approved by labor service agencies or labor bureaus (depending on the locality and/or legal entity).
Use recruiters	While international recruiters have been in China for some time, local firms have spun off and can sometimes provide more cost-effective alternative for mid-level hires. Foreign firms still rely on the international firms to fill critical positions.	Cost, not cheap. Even local head hunters can ask for 33% annual salary. Difficult to check people's references. Employees may have incurred liabilities (such as training bonds) that must be paid off in order to hire them away from other companies.
Recruit on campuses	This is mostly suitable for entry-level professional positions. Candidates have good English skills and are often placed in training programs that prepare them for eventual promotion to management positions.	Time consuming Candidates lack work experience Graduates may be required to repay their tuition fees if they join a foreign company, in amounts from RMB 15,000-20,000. Transferring students' *hukou*s can be difficult.
Use job fairs	For entry level positions, these can be efficient and effective and low cost. Experienced HR professionals can meet up to 200 people per day this way for as little as RMB 4,000 per day at the better known fairs.	Time consuming.

Chapter 13

Hiring And Firing

By Bonnie Furst, BIMBA Executive MBA Program
Professor, Beijing University

Hiring in Post-WTO China

Hiring in China post-WTO will not be much different from the hiring during the period leading up to WTO. If anything changes it will likely be in a positive direction, such as efforts the government is taking to experiment with ways such as offering a permanent visa-type of green card to encourage overseas Chinese talent and foreign experts to remain in China to assist with the technology transfer and management development efforts that are needed to improve China's competitiveness in the global market.

The main considerations to bear in mind when hiring in China are to comply with the applicable national and local labor regulations regarding employment of local and foreign employees and to be aware of the risks and costs associated with hiring in China. The following story illustrates the importance of undertaking a thorough due diligence process before selecting a joint venture partner or engaging large numbers of staff to work in any type of organization in China.

You must do due diligence before signing the contract. Sometimes what you do not know can hurt you. Bonnie Furst, one of the leading specialists in human resources management in China suggests spending a little time doing HR due diligence up front. In just a few days time, a prospective investor or employer can confirm not only what the real payroll costs will be, but also get a taste and preview of what it will be like to work with and manage the inherited workforce and local politics.

Labor policies are a moving target in China, so foreign managers need to make a conscious effort to study and stay up to speed on national and local labor developments, and not take local assessments of labor developments and costs at face value. A visit to the local labor bureau can teach foreign managers a lot about what can and cannot, and what should or should not be included in the payroll budgets and various types of labor contracts.

Local managers also often do not think in terms of future payroll costs or the impact they could have on cash flow or the bottom line. A case in point is a power plant in the interior of China that was being considered as a joint venture partner. The local managers simply added up the current salaries, allowances, bonuses and benefit costs to budget for payroll costs in the first years of the venture.

An external HR due diligence audit discovered hidden liabilities that added RMB 500,000 in costs to the bottom line for the first ten years of the joint ventures operation. A simple enquiry at the local labor bureau yielded information on a little known local regulation requiring foreign investors to pay each employee RMB 20,000 to allow them to purchase a home. Providing this unexpected benefit for all staff in the plant incurred a liability of RMB 5,000,000 which was to be paid off over a ten-year period.

As a result of the due diligence effort, the investors were able to adjust budgeted salaries to fit their overall HR budget before the individual labor contracts and the collective labor contract were signed, avoiding a disappointing result at the end of the first year, which could have negatively impacted bonuses, morale and relations with new foreign investors.

Following is a description of the general requirements related to the employment of local and expatriate staff in China.

How People Are Employed

In China, all employees must have some kind of labor contract, and the type of labor contract required depends on the type of legal entity the company has formed. For example, if the operation is a representative office, employees must be hired through officially recognized labor service corporations/labor agencies (*see Labor Agency Contracts next page*). In the case of representative offices, employees need only sign one individual labor contract with the labor agency servicing the representative office; however, many foreign enterprises prefer to supplement such contracts with their own labor agreement directly entered into with each individual employee. Joint ventures and wholly owned foreign enterprises may enter into individual labor contracts directly with employees. Collective labor contracts (union contracts) may or may not be needed depending on the wishes of the work force.

Individual Contracts

The Labor Law mandates that all individual labor contracts address the following areas:

☐ Contract term

☐ Nature of the job
☐ Workplace safety and working conditions
☐ Remuneration
☐ Discipline
☐ Conditions for terminating contract

Examples of legally acceptable individual labor contracts can be obtained from local labor bureaus, but companies should note that some of the terms provided in these contracts could be negotiated. Sample labor contracts for individual staff are provided in the appendix.

Collective Labor Contracts

Current Labor Law requires that all employers sign written contracts with their workers. Foreign-invested enterprises prefer individual labor contracts, as they are more flexible. However, the law does require that collective labor contracts be negotiated (i.e., unions must be formed) if even one employee requests it, and in SOEs (state owned enterprises) and joint ventures formed with former SOEs, there is almost always a union, even if it only consists of a union official. Currently, these unions may not be decertified.

Basically collective contracts apply to all workers and address general labor terms whereas the individual contract addresses specific wages, rewards, job duties, etc. Individual labor contracts are signed at the beginning of the employment relationship, whereas a collective contract can be signed at any time.

Labor Agency Contracts

In addition to individual labor contracts and collective labor contracts, there is a third type of labor contract for representative offices-labor agency contracts. Labor Agencies of Labor Service Corporations are the organizations established by or sanctioned by the Chinese government to provide Representative Offices with employees. They also serve other functions including the following:

- ☐ Talent agency
- ☐ Maintain personnel files (the government-required dossier on each citizen called the *dang an*)
- ☐ Transfer personnel files
- ☐ Evaluate staff credentials
- ☐ Issue passports and visas
- ☐ Handle disputes and arbitration
- ☐ Advise on labor law
- ☐ Administer and manage benefits programs
- ☐ Receive company payments for salary and pay employees salaries
- ☐ Arrange training
- ☐ Arrange *hukou* (the government-required residential housing permit)
- ☐ Arrange temporary living permits

The first and most famous labor agency is the Foreign Enterprise Service Corp (FESCO) in Beijing, which originally provided office staff to Representative Offices. However, FESCO now has worthy competition, most notably with the establishment of China International Intelligence and Technology Corporation (CIIC) which is organized as a corporation with subsidiaries throughout China. CIIC tends to offer a higher level of customer service than FESCO, although FESCO has made remarkable improvements in recent years. Most companies employee some of their workforce through one agency and the rest through another in order to foster competition among the agencies to obtain the most competitive rates, and to give their employees some choice in the matter. FESCO/CIIC fees in 2000 were around US$ 120-US$ 150 per month per person and this covered all state mandated benefits as well as a service fee to the labor agency. These rates are likely to increase given recent developments related to recent social welfare reform.

How Geography Matters (the "Hukou")

Another unique aspect related to employment in China is the *hukou* or place-of-birth-residence permit. This permit is issued at birth and transferred to the location where the person attends university or obtains employment.

The government implemented a mandatory residential registration system about 50 years ago in order to control the flow of rural citizens into the urban areas, and the system remains in effect to this day, although experiments are currently underway to dismantle the system. The system basically makes it difficult for persons to find employment in locations outside their assigned residence, and similarly makes it difficult for companies to relocate staff to locations outside their residence.

Employees may also be understandably reluctant to relocate to new locations when they already possess a *hukou* in a desirable location. The best option in this case is to pursue getting a temporary work permit and/or use local labor agencies to address the problem. Regardless of strategic considerations, it is still a procedural headache to transfer personnel files, although the labor agencies can be enlisted to handle these activities for nominal fees.

Local vs. Expat and Foreign Local Hire

Despite the economic and business reasons for localizing in China, few companies will do away with foreigners altogether. Most multinational companies doing business in China are global enterprises, and as such, usually have managers from a variety of national backgrounds. Expatriates and foreign local hires are also useful to train PRC managers and to facilitate technology transfer, and in some cases, customers and investors prefer to do business with, or at least see some foreigners on the management team, particularly those who understand their language and cultural backgrounds.

Expatriates are generally considered to be people who are taken directly from their home country and relocated in another country to work at the request of the company. Foreign local hires are foreigners who already live in the local labor market and who are hired to work in the companies operating in that country.

The decision to staff a position with a local versus foreigner is usually based on the requirements of the business and the budget available to cover the costs as well as the entity that will be required to bear the payroll cost. Investors are advised to not pay foreign staff directly from local joint venture budgets to avoid triggering the equal pay for equal work rule.

To date it has been relatively easy to staff positions with foreigners, but it should also be remembered that Chinese labor law requires that all positions in a foreign invested enterprise (FIE) be filled first with Chinese employees. Companies must prove that a special need exists for a foreigner to fill a position, and this must be reviewed each year when the working visa is renewed. Applicable labor law is provided in the Provisions for the Administration of Foreigners Working in China, effective May 1, 1996. Special regulations exist for expatriates from other areas such as Hong Kong, Taiwan or Macao travel-document holders. These regulations apply to both expatriates and foreign local hires.

Following are some of the criteria included in these regulations:

☐ Be at least 18 years of age and in good health.
☐ Have expertise and relevant experience.

☐ Have no criminal record.

☐ Have a confirmed position.

☐ Have a valid passport or equivalent international travel document.

Besides the cost issue, companies should carefully evaluate expatriate and foreign local hire candidates to determine their ability to work with local staff and help the firm achieve its goals, language ability, affinity for and understanding of local culture, flexibility and adaptability, mentoring abilities, and in China, in particular, the foreigners must be able to go with the flow, be patient, polite and open-minded.

Work Permits and Immigration Requirements

All foreigners entering China require a visa. Foreigners working in China can apply for single-entry visas, which are valid for 30 days, or multiple-entry visas, which are normally issued for six months and allow visits of up to 30 days each time. A foreign assignee who has commenced work in China and acquired the necessary registration and health documents may apply for a Z visa, which will usually allow the foreign employee to stay in China for a period of six months to a year. Z visas can be renewed.

Foreign personnel who travel to China for short periods of time for business purposes do not require residency or work permits. However, personnel who are to be stationed in China for any length of time are required to obtain foreigner residence permits. In Shanghai, the government has started experimenting with longer-term arrangements similar to permanent resident green cards issued in the U.S. to encourage overseas Chinese and foreign experts to stay in China.

A foreigner working for a representative office is also required to obtain a resident representative card. The first step is to acquire a letter of introduction from the sponsoring Chinese entity, as this will be required for registration with the relevant authorities.

The foreign employee of a representative office must then register with the local authority to obtain resident representative cards, but they must acquire foreigner residence permits. The procedures for obtaining these permits and the Z visas are the same as for representative office employees.

Restrictions on Employment

Although there are no restrictions on the number of foreign personnel that may be employed by a foreign investment enterprise or foreign business in China, nor is there a time period imposed on their employment. FIEs are required to submit resumes of their foreign employees to the local labor bureau for assessment. Should the labor bureau determine that there is local talent available with similar backgrounds and skills to deliver comparable services, the application for obtaining employment permits for foreigners may not be approved. In addition, joint ventures are now required to obtain permission from the local labor bureau if they want to take on foreign personnel that are not in the original investment contract.

Role of the Local Labor Bureau and Union

Local labor bureaus exist to implement and interpret national labor law at the local level. They provide companies with information on amendments to labor laws, albeit almost always on a belated basis, and they are responsible for collecting various statistics, such as marital status, pregnancies, religious affiliation, etc. on workers within their jurisdiction. In rural areas they should almost always be consulted for before undertaking major hiring and firing actions, since such localities have been known to modify or in some cases even add labor requirements beyond those promulgated at the national level.

In some localities, the local labor bureaus are pro-investment and try to interpret labor law requirements in a manner conducive to trade. In other localities, however, the local labor bureau can be neutral or even anti-investment. It behooves foreign investors to investigate the local politics of the relevant labor bureau before making a decision to invest in any location in China.

Unions are labor representative organizations provided by legislation to look out for the interests of the workforce. All unions are governed by the government-sanctioned All-China Federation of Trade Unions (ACFTU). When a company has a union they must pay 2% of payroll into a union fund to be administered by the union. Companies without a formal union must pay the 2% dues to the local labor bureau.

Joint ventures are required to provide appropriate facilities for the union to carry out its work. The extent to which unions exercise their influence varies from company to company and locality to locality. Some limit their involvement to social, cultural and political activities and resolving employee disputes, while others become more involved in company affairs, particularly during times of restructuring and downsizing.

Employees are encouraged to seek various dispute-resolution methods such as mediation and arbitration as opposed to legal actions. Recently, however, more and more employees are availing themselves of legal recourse and companies are advised to pay attention to how well they handle employee relations and maintain positive union relations.

Salary Disputes in IT Company

Ms. Fan Doudou, a senior executive at an Internet company in Beijing, recently won a lawsuit against her employer for delaying her salary, *Beijing Daily* reported yesterday.

The company had promised Fan a high salary and options when she was hired, but the firm later decided to cut executive salaries due to less-than-expected profits. The local court ruled that the company should give Fan the salary originally agreed to.

Analysts said with the reshuffling of the Internet industry, more Internet companies would face bankruptcies or mergers, which will give rise to similar disputes.

China Daily, September 15, 2000

Compensation and Benefits as Attraction, Motivation and Retention Tools

In China, compensation approaches differ for local versus foreign staff. Compensation for local staff is a function of the local labor market and historical pay practices whereas compensation for foreign staff is usually tied to pay practices in the home country.

Local Pay Practices

Local pay practices vary from: (a) a fixed salary with no allowances, (b) a salary that is part fixed and part variable, (c) the old SOE system of a base salary plus allowances, bonuses less deductions for income taxes, statutory benefits contributions and penalties for violating company policies.

Base Salaries

Salaries usually refer to the amounts paid for performing the basic

---

Typical Chinese Compensation Structure

- ☐ *Base Salary*
- ☐ *Bonuses, Variable Bonuses*
- ☐ *Incentives, Sales Incentives, Commissions*
- ☐ *Allowances*
- ☐ *Profit Sharing Payments*
- ☐ *Less Deduction for Income Taxes, Statutory Benefit Contributions and Fines and Penalties*

Benefits-related payments are considered separate from compensation in China (*see Benefits section below*).

---

duties of the job. It can be paid on any basis, although hourly, monthly and annually are most common. In production environments, salaries or base pay can also be paid for quantities of work produced. In many state owned enterprises, base pay is a function of seniority, political record, etc. In state enterprises labor rates are generally standardized according to job grade. The labor regulations governing foreign investment enterprises allow these enterprises greater freedom in establishing their own wage scales and incentive schemes. The board of directors is responsible for determining the salary levels to be paid to the enterprise's local senior personnel, which must be higher than those paid in state enterprises. The Chinese partner may want to implement the same pay scales for foreign and local workers of the same grade; this is subject to negotiation between the partners.

Foreign representative offices operating in China may either pay their employees directly or pay a labor agency such as FESCO for the staff they hire. When paying through FESCO the staff will receive only a percentage of the salary, with the percentage increasing on the basis of their seniority and years of service with the labor agency. To make up for the shortfall in wages, most representative offices pay the difference to their staff. Recently, most representative offices have modified their arrangements with the labor agencies to allow the firms to directly pay all staff compensation directly to the staff themselves. In these cases, the foreign investment enterprises will pay an additional fee to the labor agency for the other services they may render such as handling personnel files, handling statutory labor benefits, etc. Minimum wages are also in effect in China for full time workers and in some localities for part-time workers.

Allowances

Chinese employees still expect to receive allowances, a practice inherited from the SOE system which. While not material, allowances are seen as a demonstration of the extent to which the company cares for employees and as such should not be eliminated or folded into salaries without first considering the impact or how best to communicate such changes to the work force.

In one foreign company, employees reacted negatively to the consolidation of allowances into a fixed salary payment, which they viewed

Chinese Allowances

The types of allowances offered staff vary from company to company and between staff depending on company policies and employment contracts. Following is a list of typical allowances offered in China:

- ☐ *Transportation Allowance*
- ☐ *Meals Allowance*
- ☐ *Tuition/Education Allowance*
- ☐ *One Child Allowance*
- ☐ *Day Care Allowance*
- ☐ *Price Subsidy Allowance*
- ☐ *Housing Heating Allowances*
- ☐ *Haircut, Laundry, Sanitary Allowances*
- ☐ *Housing Allowance*
- ☐ *Auto Allowance*

as an elimination of the allowances for clothing, summer cooling allowances (money for watermelon) and the winter heating allowances. So the HR department decided to state in the Employee Handbook the portions of employee salaries that could be considered allocable to the various former allowances. Employees felt better about the company afterwards.

Bonuses

Bonus usually refers to extra pay that is not a fixed amount. It is usually paid in relation to some criteria such as achieving certain results or achieving a certain level of performance. In China, some companies award an automatic 13th or 14th month bonus. This, however, is not a legal requirement, and many companies are changing their employment agreements to switch to performance-based rewards to be paid based on company performance and employee performance at year end.

Incentive Pay

Bonuses are one type of incentive pay, that is, compensation which is not fixed and is dependent upon performing beyond normal expectations. The word incentive is used to imply that the extra payment is being offered to encourage or motivate a person to do something. The usual types of incentive pay used in China include merit/performance-based bonuses, profit-sharing or gain-sharing payments, sales incentives and stock options.

In foreign companies, variable pay is most often based on measurable financial results, such as achieving profits or sales targets. Recently, variable pay has also been tied to improving quality, customer satisfaction, productivity as well as reducing costs, improving safety and attendance, even in state owned enterprises.

Commissions

Commissions refer to payments staff receives as a result of selling company goods or services. They are not usually paid until the company has collected payment for them from their customers. This is especially relevant in China where collecting on contracts can be problematic.

Salary Increases

While the Chinese government does issue guidelines regarding inflation, general salary increases are primarily market driven. In China, salary increases are based on developments in the economy, the market and company and staff performance. Companies try to keep up with inflation when considering how much to increase salaries, and in heated economics, profitable companies usually offer increases that keep pace with inflation.

There are basically two ways salary increases are awarded: the same increase for everyone or individual increases awarded to staff on the basis of performance and/or their position in their pay range. Both approaches are used in China, although uniform increases are culturally more acceptable and easier to administer.

As global competition comes to China, many companies are feeling greater pressure to produce profits. As a result, they are finding they cannot always offer salary increases commensurate with inflation, as has been the case in the past. SOEs have also paid out bonuses in years when there were no profits. This practice is being eliminated in as many locations as possible, understandably to worker chagrin.

When it comes time to decide on increases and inform staff about them, managers usually consult union heads or Party leaders before deciding on the final amounts or announcing them. Some companies announce increases around Chinese New Year, others in accordance with their fiscal year ends, which tend to fall around December or June.

Stock Options

Stock options are still not quite legal in China, but companies have found ways to try to offer them, or at least approximate their benefits.

Employee share-ownership programmes are being used by foreign companies in China with increasing frequency by foreign companies to retain and motivate local professional staff – especially in high-tech industries. Chinese companies have also started to employ stock options for their incentive value especially in high-tech firms.

Western companies often compensate different groups of employees differently, and some companies in China are adopting some of these practices.

For **executives**, for example, they usually receive a greater percentage of their total compensation in the form of incentive pay than other employees. Their compensation tends to be based on the performance of the business. Their packages may consist of: base salary, annual incentives, long-term incentives, perquisites (special privileges such as company cars, special parking places, club memberships, etc.), and financial protection in case their company is acquired or taken over by another company.

For **sales people**, there are three ways to compensate:

☐ straight salary
☐ straight commission
☐ combined salary plus commission and/or bonus

As in western countries, the straight salary approach is only used when 1) it is too difficult to measure sales performance, 2) the selling process

Stock Plans Come to Shanghai

In 1999, at the height of high-tech stock issuance in the west, Shanghai companies started offering stock option programs as incentive compensation as a way to attract and retain staff in new industries and to reform old ones. According to the *Wall Street Journal*, Legend Holdings Ltd. distributed 17% of its annual profit in 1999 to employees in the program and started to transform its shareholding structure to allow employees to convert the profit distribution to equity. This program dealt with two problems the company struggled with in China: retaining talented workers and helping the executives feel that they are owners of the company.

As of November 1999, 32% of high tech companies in China offered stock options, 8% stock purchase plans, 8% both and 52% no type of stock program, partly in imitation of Silicon Valley, and partly to keep employees from trying to join companies in Silicon Valley.

Microsoft's research and development laboratory uses stock options to attract new recruits and keep experienced engineers on board. Microsoft awards more shares to good performers resulting in a low turnover rate of 3%.

Intel offers employees stock options and purchase plans at a 15% discount of market prices.

Options are awarded to people at most levels of the company based on performance. Most programs require employees to be with the company for a specified period of time before they are vested or have the right to the full value of the stock, thus making it a valuable retention tool.

Recently, low-flying companies in the chemical and textile industries are also offering stock option and stock purchase plans.

involves too many people to be able to separate the efforts of the sales person from what other people involved in the sale have done, and 3) when the sales person does not spend much time selling, and spends most time helping customers, training distributors, doing trade shows, etc.

The straight commission approach is used when 1) the cost of sales must be strictly controlled, 2) it is the standard practice in the industry, and 3) the company must achieve sales volume (even at the cost of service). In China where it tends to be hard to get paid, straight commissions are usually considered too risky.

Administrative and blue-collar compensation is fairly uniform from location to location consisting of the standard base pay plus allowances plus monthly bonuses/cost savings payments, etc. described above.

Technical and professional compensation usually includes the standard package plus additional incentives such as training or education allowances, club membership, etc.

There are also **minimum wage** and **overtime** regulations that must be followed, published in English and Chinese and available from local labor bureaus as well as labor agencies.

Expatriate Packages

Packages for expatriate staff in China include basic salaries, foreign service premiums and hardship premiums depending on the location in China, cost-of-living allowances, housing allowances, medical insurance, children's education cost, tax equalization in the home country, completion bonuses (for localizing positions, e.g.), home leave for expatriate and their family, rest and relaxation vacations and club memberships. As could be imagined, expatriate packages for executives can run as high as US$ 250,000 to US$ 650,000 a year. Thus the tendency is to localize as quickly as possible.

Salary Level Information

In China, salary levels in FIEs are a function of the employee's residence, level of international experience and technical expertise acquired: expatriates from the most developed countries tend to have the highest salaries, followed by internationally experienced top/senior PRC executives, foreign local hires/returnees and local PRC staff in that order. Companies in China rely on several sources to determine pay levels: published surveys, informal surveys with colleagues in other companies and new hires from other companies and government guidelines, which are estimated to be around 5% for 2001.

Specific salary level information can be obtained for most locations from HR consulting firms. Following are samples of the types of information typically available for some IT positions in Beijing, for example, who are paid significantly less in China than Asia in general. Annual labor costs (salaries and benefits) for IT personnel in Asia can run around US$ 72,000 per employee compared to US$ 18,000 to US$ 30,000 per employee in China *(see next page)*:

Until recently, salary increases were hefty, in the 20%-30% range. With recent deflation and the slowed economic growth, increases have dropped to 8% and less.

Taiwanese FIE Salaries Dropping in China

Working in mainland China is getting less attractive for Taiwanese executives employed on the mainland. Wages drop, bonuses are scrapped, and demand for talent decreases. Still, many Taiwanese workers are eagerly eyeing a career on the mainland, reports *Taipei Times*.

The persisting enthusiasm is caused by the economic slowdown in Taiwan and the business migration to Mainland China, writes the

Salary Info for Local PRC Staff	MIS Manager	MIS Analyst/ Administrator	MIS Analyst/ Administrator
Other Titles	Advanced Information Technology Specialist, Assistant Systems Manager, Information Technology Manager	Information Technology Specialist, Systems Supervisor	Systems Supervisor, Information Systems Specialist, Information Technology Engineer
Average Age	30 years	28 years	23 years
Average # of Years in Position	2 years	1.7 years	1.1 years
Average Years in IT	5 years	4.2 years	1.5 years
Average Annual Years Work Experiences	7 years	5.5 years	2.9 years
Highest Education: PhD/Master/BA/ College/High School/Tech School	0%/0%/67%/33%/0%/0%	0%/11%/66%/6%/6% 11%	0%/0%/33%/0%/0% 50%
RMB Average Annual Base Salary	137,567($16,500)	76,948($9,300)	43,625($5,200)
RMB Average Annual Guaranteed Pay	164,973($20,000) (50% companies offer allowances at 25% of salary)	84,387($10,000) (40% companies offer allowances at 13% of salary)	48,539($5,848)
RMB Average Variable Pay	0	12,247($1,745)	0
RMB Average Annual Total Cash	174,418($21,000)	89,052($11,000)	49,822($6,000)
Getting Stock Plans	0%	5%	0%
Getting Education Benefit	0%	14%	14%
Getting Club Membership	25%	9%	0%

Source: Amcham Beijing 2000

newspaper. Between January and May this year Taiwanese investment in China grew by a third to US$ 1.06 billion. Meanwhile foreign investment in Taiwan dropped by a fifth, partly due to the harsh competition of the mainland market, with its promising consumer size and low labor costs.

The demand of mainland-based companies for Taiwanese talent is falling, as the market is filled with Taiwanese workers who move across the strait to find their luck. Reliable figures are lacking, but some estimate that up to half a million Taiwanese might already be working in China's eastern provinces. Because of that salaries are dropping significantly. Where Taiwanese working in mainland China could a few years ago count on a salary twice as big as back home, and many additional bonuses and benefits, they now have to do with an 1.5 fold salary or less, and mostly forget about the extras. Several Taiwan-based companies are said to plan a decrease in the salaries for China-based staff, like Acer Communications, Arima Computer Corp. and Quanta Computer Inc.

Personal Income Tax

Personal income tax is estimated and withheld by the employer and delivered to the local tax bureau on the employee's behalf on a monthly basis. The following demonstrates how income is calculated in China, also on a monthly basis:

Benefits and Social Security

Given the legacy of the iron rice bowl, and the government's desire to maintain social stability, the Chinese government exerts more control over social welfare than in the United States. Basically, the government provides state-mandated benefits, such as unemployment insurance, maternity leave, pension, medical insurance and accident insurance. All of these benefits programs are in various stages of reform and should therefore be watched closely by HR managers.

The government requires the employer to contribute set percentages of payroll for each benefit program and the employee to contribute a percentage of payrolls. Following are some indications of benefit costs in the four cities under consideration. As can be seen, companies are expected to contribute from 30-45% of payroll:

The way these payments are made depends on the legal entity the enterprise has chosen to form. Representative offices may pay a fixed consolidated fee to their labor agency that will in turn pay the various benefits agencies. Joint ventures may make the payments directly to the benefits agencies or use the services of labor agency for convenience sake or to reduce employee personal income tax.

How to Calculate Chinese Personal Income Tax

Table a: PRC Tax Calculations

PRC Tax Rate	Factor	Range	Applicable Tax Rate
5%	0	<500	20%
10%	25	500-2000 *	
15%	125	2000-5000	
20%	375	5000-20000	
25%	1375	20000-40000	
30%	3375	40000-60000	
35%	6375	60000-80000	
40%	10375	80000-100000	

2,000	USD/mo			
8.30	Exchange Rate			
16,600	RMB/mo			
-1000	Applicable deduction for bj			
15,600				
20%	Tax Rate			
3120				
-375	Factor	$2,000.00	$24,000.00	Annual Gross
2745	RMB Tax	$331.52	USD Tax	Per Cal Month
		$1,668.48	Net Mo	
		$20,021.74	Net Annual	

Unemployment

The first component of the reformed social security programme was put in place in December 1998 when the State Council passed the Unemployment Insurance Regulations. This benefit currently covers all urban workers including those of foreign-invested enterprises, although the government has plans to create communal pools to provide some type of minimal benefits to workers living outside urban areas as well.

About 80% of China's population lives outside the urban areas and they do not participate in these national benefit programs yet. Therefore, the national and local governments tend to be happy to encourage foreign enterprises to invest in localities to help alleviate this social burden that the government has not yet been able to handle on its own.

Social Insurance Schemes in Four Cities in China

City	Retirement Pension Employer	Employee	Basis	Medical Employer	Employee	Basis	Housing Employer	Employee	Basis	Unemployment Employer	Employee	Basis
Hangzhou	23%	6%	4323	Social insurance			9%	9%	actual	2%	1%	4323
Shanghai	22.50%	6%	3855	2%	2%	3855	7%	7%	3855	2%	1%	3855
Xi'an	20%	6%	1919.5	7%	2%		5%	5%	actual	2.50%	1%	
Beijing	19%	7%	3444	6%	1%	1311	8%	8%	1375	1.50%	0.50%	3444
							10%	10%	actual (future)			

Note: Base salary is three times the monthly average salary of employees in that city.

Housing fund for Hangzhou, Xi'an, and Beijing is calculated based on actual monthly salary.

Pension

In 1997, the State Council issued regulations to reform and create a unified pension system by 2000 throughout China. This program has only begun and already the amount of pensions paid out exceeds the amount of contributions collected. The government is working on various initiatives (including a Lottery for the Elderly) to address this crisis including enforcement efforts to collect past due amounts from foreign and domestic companies that have not complied.

In the past, many foreign enterprises were lax about participating because the government had not communicated the requirements clearly and there were no enforcement mechanisms. Now, compliance is being monitored and penalties levied. It won't be long before employees take action with their unions or in courts to ensure companies are providing for their futures, so it is a good idea to budget to meet these mandated obligations, despite the fact that these programs are in their infancy and fraught with problems including graft and neglect. For these reasons, it is a good idea for companies to only pay the minimum required by law and investigates how to meet staff needs through various supplemental programs.

Supplementary Insurance Benefits

The new national pension and medical insurance schemes are designed only to provide a basic, subsistence level of benefits, and the expected levels of pension benefit will be less, as a percentage of income, than they were under the iron rice bowl. For these reasons, more and more companies are offering some type of supplementary insurance benefit, such as life insurance. The lack of effective investment vehicles precludes self-funding pension programs at this point in time.

Medical

In December 1998 the Chinese government set up a unified medical insurance scheme to provide minimum medical coverage for workers in urban areas and the foundation for some minimal coverage for rural citizens as well. Employees participating in the government programs see doctors in government hospitals and get reimbursed for the covered expenses. The percentage of expenses covered is generally higher than in the United States.

Supplementary Medical Benefits

These are medical plans that are offered to local professional staff as an extra benefit. These programs cover outpatient care and supplemental coverage for the full cost of hospitalization – neither of which are covered by the national medical insurance system-and allow Chinese managers to receive care in the growing network of foreign and international medical facilities in China.

Housing

Housing is not considered a benefit in the United States, but given the fact that the government has historically provided everything – food, housing, medical care, etc. – it is considered a benefit in China.

The government has set up housing funds to encourage investment in real estate and stimulate construction, and is beginning to require hefty contributions from employers and employees in some cities, including Shanghai and now Beijing. Employees are entitled to 100% of their individual contributions but not necessarily 100% of the company contribution that has created some controversy in the foreign community.

Some companies offer **Supplemental-housing benefits**, such as matched savings programs, interest-free housing loans, rental allowances, etc.

Others

Employers are also often required to make other payments for workers compensation, education-training and maternity leave. In all, foreign employers in cities that conform to the unified model can expect to pay 30-50% of employees' wages in aggregate social security contributions. Following are other supplemental benefits sometimes provided by companies in China: tuition refunds (companies may pay university tuition fees which can amount to RMB 20,000 in China or substantially more for study abroad, which is a strong retention tool, ironically), travel allowances and educational assistance for employees transferred away from their home-town (on a semi-permanent basis are also provided for inpats or employees on secondment to locations outside their place of residence), car loans or access to company cars, and education loans for children of employees.

Chapter 14

Training

By Bonnie Furst, BIMBA Executive MBA Program
Professor, Beijing University

Training and Development in China

Training in some western companies is considered a luxury or an option to be provided to staff in good times when funds are plentiful. In hard times, training is often the first thing to go. This is generally not the case in China. There are labor laws governing joint ventures and wholly-owned foreign enterprises that require efforts be made to provide professional and technical training to workers. It is also often difficult to recruit staff who possess all the required qualifications, especially in the management and advanced technology areas, making training a real need that must be addressed.

Training and development is also one of the most important functions for developing companies in developing countries, and for localizing, filling expatriate positions by local staff that have been trained and prepared to take on new responsibilities, in particular.

Many investors think localizing just happens by osmosis but find out the hard way that this is not true. The most successful localization efforts are the results of careful selection of the incumbents to fill the position and plans to help the person master the technical requirements of the job as well as the social and political aspects. As shown in the above chart, good localizing plans can be pictured as a type of see saw, where the expat and the local take turns observing/shadowing each other over a period of time of about two years.

During this time period, several important milestones must be achieved, none of which can be done in a rush under normal circumstances:

In the first months, after the assignment is announced, the local shadows and observes the expat to confirm interest and potential to do the job. The expat documents the procedures and policies involved and lets the local study the technical requirements of the job. This may require sending the local out for formal training to remedy specific skill gaps.

In the middle of the period, the local works and studies in the country of the headquarters to both become acquainted with and fluent in the home country culture and work ethic, policies and strategies, and to begin establishing the network of contacts he or she will need to succeed in the new job back on the mainland when the expat returns to HQ.

The local then performs assignments or parts of the job under supervision of the expat and then without supervision of the expat, and eventually is doing more or all of the job, first with the expat shadowing him or her and then completely independently. This model provides just the right amount of time to build self confidence and the confidence of others in the local's ability to do the expat's job very well.

What Training Means to Chinese Employees

Training is critical both to enable employees to do their jobs and to retain employees. Training is extremely important to the average upwardly mobile employee in China. Education is seen as the key to the future, providing employees with skills needed to earn promotions, higher levels of pay, more interesting job opportunities and opportunities to travel. Training that is provided outside China is particularly valuable both for its value in helping employees develop international perspectives and skills, and for the opportunity to see the world. Training is translated into promotions, increased income, more interesting work and not least, travel opportunities, especially abroad.

Chinese employees are both hungry to learn new skills, but many unfortunately have inherited some bad habits from college days where rampant cheating got them through school and helped them obtain degrees. Employees have been known to pay for grades and certificates, and the tradition of cheating the system has made its way into company offices and training classrooms.

For this reason, companies should be careful to invest only in programs where competency must be demonstrated and should take care to investigate the quality of training programs they invest in and send employees to.

Management and technical training is available from many sources in China. The *Directory of Training Services* in China provides a fairly comprehensive guide to training offerings in China, which are organized into the standard categories of management training, technical training, communications skills, cross-cultural training, etc. The directory lists external training firms and international MBA programs. The Universal Ideas Consultancy Group in Beijing can also provide lists of foreign and domestic universities in China. Large corporations, such as Motorola, Nokia, etc., also provide extensive internal training programs.

Multinational companies often provide cross-cultural training to help their management teams function effectively and to expose their PRC staff to other points of view. Such courses range from general orientations, to Chinese history and culture as well as practical advice

Successful Localization Strategies

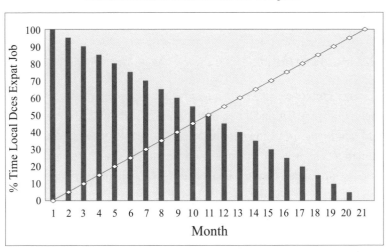

Localization Process – 10 Steps

1. Local observes while expat trains, then local works while expat supervises to build confidence on both sides
2. Local observes and shadows expat 100%
3. Expat documents work in expat language
4. Local studies procedures policies
5. Local studies and works abroad at HQ
6. Local returns works assignments w/ expat
7. Local works abroad at HQ
8. Expat documents work in local language
9. Expat supervises work of local
10. Expat observes shadows local 100%

on dealing with management issues that commonly arise in multi-cultural workplaces.

On the job training includes every day tutoring and training done formally to implement localization plans such as described above and informally between supervisor and staff, as well as self study now through the internet from sources such as **Online Education** – now available in Chinese and English from **BeiDa University www.beida-online. com**.

Degree Assistance

Younger employees often wish their foreign employers would provide them with an MBA and a passport to the United States to cash in on it, and employers in China should be careful not to promise either. The American embassy frowns on American employers who promise visas or passports when hiring Chinese staff, and considers it abuse of the privileges it extends to AmCham members to use the express lane visa program. In extreme cases, managers have been found selling visas or passports, and disciplinary action has been taken.

Practically speaking, it is not possible to promise Chinese staff that they can study abroad, so employers should exercise prudence when describing their training programs and opportunities to study or work abroad. Visas are becoming increasingly hard to get given the growing numbers of people who get them and don't return.

MBAs are still a bargain in China but employers often get what they pay for. The international programs such as those offered in China by Rutgers and CEIBS are quite good, but so is B MBA, the international MBA offered by *Beida*.

More and more graduate school teachers have studied abroad, use imported text books from the top schools and invite professionals with practitioners to enhance the value of their business school programs. The best way to find a good program is to ask fellow HR executives who have already sent their employees to various programs to find the ones that best meet the company's needs and budgets and the employee's expectations.

Providing employees with degrees can be an effective retention tool as well as reap benefits for the company. But they can present a considerable cost both in terms of tuition and fees and employee time away from the job. Some companies therefore ask employees to sign training bonds or promises to stay with the company or repay the company the tuition if they leave the company before some specified period of time, usually two to three years.

Since finding qualified managers is a challenge and top employees expect employers to fund some of their graduate education, we provide below a list of the better known available MBA programs:

Beijing International MBA (BIMBA) Programme – degrees awarded by Fordham University and the prestigious Beijing University China Centre of Economic Research
China Centre of Economic Research
Beijing University
Beizhao No. 17
Beijing 100871
People's Republic of China

Rutgers University School of Managements Beijing Executive MBA programme – degrees awarded by Rutgers University and the Dalian University of Technology, located at Motorola University
Tel: (86 10) 8526-2528,9
Fax: (86 10) 6500-7299
www.uichina.com

Kellogg-Hong Kong University of Science and Technology (HKUST) Executive MBA programme – degrees awarded by Northwestern University's Kellogg School and HKUST
Office of the EMBA Programme
Hong Kong University of Science and Technology
Clear Water Bay
Kowloon, Hong Kong

Nanyang Business School (Singapore) – degrees awarded by Nanyang Technological University and Massachusetts Institute of Technology.
Tel: (65) 874 4474
Fax: (65) 775 2920

Motorola University
Tel: (86 10) 6564 2288
Fax: (86 10) 6566 8457

State University of New York (SUNY) at Buffalo School of Managements China Executive MBA programme – degrees awarded SUNY Buffalo and Renmin University in Beijing
Professor Erming Xu, Dean, School of Business Administration
Renmin University of China
175 Haidian Road
Beijing China 100872
Tel: (86 10) 6251 2823

Supervision and Performance Management

Creative Management in China

You have to think out of the box when you manage IT people,

especially developers, says one China hand who is a manager of a software development firm in China. IT people are almost like artists in a way, they are not punching clock folks.

Their organization is flat, with a minimum of bureaucracy, and few job grades. Titles are creative, too, since face is so important in China. This firm lets employees pick the title used on their business card. Their goal is to have a creative organization, one that is flexible enough to bring out programmers' and developers talents. One way to create this type of organization is to have HR policies that foster this type of creativity, such as allowing developers to come into work anytime before 3 to play computer games before starting work which goes until about midnight. The company also provides a dinner allowance to buy dinner but does not pay overtime.

Trends in Supervision

Approaches to supervision are flexible. Managers tend to use the styles their bosses used or that they learned in their home countries or formative years. Enterprises in China suffer from the same lack of systematic people-management training that their counterparts suffer from outside China. The result is that some people manage and supervise well and others need improvement but stronger leaders tend to be more respected in the paternalistic environment of Chinese culture.

In addition, foreign companies in China are relatively new and often suffer from poor control systems, making them more vulnerable to theft and fraud than they need be if they invested some time up front to establish clear policies and firm operational and financial controls. Without such aids, supervisors have an unnecessarily heavy burden, and in some cases, end up relying on archaic penalty and punishment systems to enforce staff compliance with company policies and procedures.

HR Practices Improve Company Control

Kevan Bradshaw, the leader of PricewaterhouseCooper's Global Risk Management Solutions practice in China, has been advising companies on risks such as these for a number of years: "Companies at all stages of development in China – from start-up ventures to well-established companies – are well-advised to take stock of their risk management abilities. There are many HR practices that unwittingly increase a company's risk of fraud and corruption, such as matrix management, downsizing and expatriate management rotations. One program that we have successfully implemented in China to deal with these risks is our Employee Integrity Programme which is designed to select the most suitable candidates based on genuine qualifications, protect assets against fraudsters and screen out employees who have a history of antisocial behavior.

Performance Management Practices

Not all western HR practices and tools are appropriate for China and one of the most controversial has been the one-on-one performance appraisal. In the early years of investment in China, people were genuinely fearful of implementing individual performance reviews for fear of employees viewing them as the dreaded pi pings and self-criticisms imposed on them during the Cultural Revolution.

But this has tended not to be the case. As is usually the case when anything is imported to China, the Chinese consider it, tailor and dilute it to make it suitable for use. Consequently, in foreign companies in China, one can find a variety of approaches to performance appraisal ranging from the traditional Chinese approach of writing and sharing self-assessments with one's unit or department head, to group evaluations and discussions of the departments performance to the use of American style top-down performance reviews and even 360-degree appraisals.

What seems to matter more is the skill with which the persons involved in the review perform the review. Communication skills, cultural sensitivity and politeness go a long way to conducting an effective and productive review session. Of course, if financial rewards can be tied to good performance, they are even more effective.

Rewards

Profitability allowing, companies in China make liberal use of annual bonuses and profit sharing schemes which can take such forms as awarding shares of stock, matching savings programs, high-potential study-work-abroad programs, etc. Employees in China who work hard appreciate getting recognition, promotions and financial rewards when they have earned it, and are becoming less nervous about being singled out for such distinctions than they may have been in the past.

Punishments

Amazingly, despite the proliferation of western profit sharing methods, penalty schemes still abound particularly in the factories and facilities of joint ventures formed by taking staff from former state owned enterprises.

Employee Handbooks and Personnel Policies

A very important tool in China to providing appropriate supervision, managing employee morale and preventing the need to terminate employment is the Employee Handbook. As one manager at FESCO said, if it isn't written down, you can't fire someone for it. Chinese employees are used to working in environments with books of rules, and are also notorious for learning how to work around them.

A cultural predilection to be fluid and try to get around things makes it difficult for managers to manage behavior, and almost impossible to terminate employment for poor performance on the job.

So at the very least, Employee Handbooks should provide a clear picture of what is considered acceptable behavior and what will be considered grounds for termination of employment, and all new hires should be required to read the policies and sign a statement that they have done so and accept the company's terms of employment. Labor contracts should reference the handbook as well as applicable job descriptions so there is no doubt what the employee is being paid to do and not to do.

Handbooks usually cover policies on the following topics (*see next page*):

The Chinese government has been notorious for the fragmented state of its labor and tax administration systems. As a result, labor regulations are issued not only at the national level but at the provincial and local levels as well which makes it difficult to find out what the rules of the game are in any particular locality or to implement efficient and consistent China-wide HR practices. It has even been difficult to know how to plan work, because the government doesn't announce its public holidays until shortly before the holiday itself, even though it could easily publish such a calendar.

As for public holidays, China now has ten, although exactly when they fall could vary from year to year:

Holiday	Number of days	Dates
Chinese New Year	3	Late January to mid-February
International Labour Day	3	May 1st approximately
National Day	3	First two weekdays of October
New Year's Day	1	First weekday of the New Year

Employee Handbook Topics in China

1 Outside Employment
2 Working Hours
3 Office Hours
4 Absenteeism, Tardiness
5 Timesheets
6 Overtime
7 Confidential Information
8 Business Ethics
9 Conflict of Interest, Gifts
10 Corruption
11 Recruiting, Hiring and Probation
12 Confirmation of Employment
13 Training and Career Development
14 Termination
15 Disciplinary Action
16 Resignation
17 Settlement of Employee Accounts
18 Grievance and Appeal
19 Salary Administration
20 Payment of Salaries
21 Salary Adjustments
22 Performance Plans
23 Performance Reviews
24 Performance Bonuses
25 Benefits
26 Insurance
27 Annual Leave
28 Public and Company Holidays
29 Work Related Sick Leave
30 Non Work Related Sick Leave
31 Marriage Leave
32 Maternity Leave
33 Bereavement Leave
34 Work Meal Allowances
35 Stock Ownership Program
36 Clean Desk Clean Office Policy
37 Image and Dress
38 Office Safety and Security
39 Company Computer Equipment
40 Company Software and Systems
41 E-mail, Internet and Our Website
42 Computer Filing Systems
43 Office Telephones and Fax
44 Company Mobile Phones
45 Business Travel
46 Business Entertainment
47 Expense Reporting
48 Use of Logo
49 Business Cards
50 Use of Conference Rooms

Confidentiality Policies and Enforcement

In high tech companies, the handling of confidential information and company secrets, records, etc. are extremely valuable assets. Employee training and Employee Handbooks should include language along these lines:

Sample Employee Handbook Language–Handling of Confidential Information

In order to perform your job efficiently, from time to time you will be entrusted with confidential and commercially sensitive information. You shall not at any time, either during or after the period of your employment, disclose to any person whomsoever any such information, whether relating to the Company and its business or its related companies, customers, suppliers and personnel or any of the Company's proprietary documentation, risk mitigation structures, or other trade secrets.

You are obliged to ensure that all business and Company operational documentation is safeguarded and that said documentation is returned to the Company on termination of employment or at the request of the Company during the course of employment.

Upon joining the Company, all Employees sign an agreement regarding confidential information. As provided in our Employment Contract and Confidentiality Agreement, each Employee is responsible for following the Company's procedures for handling and protecting confidential information.

Our Company considers all information (including contracts, documentation, structures) related to our Employees, customers, business partners, investors or competitors. All passwords as well as Company policies and procedures are confidential information.

Confidential material in hard copy should be locked away at the end of each business day. Confidential information in computer files should be password protected. Extremely confidential information should either be sent as an attached password protected file or an encrypted file when using e-mail.

Business Ethics

All Employees are expected to uphold a high standard of integrity and business ethics in all dealings with customers, suppliers and each other.

Employment Termination, Restructuring, and Managing Headcount

Easy or Hard

As the story below suggests, terminating employment is not as easy to do in China as it is in the United States. Except in cases where employees have signed fixed terms contracts where the term has expired, or when they are in their initial 3 months probation period, the employee must usually have committed a serious crime, been caught red handed violating a documented company policy, or the company must have a well document case against the employee in terms of poor performance that is backed up with lots of incontrovertible and tangible evidence, and the employee should not be politically connected to anyone important affecting the company.

Specifically, national labor law explains certain circumstances under which people's employment may be terminated, but most of these must have concrete evidence to support the action:

☐ The employer can demonstrate the employee's failure to comply with the job requirements during the probationary period

☐ The employee has violated company operating policy or any provisions in a foreign-invested enterprise's labour-procedures manual

☐ The employee has committed a serious dereliction of duty, or undertaken activities such as favouritism or graft resulting in serious financial losses for the employer

☐ The employee has been charged with a crime

Employers are also entitled to terminate an employment contract provided 30 days prior written notice has been given to the employee and provided that one of the following has happened:

Power Struggles in the Provinces

The electricity was off and a few workers were milling about on the factory floor. Notices were posted on the walls awarding everyone an impromptu day off. It was not the sort of welcome the boss expects when he visits a rural subsidiary that cost him US$ 18 million. For Jack Perkowski, 51, it marked a nadir in his experience of running 17 Chinese manufacturing ventures employing nearly 16,000 people. He soon found out the reason for the slapdash state of affairs: the factory's local manager had heard that Mr. Perkowski's investment company was going to fire him. He had turned off the power and sent workers home in an effort to show his new master who was really in charge.

What happened next Mr. Perkowski regards as evidence of real change in the tide between old and new China. He rang the Communist party chief of Ningguo, the city where the factory was located, and was invited to lunch. "I saw the factory at 9 a.m. and by 11 a.m. I was with the Communist party secretary. I told them of our desire to make the joint venture work, that we were a long-term investor in China but that in order to achieve our aims, we needed the power to be turned back on." Party officials' subsequent decision to restore the electricity represented a triumph of commercial realism over local politics. By siding with a foreigner against a powerful local, the Ningguo government was taking a risk.

In the old China of the 1980s and early 1990s Mr. Perkowski says local government officials regarded themselves as the guardians of state assets, and foreigners in joint ventures with state-run companies were rarely given the power to select senior management. But now, officials are more likely to be focused on generating employment opportunities and tax revenues.

Mr. Perkowski says that his company will post its first net profit this year with earnings of US$ 5 million on sales of US$ 200 million. He believes the key is to recruit new China managers, people between 30 and 50, with some formal management training and experience in a multinational in China and a state-run company. These people understand both worlds and now what has to be done, and most importantly, how to connect the two.

Financial Times, June 22, 2000

☐ The employee has not performed his job satisfactorily following the completion of medical treatment for illness or non-work-related injury

☐ The employees performance has remained unsatisfactory after further training or a transfer to another position

☐ The objective circumstances that provided the basis for the employment contract have changed substantially, making it impossible for the terms of the employment contract to be fulfilled and, after consultation, the employer and employee cannot agree on amendments to reflect such change

Employees may usually terminate their employment with only 30 days' notice, except where a signed legal agreement allows otherwise, and the employee may leave without giving notice under the following circumstances: during the probationary period, the employer has used violence or threats to coerce the employee into work, the employer fails to provide working conditions as stipulated in the employment contract.

Furthermore, the following workers may not be laid off under national labour law:

☐ Workers who suffer from a work-related injury who are totally or partially unable to work.

☐ Ill or injured workers undergoing medical treatment.

☐ Female workers who are pregnant or on maternity leave.

☐ Other conditions as stipulated by supplementary notices or local regulations.

Protecting Your Company

For these reasons, it is imperative that companies document their policies and rules in writing such as in Employee Handbooks and make them easily accessible to all staff. Clear contracts in writing and signed and filed with the relevant labor bureau, union and/or labor agency also help, as does doing good pre-employment screening.

Downsizing or Ramping Down

Finally, it is not easy and can be costly to downsize. Exactly how much grief and money it will cost depends on the nature of contracts and years of service the employees involved have put in. Generally employers must pay at least one month's wage for every year of service, but companies often pay more to have a peaceful ending. Given recent pension reform, many employees complain that their severance packages and pension benefits will leave them destitute, so downsizing and plant closings must be handled delicately, preferably outplacing workers as much as possible.

Companies should also be aware of the Double Ten Rule – if a worker has been employed by an enterprise for ten or more years, or if he or she is within ten years of retirement age (60 for men, 50 for women), the employee has the right to demand an open-ended contract. Since workers remaining in service after a state-owned enterprise is converted to foreign-invested status are considered to be in continuous service, foreign employers could find themselves with lifelong obligations to certain employees acquired from the local partner. Lifetime employment really is lifetime. Companies in these situations must continue to pay housing, medical, pension, etc. To simplify things, some companies just send redundant staff home and pay them a nominal wage to not come to work and avoid the issue altogether.

Managing Employee and Union Relations

National labor law requires foreign enterprises to provide for the welfare and safety of their employees. Until recently, firms were allowed to decide pretty much for themselves to what extent and how this would be handled. Unlike western companies, Chinese companies do not normally have employee relations functions per se. Instead the Party and union leaders, and the general managers per se have been expected to attend to matters of employee safety and morale.

Recently the government has issued various laws covering many areas impacting employee welfare including individual and collective labor contracts, working hours, holidays, wages, occupational health and safety, the protection of women and minors, vocational training, social insurance and welfare, labor disputes, and supervision and inspection.

In general, employer/employee cooperation and the efficient operation of the venture are influenced by the chemistry between the Chinese and foreign partners and among the leaders on the management team. Foreign partners of newly established joint ventures often experience problems arising from the different management techniques and business procedures practiced in China and the West, as well as from cultural and linguistic barriers.

For the most part, both foreign and domestic firms comply with the spirit of the laws affecting employee welfare and employee relations. However, the government has recently given more power to the unions and other watchdog positions such as party officials in order to improve compliance overall and to shift responsibility for citizen welfare away from the already over burdened government which can no longer provide the cradle-to-grave security it once was able to provide.

Unions on the Rise in China

The word union in the U.S. could conjure up images of workers picketing in front of a factory or endless wage negotiations between the employer and employees. If you have worked in China for any length of time, the word union more likely brings to mind company karaoke outings, handling of minor infringements of company policy and possibly CCP education classes.

From 1992, when the Labor Union Law was enacted until 2000, there wasn't much new union legislation, but not so any more. Now five of the 15 labor laws likely to be promulgated soon will give unions more power in their role of the protector of the workers (*see insert at end of this newsletter*). And while it has not been entirely clear whether or not a company had to establish a union, it should be soon – possibly in July 2002 – at which time it could become mandatory according to a recent announcement in *China Daily*, August 31, 2001. If a union shows up and convinces staff to unionize, companies will have to say yes.

The likely causes for the government's turning up the heat on the union front are a combination of 1) pressures building up in the ranks of the unemployed and under protected in terms of social welfare benefits such as unemployment insurance and pensions, and 2) recent instances of bad management among both local and foreign firms in China. Examples of misbehavior include preventing workers from joining trade unions, illegally hiring workers without signed contracts, forcing people to work longer than the required hours, irregular salaries, not making contributions to statutory benefit funds, safety violations and most recently harassment of female workers:

What does this mean for foreign companies trying to do business in China? While the union has often been the employer's friend, the change will likely also make it more difficult to negotiate salary increases and employment terminations with staff. Labor costs could increase for foreign enterprises currently without unions, due to a requirement to contribute 2% of payroll to a labor fund, higher wages, and increased legal and administrative costs to deal with union management. In

Korea when unions were finally legalized, salaries went up 25% to 30% a year for several years, in some cases to levels higher than their U.S. counterparts. While China is not Korea, it is worth taking note of the possible implications.

In most cases, where the foreign employer is already a good corporate citizen and perhaps a generous employer, cordial relationships will likely continue. For companies not following the requirements of labor law, however, it will mean making painful changes. The year 2002 will be the Year of the Horse and a good time to see how prepared your organization in China is to run the race.

As can be seen above, for all practical intents and purposes, it is no longer a good strategy to assume one's firm will not have to form, fund and cooperate with a union. The best of all possible worlds is to create the kind of work environment where employees no longer see the need to have a union, but where this is not possible for political or other reasons, the next best strategy is to pro-actively take steps to clean house in terms of labor and safety practices and staff union positions with the most capable and business-minded personnel available.

Developing or Outsourcing the HR Function

Until recently, there was a shortage of globally trained and experienced human resources professionals in China. Senior executive HR positions were almost all filled by expatriates or repatriated overseas Chinese and HR conferences were attended primarily by expatriate HR Directors and General Managers who were accompanied by their Office Managers.

However, in the last year and a half, Human Resource Management as a profession has become better established and the tables have turned. Chinese is the language used in most professional HR gatherings today and the ranks of mainland Chinese HR professionals with five years or more experience are swelling. Mainland Chinese view a career in human resources management and/or consulting as attractive and HRM-oriented courses of study and certificate programs are on the rise.

Nevertheless, there still exists a need to train more people to fill this critical function and improve their global business perspectives as the competition for skilled HR professionals intensifies.

One temporary solution that foreign investors are turning to is HR Outsourcing.

The Case for Outsourcing

Human resource (HR) management is a strategic component of a successful business in every country including China. The development and maintenance of effective HR management has greater impact in a developing country like China where transparency and rule of law may not be as evident as in more developed economies.

The following case study will illustrate the possible consequences of not having effective HR management in China and provide an example where HR outsourcing can help.

A global 1,000 consumer product company had launched its products successfully in China and was contemplating a major expansion. Recently however, assistance from the home country management team was required to resolve a dispute between the host country General Manager and Deputy General Manager. The General Manager decided to resolve the dispute by terminating the employment of the Deputy General Manager.

During the implementation of this termination, the company was faced with the following events and circumstance. First, even though there was a physical altercation, the Deputy Manager's employment could not be terminated as sufficient documentation and direct proof was not available. Therefore, the company had to propose a termination package that was far in excess of the legal requirements which created a precedent for future termination packages. Second, the company then realized that the inventory in China was legally registered under the name of the Deputy General Manager. The company was faced with the possibility of having to purchase their inventory from the former Deputy General Manager. Third, many of the key distributors in China hesitated to further conduct business with the company due to their long-standing relationship with the Deputy General Manager. Due to this confusion, important orders from key customers could not be fulfilled which resulted in a material decline in market share. In a very short time frame, the company's profitable operation in China was facing a substantial decline in revenues and possible damage to their brand image as well as legal difficulties.

Although hindsight is 20/20, there may have been human resources management steps that the company could have undertaken to reduce or eliminate the risks and liabilities relating to the above incidents. There was no formal HR policy or employee handbook that was specific to China. Although the company's home office policy and handbook were available, it had not been reviewed properly for its applicability to China. The company lacked a formal evaluation process for all staff including the General Manager and Deputy General Manager. It also did not have an objective third party familiar with the China labor conditions to develop and enforce the evaluation process.

In addition, the management did not properly examine the various relationships between their employees with vendors, customers and other key parties. Company management also had not prepared an impartial channel of communication for employees to express their concerns and grievances. Prior to undertaking the termination process, independent third party legal counsel and HR professionals had not been consulted. There was never a systematic audit of its HR function during the company's ten year history in China by third parties familiar with China and its business practices. Due in part to the meteoric rise in revenues and profits in China, company management neglected key HR issues.

In a perfect world, it would be desirable to have a full complement of HR executives and staff in every market to resolve a company's HR issues. This resource, however, may not be possible in every country; even if a company does have an HR department in a specific market, it may not be able to handle every complicated HR issue relating to both expatriates and PRC nationals. This dilemma is further complicated by exogenous economic events that may decrease the company's internal HR resources to deal with the above events. To augment a company's HR resources, outsourcing their HR functions to independent third party HR professionals may represent the most optimal and economic solution.

PART V

TELECOMMUNICATIONS AND INFORMATIZATION

The Chinese government attaches great importance to the development of the information industry and is striving for the informatization of the national economy and society. As a developing country, China has not finished its industrialization process and is faced with the huge task of realizing an informatization economy. A national strategy has been adopted to make use of the information technology in the process of industrialization so as to reach a higher standard and renovate traditional businesses with information technology. Information technology will be used to push industrialization in a bid to leapfrog development. With WTO unprecedented opportunities will open for foreign participation in this bold and dynamic growth sector.

Chapter 15

Telecommunications

By Peter Lovelock, Director of Insight
and Tara Tranguch, Buzz Director, MSC Insight

Deregulation/Liberalization

The information economy has become an ever more central part of, and is playing an ever increasing role in, China's national economic development. Communications networks provide the infrastructure of the national economy, constituting the basis and major driving force for what in China is known as national "informatization. "

Information and communication technologies (ICTs) have become a focal development point for almost all countries due to their impact upon – and significance to – the national economy. In China they have been given particular strategic importance. The Fifth Plenary Session of the Fifteenth National Congress of the Communist Party of China held in October 2000 made it clear that the development of the information industry should be the driving force for industrialization and the late-take-off advantage should be taken to achieve a leap-forward (or "leapfrog") development of social productivity. Based on this requirement, in the next five years, China's information industry is expected to continue to grow at a speed higher than 20 percent.

MII Minister Wu Jichuan has stated that during the current 10th Five Year Plan (2001- 2005), the scale of the market will be doubled, and that both the scale and capacity of the fixed mobile telecommunication networks are to become the largest in the world. However, in order for this goal to be met, effective development strategies and measures oriented to the new economy communications networks need to be adopted.

According to Minister Wu, China will pursue five strategies in order to achieve its goals:

☐ Advanced technologies will be adopted to upgrade the information infrastructure into a network with super high capacity and the ability to integrate voice, data and video.

☐ The ICT manufacturing industry and software industry will be fully revitalized so that China can become technologically self-reliant and emphasize locally manufactured equipment.

☐ Information services to promote industrialization, such as e-commerce, must be developed.

☐ A regulatory system must be established to clarify foreign investment in the telecommunications sector.

☐ China will continue opening up to the outside world in order to bridge the digital divide with other more developed countries.

China's rate of opening in telecommunications and high-technology is thus, once again, accelerating, and 2002 appears to be a year of tremendous transition – due to domestic reform and industry development, but also as a result of WTO accession.

During this year of transition, how should outside players view China's telecom market and how should they prepare to enter the market? This chapter provides an overview of China's telecom market by briefly reviewing the past decade of deregulation and liberalization; looking at the current rate of growth and where that growth is occurring; and then examining how WTO will impact China's telecom market in terms of foreign investment and licensing. An appendix of detailed information on China's telecom administration and regulation bodies and legislation has also been provided for reference.

Domestic Competition

As with most countries, China's telecommunications sector was state-owned for decades. To build a communication infrastructure that could connect all areas in China required a large amount of investment that only the government could provide. As such, up until the early 1990s, the government's development and reform objectives in telecommunications were fairly straightforward and far from unique – to provide affordable basic telephony and information services to as large a population as possible, and to attract the necessary capital to further expand and modernize the network. From the mid-1990s until today, China's market has been rapidly opening up with the entrance of new carriers. Today, there are six operating carriers in China with more on the verge of launching services including China Telecom, China Mobile, China Unicom, China Netcom, China Jitong and China Railcom.

In 1994, the then Ministry of Electronics Industry (MEI) sponsored the introduction of two new carriers to enter the market – China Unicom and China Jitong – in direct competition with the incumbent China Telecom (supported by the then Ministry of Post and Telecommunications (MPT), now a part of the MII). Since competition had emerged from outside the conservative MPT and the new network pluralism required explicit State Council approval, observers saw what they wanted to see: China adopting the worldwide trend towards telecoms liberalization and sector competition. This was an overly simplistic interpretation. The introduction of the two new carriers (China Unicom and Jitong) started something close to network competition, but perhaps the best way to describe this is "telecommunications, with Chinese characteristics."

Before the MII was formed in 1998*, turf wars between the different ministries provided the defining context for competition and liberalization. (This is still the case, just between different entities, so it is a worthwhile lesson to understand.) While the introduction of Unicom and Jitong appeared to many to break the MPT's monopoly it would be more correct to see Unicom and Jitong as rounding out China's telecom sector in the hopes of preventing strong foreign intrusion while also accessing capital and expertise, increasing domestic competitiveness, and both protecting and strengthening the domestic telecom industry in the long run.

What determined China's policy framework was not a desire to liberalize the sector, but an overall objective to develop a strong telecommunication industry because this was important to Chinese modernization. The tenets of telecommunication industry policy were:

☐ the need to rapidly develop the telecommunication/ information infrastructure;

☐ the need for capital to fund both the build-out and industry development;

☐ the need to encourage and encompass nascent market-demand;

---

* In March, 1998, the Ninth National People's Congress ratified a wide-ranging restructuring of China's state bureaucracy. The MII absorbed the former Ministry of Posts & Telecommunications (MPT), the Ministry of Electronics Industry (MEI),parts of the Ministry of Radio, Film and Television (MRFT) and segments of other government bodies.

and

☐ the desire to maintain control and centralized power.

Specifically, this resulted in a focus upon: teledensity growth, finance and supplementary (or, "value-added") networks, which included the paging and mobile telephony sectors, the cable TV networks, the development of the Internet, and the subsequent issues of interconnection and interoperability.

Break-up of the Monopoly

By the end of the 1990s China's telecom industry was undergoing its most dramatic changes. First, competition was pushed rapidly along and, having debated many different options (including splitting the incumbent along geographic lines), China Telecom was split into four different business units: China Mobile Communications Group, which received the mobile license; China Satellite, given the satellite license; Guoxin Paging, which was gifted to China Unicom; and China Telecom, which held its basic telecom license. (Interestingly, at this point in time, Unicom became the only fully-licensed carrier in China.) Beyond enterprise reform, China's government underwent a significant restructuring and the MEI and MPT were dissolved into the so-called "super-Ministry", the Ministry of Information Industry (MII).

The provision of experimental IP telephony licenses in 1999 to Unicom, Jitong and Netcom effectively served to erode China Telecom's international monopoly because it allowed the three other carriers to transmit international traffic without having an international license. This expanded all the carriers' coverage enormously and as a result, Jitong, Unicom and Netcom all began building international gateways in anticipation of being awarded international licenses. VoIP licensing essentially allowed other licensed carriers to get a solid foothold in

China's telecom market with the ability to carry voice transmissions outside the country's borders, provide competition to China Telecom, and earn revenues.

Emergence of Netcom

In 1998, the State Radio, Film and Television Bureau of the State Council in conjunction with the Ministry of Railways, Chinese Academy of Science and the Shanghai Municipal Government established China Netcom Corporation (CNC). Netcom was conceived to be a model of China's new telecom enterprise. Premier Zhu Rongji asked Edward Tian Sunning to leave the systems integration company he had founded with partner, James Ding, AsiaInfo, to head Netcom. With Zhu's backing, Tian took to managing Netcom like a private firm – complete with Western-style corporate by-laws.

One of the unique qualities about Netcom's development was its ability to secure private foreign investment. The company closed its first round of private equity solicitation in February 2001, raising US$ 325 million from a group of high-profile international investors, including Dell Corp., News Corp. Digital Ventures, Goldman Sachs Private Equity, and other leading Hong Kong and Chinese financial institutions. Netcom claims to be the first direct private investment in a Chinese telecom firm by international financiers; it gave up 12 percent of its equity to investors that also included state-owned banks.

New Entrants

In 2000, China Railway Telecom (Railcom) was approved by the MII and the State Council to be China's sixth licensed telecom operator. Railcom has been licensed to provide all communication services excluding mobile. Railcom spent the entire year of 2001 contending with bureaucratic issues such as interconnection with other carriers and the allocation of number resources from the MII. As of early 2002, the only service Railcom had officially launched had been VoIP services in Beijing and a handful of other cities.

In 2001, the liberalization agenda increased further with the issuance of China's eighth telecom license going to a firm named CNet, the first privately owned enterprise to be given such a license by the MII (*see table*). This new license is remarkable not only because it is further evidence of the rapid increase in competition in China's telecom marketplace, but also because it illustrates the perspective of the authorities in the lead up to WTO. Once WTO accession occurs foreign investment will need to partner with Chinese entities under the current restrictions. This new license indicates that China's government is preparing the groundwork for that next wave of foreign capital.

China's Telecom Carriers

	Fixed	IP	Internet	Data	VAS	VSAT	Mobile	Satellite	Paging
Telecom	Y	Y	Y	Y	Y	Y	-	-	Y
Unicom	Y	Y	Y	Y	Y	Y	Y	Y	Y
Mobile	-	Y	Y	Y	Y	-	Y	-	-
Jitong	-	Y	Y	Y	Y	Y	-	Y	-
Netcom	-	Y	Y	Y	Y	-	-	-	-
Railcom	Y	Y	Y	Y	Y	Y	-	Y	Y
ChinaSat	-	-	Y	-	-	Y	-	Y	-
China CNet	-	Y	Y	-	Y	-	-	-	-

VAS= Value-added Services
Source: MFC Insight

Another notable move in the last year (in this regard) was the formation of a joint venture between China International Trust and Investment Corporation (CITIC) and China Telecommunications Broadcast Satellite Corporation (ChinaSat). Because ChinaSat is one of eight basic telecom operators in China, CITIC has essentially received a license for basic telecom operations. The license is not a sure thing, however, since China recently passed the *Implementing Regulations for the Law of the People's Republic of China on Equity Joint Ventures* stating that license operators holding less than a 51 percent share of their joint venture will **not** be able to pass their license on to their joint venture. If CITIC had received China's ninth license, this would have been quite dramatic news since CITIC has been on a remarkable fiber buying spree around China since the end of 1999 and would have immediately become the biggest fixed-line competitor to China Telecom.

Carrier Restructuring, 2002

At the end of 2001, the MII announced that China Telecom would be restructured along geographic lines into northern and southern entities with the northern portion absorbing China Netcom and Jitong (*see table*). This carrier restructuring was summed up as a "5+1" solution, whereby China Telecom, China Netcom, China Mobile, China Unicom, and China Railcom were seen to be the dominant domestic carriers, and ChinaSat was the vaguely anointed "+1"(further confusing CITIC's place in the market). Then, in early 2002, MII Minister Wu further complicated these developments by stating that China would have *four* fully integrated carriers, although it would take roughly two years for the carriers to be fully licensed. It was widely expected that the four full carriers would be China Telecom, China Mobile, China Unicom (already fully licensed), and China Netcom (thus leaving China Railcom in a somewhat confused position) – although nothing official had been

"5+1" Solution

Carrier		Advantages	Mobile Experience	Potential
China Telecom	(China Telecom south)	70% of nationwide trunk lines Fixed line services Largest Internet network Data comms Trunk line leasing	"Little Smart" Fixed CDMA	"Little Smart" to 3G Fixed CDMA Fixed wireless access
China Net Comm. Group	(China Telecom north)	30% of nationwide trunk lines Fixed line services Data comms Trunk line leasing	"Little Smart" Fixed CDMA	"Little Smart" to 3G Fixed CDMA Fixed wireless access
	Netcom	12,000 km DWDM backbone Broadband wholesale	Fixed wireless access	Fixed wireless access Broadband access
	Jitong	2nd largest satellite network 2nd largest Internet network in China VSAT business VoIP business		Satellite data
China Unicom		Fully licensed carrier	CDMA,GSM	2.5G and 3G CDMA Uni-Info
China Mobile		Mobile Mobile data	GSM, GPRS	GPRS and W-CDMA Monternet
China Railcom		Fixed line Data comms Line leasing		Large national service demand
China Telecom Satellite		Largest satellite network providing data, Internet, ISP services	Satellite mobile	Satellite data, Internet services

Source: MFC Insight

said to confirm this. There are also persistent rumors that Railcom and China Unicom could be forced to merge within three years.

The carrier restructuring is partly the result of friction between the various factions within the government and is still in the negotiation stage with regards to how China Telecom will be restructured and who will lead the new carriers. Similarly, China's other carriers are also unsure as to who will receive what license and when. *What does appear to be clear is that the new telecom service industry currently emerging is being formed to receive foreign investment and simultaneously dominate the sector against foreign entrance.*

The Telecommunications Market

Sheer numbers alone make China's telecom market, and especially the mobile market, an attractive proposition. According to the official government numbers, by July 2001, China had become the world's largest mobile market, and by year-end 2001, total fixed-line and cellular subscribers had reached 323.8 million and 145 million, respectively. Despite these big numbers, penetration is only at 13.9 percent for fixed line and 11.2 percent for mobile, revealing that there is still ample room for growth. In addition, China's cable TV market is also the world's largest with 100 million subscribing households as of the end of 2001, growing at a compound growth rate of 6 percent since 1996.

China is a big country, however, and growth and market size are unevenly distributed throughout the country. Unequal growth has prompted the government to promote development of the western regions and to establish a universal service fund to ensure access and improve teledensity rates.

Provincial Disparities

A big market overall, but there are many regional differences that must be considered when determining the robustness of the market. Development is focused predominantly on the three large urban hotbeds: Beijing, Shanghai, and Guangzhou, and then, perhaps, one more notch back, the eastern seaboard linking these three cities together. China's more remote and rural areas – predominantly the western regions – still require basic access. As shown in the table (*see next page*), provincial capacity for both fixed and mobile subscribers is considerably lower for the more underdeveloped western regions than for the eastern and southern regions. The north and northeastern regions also enjoy significantly less capacity although there are exceptions such as Beijing, Hebei and Liaoning.

Nevertheless, China has been focused on equalizing teledensity across all regions, and this has now been combined with an overall economic push out into the Western region. At the 15th Plenary Session in October 2000, Ministry of Information Industry (MII) Vice-Minister Lu Xinkui said that the central government would invest some RMB 120 billion (US$ 14.5 billion) over the next five years in telecom infrastructure in the autonomous regions (Ningxia, Xinjiang, Inner Mongolia, Tibet, Guangxi) inhabited by minority nationalities. The MII aims to have fixed-line penetration hit 25 percent and mobile penetration to reach 10 percent in the autonomous regions within the next five years.

Universal Access

Average teledensity by 2000 was 30 percent for China's urban areas, and was as high as 50-60 percent in cities such as Beijing, Guangzhou and Shanghai. With nationwide teledensity estimated to be approximately 12 percent, the gap has prompted the Ministry of Information

China's Provincial Capacity, December 2001

Location	Fixed ('000s)	Mobile ('000s)	Location	Fixed ('000s)	Mobile ('000s)
NORTH			**SOUTHWEST**		
Beijing	6,302	7,900	Chongqing	3,474	4,794
Tianjin	2,964	2,870	Sichuan	7,069	8,696
Hebei	9,420	8,348	Guizhou	2,233	3,043
Shanxi	4,495	3,803	Yunnan	4,316	5,565
Inner Mongolia	2,764	3,769	Tibet	164	243
Total	25,945	26,690	*Total*	17,256	22,341
NORTHEAST			**SOUTH**		
Liaoning	9,100	9,202	Henan	11,062	8,380
Jilin	4,574	4,730	Hubei	6,892	8,573
Heilongjiang	5,860	5,596	Hunan	7,132	7,000
Total	19,534	19,528	Guangdong	19,798	29,477
			Guangxi	4,349	4,262
			Hainan	1,297	1,275
			Total	50,530	58,967
EAST			**NORTHWEST**		
Shanghai	8,187	11,462	Shaanxi	4,393	6,075
Jiangsu	23,000	15,613	Gansu	2,609	3,286
Zhejiang	17,801	18,460	Qinghai	491	888
Anhui	6,544	6,381	Ningxia	770	788
Fujian	8,268	9,790	Xinjiang	2,695	2,873
Jiangxi	4,489	4,838	*Total*	10,958	13,910
Shandong	15,644	13,224			
Total	83,933	79,768			

Source: *Ministry of Information Industry (MII)*

Industry (MII) to address the uneven pace of development between rural and urban areas – between the eastern and coastal regions (where most of the industrial and urban centers are to be found), and the land-locked central and western regions. Figure (*see next page*) shows what was a gradually narrowing gap in the shares of national telecom revenues coming from the three regions with the share of the eastern region falling from 74 percent to 66 percent (left side), and then 60 percent to 54 percent (right side); the central region rising from 17 percent to 23 percent, and then 24 percent to 27 percent; and the western region rising from 8 percent to 11 percent, and 16 percent to 19 percent.

The mandate to provide basic connectivity and universal access is an important one – not only for political or social reasons, but also for long-term economic reasons and the network development issues it is seen to support. In January 2002, the MII announced that it would establish a universal service fund (USF) using contributions from telecom operators, including foreign firms, to develop networks in rural and western areas. Now that China is a member of WTO, all telecom operators – foreign as well as domestic – will be required to participate in national development.

Should the government meet basic telephone access needs via fixed-line network rollouts or through increasing mobile capacity? Mobile networks are cheaper and faster to rollout, especially in terrain that is mountainous and hard to reach, such as parts of western and northwestern

Regional Revenue Diversity

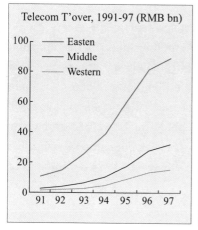
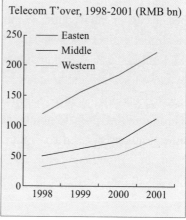

China. Could cable networks be used to achieve universal service, and if so, would the individual provincial cable transmission groups be made to contribute to the fund? It still remains to be seen what services the MII defines as constituting universal service and how it plans to administer the utilization of the funds.

Telecommunications and Mobile Development

Since the early 1980s, the scale of China's telephone network has evolved from millions of subscriber lines, to tens of millions, to hundreds of millions at a remarkably rapid rate. In the 13 years from 1979 to 1992, the total number of fixed line telephone and cellular telephone subscribers grew from 2 million to 10 million. Six years later, in 1998, this figure had reached 100 million and by September 2000, the 100 million figure turned to 200 million – a doubling in less than two years! As of December 2001, China had 323.8 million total subscribers.

The growth of the mobile sector, and its impact upon both the telecommunication industry and, more generally, society, has been an astounding and unforeseen phenomenon. At the turn of 2000, wireless growth became exponential adding 42 million new mobile subscribers in 2000 to almost double the year-end 1999 mobile subscriber figure from 43.3 million to 85.3 million. Over 2001, mobile subscribers increased by close to 60 million to reach 144.8 million. A huge boost to mobile uptake has been the introduction of prepaid tariff options in late-1999. Through 2000, prepaid uptake accounted for 17 million of the new mobile subscribers, and 17.5 million of new mobile subscribers in 2001, bringing the total number of prepaid subscribers to 34.5 million as of December 2001 (*see figure*).

Prepaid & Postpaid Market Share, 2000-01

From postpaid...   *... to prepaid*

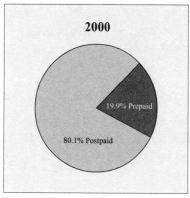

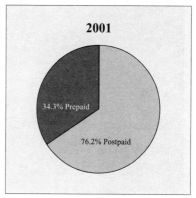

Source: MII

There is no obvious reason to believe that mobile growth will slow dramatically over the next few years. Indeed, given the importance (both political and economic) attached to this sector and the resources being allocated, **MFC Insight** believes that the government's projections continue to be conservative (*see table, next page*). The MII had earlier forecast that mobile subscribers would total 120 million by year-end 2001 (a number already surpassed in July 2001) and 260 million by 2005. **MFC Insight** believes China's total mobile population will exceed 260 million before year-end 2003, and some 418 million by 2005.

China's mobile (and fixed) penetration is still low enough to assume that there is plenty of room for growth. Nevertheless, mobile penetration has been increasing far faster than fixed penetration, and in certain areas mobile penetration has already well exceeded fixed. In Shenzhen, for example, as of the end of June 2001, mobile penetration was at 75 percent and fixed penetration was at 50 percent. The introduction of a new 2G network – China Unicom's CDMA networks – appears set to contribute to further boosting China's mobile growth.

China's 2G Provincial Numbers, 1998–2003

	1998	1999	2000	2001	2002	2003
Beijing	1,033	1,755	3,365	6,174	6,795	7,584
Tianjin	438	707	1,165	2,155	2,820	3,926
Hebei	543	1,199	3,189	5,434	10,203	13,696
Shanxi	290	539	1,532	3,030	5,396	7,286
Inner Mongolia	100	398	1,169	2,276	2,721	3,529
Liaoning	1,084	2,360	4,975	7,038	10,741	14,918
Jilin	505	944	2,037	3,365	5,335	7,860
Heilongjiang	867	1,312	3,421	4,894	6,968	8,843
Shanghai	970	1,807	3,585	6,147	7,622	8,517
Jiangsu	890	2,487	6,240	10,264	14,473	18,494
Zhejiang	1,251	3,073	6,742	11,205	15,424	18,781
Anhui	500	951	2,571	4,192	5,803	7,887
Fujian	1,198	2,656	4,208	6,200	8,512	12,060
Jiangxi	313	626	1,408	3,183	4,744	6,581
Shandong	1,068	2,071	4,485	8,138	13,587	18,006
Henan	935	1,623	3,159	4,940	8,514	10,700
Hubei	531	974	2,297	4,285	6,425	7,886
Hunan	434	946	2,521	4,104	6,243	7,759
Guangdong	3,142	6,388	13,472	23,847	31,370	35,173
Guangxi	331	584	1,675	2,710	4,247	6,117
Hainan	168	284	585	812	1,511	2,070
Chongqing	322	713	1,570	2,705	4,389	5,961
Sichuan	632	1,531	3,324	5,687	9,526	12,443
Guizhou	144	300	795	1,699	3,065	4,298
Yunnan	418	743	1,929	3,386	6,045	78,58
Tibet	7	24	60	113	252	314
Shaanxi	334	659	1,530	2,914	4,313	4,924
Gansu	57	172	638	1,430	3,215	4,696
Qinghai	26	59	195	457	580	836
Ningxia	48	103	215	431	656	972
Xinjiang	102	304	731	1,809	3,507	5,023
National	**18,676**	**38,289**	**84,790**	**145,024**	**215,000**	**275,000**

Source: MII (1998-2000) and MFC Insight (2001-2003)

WTO: Impact and Opportunity

On December 11, 2001 China became a full member of the World Trade Organization (WTO). Entry into the WTO does not in itself rectify China's legal vacuum, but accession has spurred the drafting and issuing of new laws and regulations all attempting to fulfill three goals: protect China's domestic industries, prepare for foreign entrance and help make China's legal environment more transparent. Since accession to the WTO, China has issued several regulations aimed at making the sector WTO-compliant: *the Provisions on the Administration of Foreign Investment Telecommunications Enterprises (FITE Provisions), the Measures on the Administration of Telecommunication Operating Permit, and Beijing's Provisional Measures for the Administration of Mobile Network Value-Added Telecom Services.* One word of warning we would like to stress: *do not expect China to simply increase liberalization following WTO accession. As much as there are moves to open access and market interaction, this is a different agenda from creating a "level playing field." Chinese authorities have been working diligently to take control of industries before the government is forced to open these industries up.*

Under the final deal struck over the country's accession to the WTO, in basic telecom services, foreign investors will still be blocked from controlling telecom joint ventures in China. According to a briefing paper from Geneva outlining the rules for telecoms, foreign service suppliers will be permitted to establish joint venture enterprises, without quantitative restrictions, and provide services in several cities, but originally foreign investment in the joint venture shall be no more than 25 percent. This situation will be progressively liberalized over the following five years: within one year, the areas will be expanded to include services in other cities and foreign investment shall be no more than 35 percent; within three years of accession, foreign investment shall be no more than 49 percent; within five years of accession, there will be no geographic restrictions (*see next page*).

The general provisions include that:*

☐ China will give non-discriminatory treatment to all WTO Members.
☐ China will eliminate dual pricing practices, as well as differences in treatment for goods and services produced for sale in China and those produced for export.
☐ Price controls will not be used to protect domestic industries or domestic service providers.

Agreements are one thing, but China's WTO accession is only the beginning of a long and arduous process of implementing the commitments China has made in its bilateral and multilateral agreements.

The four major challenges stated by the government for China's telecom sector after WTO entry are:

☐ regulatory and enterprise restructuring
☐ two-way versus one-way billing for mobile calls
☐ the enactment of a Telecom Law
☐ universal service

As for tariffs, China will implement the Information Technology Agreement (ITA), which will reduce tariffs from present levels averaging 13. 3 percent to zero for semiconductors, computers, computer equipment, telecommunications equipment and other information technology products. Most of these tariff eliminations will be phased in by 2003 with some exceptions until 2005. All other ITA participants will have implemented tariff cuts by 2005.

---

* China will unify tax rates for both domestic and foreign companies after WTO, but will continue to grant preferential policies to foreign-invested enterprises for infrastructural and high-tech projects and for western development.

The WTO Schedule for Telecoms

Domestic and International Fixed-line Telecommunications
*(including voice, data, circuit and packet-switched, public
services and closed-user groups)*
⇨ Up to 25 percent equity in limited cities Beijing, Guangzhou
and Shanghai three years after accession;
⇨ Up to 35 percent equity five years after accession Beijing,
Guangzhou, Shanghai, Chengdu, Chongqing, Dalian, Fuzhou,
Hangzhou, Nanjing, Ningbo, Qingdao, Shenyang, Shenzhen,
Xiamen, Xi'an, Taiyuan, and Wuhan; and
⇨ Up to 49 percent equity throughout China after six years.
⇨ No geographic restrictions six years after accession.
⇨ China also merely stated that gateway facilities would be
established according to the approval of an independent tele-
communications authority in accordance with the principles of
the WTO's Basic Agreement on Telecommunications (BAT) Ref-
erence Paper.

Mobile Voice and Data Services
*(analog/digital cellular services as well as personal commu-
nications services)*
⇨ Up to 25 percent equity in Beijing, Guangzhou and Shang-
hai upon accession;
⇨ Up to 35 percent equity in Beijing, Guangzhou, Shanghai,
Chengdu, Chongqing, Dalian, Fuzhou, Hangzhou, Nanjing,
Ningbo, Qingdao, Shenyang, Shenzhen, Xiamen, Xi'an, Taiyuan,
and Wuhan one year after accession; and
⇨ Up to 49 percent equity throughout China after three
years.
⇨ No geographic restriction five years after accession.

Value-Added (includes Internet) and Paging*
(electronic mail, voice mail, online information and

---

* The US-China WTO deal ultimately (according to differing timetables) allows 50 percent
foreign ownership in ICPs and 49 percent in ISPs. A footnote to the agreement calls for the
creation of an independent telecoms regulatory agency (USTR negotiators argue that this
would preclude the MII from taking this role), but this isn't binding.

> *database retrieval, electronic data interchange, enhanced/*
> *value-added facsimile services (including store and forward,*
> *store and retrieve), code and protocol conversion, online infor-*
> *mation and data processing (including transaction processing),*
> *and paging services)*
> ⇨ Up to 30 percent equity in the Beijing, Guangzhou and
> Shanghai upon accession;
> ⇨ Up to 49 percent equity in Chengdu, Chongqing, Dalian,
> Fuzhou, Hangzhou, Nanjing, Ningbo, Qingdao, Shenyang,
> Shenzhen, Xiamen, Xi'an, Taiyuan and Wuhan one year after
> accession.
> ⇨ No geographic restriction within two years after accession
> and ownership can rise to 50 percent.
> China also agreed to phase out all geographic restrictions
> for paging and value-added services in two years, for mobile/
> cellular in five years and domestic fixed-line services in six years.
>
> Satellite Services and Other Services
> ⇨ China has attached and signed "Notes for Scheduling Basic
> Telecom Services" which provides that unless explicitly
> excluded, any basic services may be provided through any means
> of technology, including satellites.

Source: Hong Kong Trade Development Council

Also worth mentioning is how WTO accession will effect the cable TV industry. Before 2005, China will implement content convergence between telecom, Internet and cable over one network. WTO agreements, however, do not mention liberalization of the cable industry, and it is unclear as to whether or not the government will encourage foreign investment in this area. As of March 2001, foreign and private capital of any kind was forbidden in the construction of broadcast & TV transmission network. In September, however, the State Council Office issued a document allowing state-owned large and medium-sized enterprises to invest in cable networks. While this document still does not allow foreign investment, the change of heart towards private funds being injected into the cable sector is promising.

In addition, in 2001 China has been allowing foreign cable providers to air programs on a trial basis in Guangdong province. These channels must all be aired from one satellite platform administered by China. As of July 2001, overseas companies are no longer allowed to run satellite transponder lease businesses directly to domestic customers without prior approval from the relevant communication department.

Venture Capital

In September 2001, the Ministry of Foreign Trade and Economic Co-operation (MOFTEC), the Ministry of Science and Technology (MST) and the State Administration for Industry and Commerce (SAIC) issued a notice announcing that foreign companies would be allowed to set up wholly-owned or Sino-foreign cooperative venture capital firms in China. Foreign-invested venture capital firms will be able to withdraw their capital through share transfers, buybacks or selling their shares in the company if and when it becomes listed on a domestic or overseas stock market.

Before applying to set up wholly owned or Sino-foreign cooperative venture capital firms in China, one of the foreign investors must have managed assets of more than US$ 100 million in total, invested more than US$ 50 million of these assets in the past three years and own at least three percent of the new firm's capital. They must also put at least US$ 20 million into the new venture capital firm.

Licensing

Licensing is the main method by which the Chinese government controls access to a sector. By controlling licensing, the MII plays the role of gatekeeper. Through 2001 the MII continued to stress mobile licensing developments particularly in the areas of 3.5GHz, broadband access, bluetooth developments, and in a number of content areas.

The problems with licensing arrangements in China are that, on the one hand, the government uses licensing as a key regulatory tool but, on the other hand, all of the transparency that that would imply actually does not exist. The reasons for this are that there are usually multiple licenses required in an area and multiple agencies issuing those licenses. A further problem is what it necessarily means in China to have a license. For example, ICPs were *supposedly* required to have IIS licenses, but even up until now it is not clear *who* has one of these licenses and how realistic a requirement it is.

Moreover, there are other ways of imitating being licensed, i.e., via a JV arrangement or a proxy license agreement. An example of the former arrangement coming under recent stress would be the *Implementing Regulations for the Law of the People's Republic of China on Equity Joint Ventures* stating that license operators holding less than a 51 percent share of their joint venture will not be able to pass their license on to their joint venture. The MII has sought to retroactively impose its will on the market through the use of more stringent adherence to licensing conditions.

Foreign Investment

Prior to December 2001, the defining element of China's telecom industry was the prohibition on direct foreign investment in the telecom infrastructure or basic telecom services, as well as the prohibition on foreign entities from owning equity in China's telecom sector. This tenant was challenged and questioned many times, but following accession to the WTO, the government passed the Provisions on the

Administration of Foreign Investment Telecommunications Enterprises (FITE Provisions) outlining the allowance of foreign-invested telecom enterprises in China's telecom market.

The FITE Provisions provide the structure for foreign-invested telecom enterprises (FITE) to be allowed in operating basic and value-added services. The geographical scope of where FITE operations are allowed as well the proportion of capital allowed is determined by the WTO timetable (*see box*). It should be noted that this timetable is not legally enforceable, and China's allowance of participation within both sectors could be either faster or slower.* While the FITE Provisions are relatively simple and clear-cut, they are ambiguous enough in certain areas to raise certain questions of interpretation. For example, how will the qualification standards for the principal Chinese and foreign investor in the basic service sector be evaluated?

Analysis of the FITE Regulations

The *Provisions on the Administration of Foreign Investment Telecommunications Enterprises* (the *FITE Provisions*) were promulgated by State Council on December 11, 2001 and will be effective on January 1, 2002. According to the 25-article *Provisions*, foreign-invested telecom enterprises (FITE) are entitled to engage in basic and value-added telecom services. The specific classification of whether a service is value-added or basic is catalogued in the addendum to *Telecommunication Regulations* released in June 2001, and the geographical scope of where FITE operations are allowed is determined by the WTO timetable and by the supervisory department for the information industry under the State Council.

In a sense, the *FITE Provisions* are similar to *Implementing*

---

* We fully expect it to in fact be significantly faster, with the exception of certain areas in which the government may feel that foreign companies would too easily be likely to dominate the local market.

Regs that the government passes in order to mandate how a previous regulation should be administered. This is because the *FITE Provisions* do not stand alone – they work in compliance with the WTO accession papers, the *Telecommunication Regulations*, and the *Provisional Measures for Administration of the Examination and Approval of Foreign-Invested Leasing Companies*. There are, however, as usual, very vague and ambiguous areas within the regulations that raise questions which will only be resolved after players in the market start to act and the government reacts.

One of these vague areas is within the application process. One of the requirements for the application process is that the principal Chinese investor turns over a feasibility report outlining the basic condition, service items, business projections, development plans, analysis of investment returns and anticipated business hours of the proposed enterprise. MII officials have stated that if there is any change in the feasibility study over the course of the application process, then the principal Chinese investor must resubmit the feasibility study and the whole application process must start again from the beginning. This creates two problems: (1) a feasibility study can be used for project approval or for investment approval, but it does not seem reasonable to require it for licensing, especially since the MII tends to be very specific with what a license allows and does not allow; and (2) the application process is so long that it seems highly probable that the feasibility study would change during the process. As such, how should potential JVs write their feasibility studies? As a general all-encompassing business model or focused on one specific aspect of the business scope? How will the MII and MOFTEC judge the feasibility reports?

Source: MFC Insight

The past prohibition on foreign investment, however, proved to be a remarkable successful aspect of China's drive to create a nationally strong telecommunications environment, and it should not be expected that upon accession to the WTO and because of the *FITE Provisions* that all aspects of telecom service will be given away to outside players too quickly. For example, China Netcom's absorption into the new China Telecom north raises the question of what happens to the foreign capital already directly invested in the carrier? Netcom's investors, including News Group, Goldman Sachs, Sun Hung Kai, Henderson Group and Dell who jointly invested US$ 325 million with the Bank of China and the China Construction Bank to attain a 12% stake in Netcom, are still in the gray zone. Will Netcom's foreign investors get a 12% stake of the new entity or will their investment be removed? An understanding of past financial arrangements is still necessary to understanding China's telecom industry.

Unicom's "CCF" Financing Structure

During the late 1990s, at a time when it was estimated that the Chinese foreign financing requirements for three sectors alone (transport, power generation and telecommunications) was in excess of US$ 233 billion, the option to minimize the state's telecom's investment by accessing foreign investment became increasingly attractive. In response, a creative means of accessing foreign capital without relinquishing control was created, known as the China-China-Foreign (CCF) (or, in Chinese, *zhong-zhong-wai*) finance structure.

Unicom pioneered CCF in an attempt to circumvent China's strict ban on foreign companies having any equity ownership or operational control over networks and network services. Early on, a major problem for Unicom's development was a lack of funding: state financing from the MPT was limited, and legislation banned direct foreign investment in telecom ventures. Via CCF, foreign telecom firms saw the possibility of entering the growing Chinese market through co-operative contracts with Unicom, while Unicom was able to receive funding and technical assistance.

The CCF structure allows for a foreign company (F) to partner with a

Chinese company (C), usually in a joint venture (C-F), which then teams with a Chinese operator (C) to establish an operational entity. The joint venture will contribute investment, equipment and telecom's management expertise in exchange for a revenue share from the network's operations (*see figure*).

Typical "CCF" Revenue Structure

Source: MFC Insight

The CCF structure, however, was as legally dubious as it was clever. Toward the end of 1998, the State Council finally required that the CCF arrangements be dismantled because foreign companies were getting too close to network operations through the back door method. In the end, the CCF structure was never declared "illegal". When the State Council decided to act, Prime Minister Zhu Rongji referred to the mechanism as "irregular". Foreign investors in CCF ventures were instructed to withdraw, leaving roughly US$ 1.4 billion owed to them across 40-odd projects.

It is important to be aware of, and understand, CCF for three reasons:

☐ It provides insight on Unicom's evolution;

☐ CCF appears to be rising up as a possible financing mechanism again – CNC looks like it has already been exploiting this mechanism, and both CITIC and China Railcom (CRC) have begun investigating possible applications;

☐ With WTO accession looming, there is a very strong chance that a variety of China-foreign relations will be pursued and variants on the CCF mechanism are likely to be revisited.

These issues are likely to be re-investigated, particularly as the value-added services area of China's telecom industry begins to really grow and develop, and the line between basic and value-added services begins to blur.* One example of this is the emergence of mobile virtual network operators (MVNOs) – which potentially provide a loophole around the restrictions on network ownership for mobile operators. Another example is in the area of Wireless-LAN developments – a region of the spectrum that was previously unregulated (as is the case across most of the world), but with increasing attention and the prospect of foreign networking and data corporations getting involved, the government has begun putting regulatory requirements into place.

Market Opening

In 2002 China will undergo rapid liberalization as the market opens up (at an increasingly rapid pace) to foreign participants and the government

---

* AT&T became the first foreign enterprise to form a joint venture in the telecom area. AT&T has joined with Shanghai Telecom and Shanghai Information Investment to form Shanghai Symphony Telecom Co., a US$ 25 million project to provide broadband value-added services to businesses in Shanghai's Pudong area.

continues to reform its regulatory and administrative duties. Market change, however, does not imply that outside companies looking to enter China's telecom service market will be entering a completely changed and brand new environment. Accession to the WTO in itself will not shift the power behind China's telecom industry from the government to the market. The government has no intention of relinquishing control over this sector of the industry, and will use WTO to fulfill its own development objectives. Examples of this are ongoing government control over China's carriers with the current restructuring and merging that is underway, as well as the government's control over the broadband access market.

The government will continue to play a fundamental role in driving ICT growth and determining the rate and direction developments take. One of the government's major objectives is to use WTO to ready domestic enterprises, the "local champions" for the international arena. As such, market opening will happen *much* faster in China-dominated sectors, and *very little* in "*strategic*" or "*competitive*" areas. And, even within sectors that the government chooses to open, licensing and project approval will still be heavily bureaucratic and difficult. To be successful, market entrants should be aware of where the government is focusing and be willing to help the domestic industry develop. Potential entrants should also find out where China *needs* help, and then provide services in those areas. For research and consultative services, please contact MFC Insight at <www.mfcinsight.com>.

Chapter 16

Internet And E-commerce

By Peter Lovelock, Director of Insight
and Tara Tranguch, Buzz Director, MSC Insight

China Internet Market

The growth of the Internet in China has been quite phenomenal. Although its history is still extremely brief, adoption rates – fueled by one of the fastest and most extensive communications network build-out programs in history – have been surprising. While usage of the Internet is still largely an elite urban phenomenon, the interest generated has spread throughout society. In this regard, the story of the Internet in China is similar to that of the Internet's development else-where – just a little more compact in time, and with substantially big-ger numbers involved. There is also the incredible market potential due to the gross numbers involved and the nascent demand still now being released as the momentum of economic reform continues to kick in. And, equally, there remain significant twists: the notable, "...with

Chinese characteristics" coming into play.

These "Chinese characteristics" can be summarized in the contradictory nature with which the Chinese government views Internet developments. On the one hand the government is rapidly pushing the infrastructure out, in what is the fastest, largest, sustained communications network build-out the world has seen; pushing it out across the entire country, with universal access a key tenet of the administration's responsibility. Two good examples of government support for China's Internet growth are the Online Projects and the Golden Projects (*see box*). On the other, the government continues to feel threatened by the possibilities that the Internet brings with it, and so attempts to restrict access to the network to all but the educated and privileged elite.

This chapter outlines the Internet's development environment and its rate of growth; the environment for Internet Service Providers (ISPs) and Internet Content Providers (ICPs) and how outside players are able (or not) to enter this sector; the current regulatory environment for China's Internet; and how e-commerce is developing in China. While the Internet has been technically closed to foreign investment both in the areas of content and access, the amount of foreign involvement has been quite extensive. As such, WTO accession will not have a significant impact on Internet developments.

Government Projects to Stimulate Internet Growth

Golden Projects
The Golden Projects are ambitious information infrastructure initiatives aimed at simultaneously developing an information economy and building administrative capabilities. The three goals behind their launch were:

☐ To build a national information highway as a path to modernization and economic development.
☐ To drive development of information technology in China.

☐ To unify the country by tying the center to the provinces and by allowing the government to act across ministerial and industrial demarcation lines.

Initially, the Golden Projects comprised three elements: Golden Bridge, Golden Card and Golden Customs, but there are now 14 Golden Projects.

Online Projects

The Online Projects are comprised of three different areas: government, enterprise and family, to be instated at different time periods. The Government Online Project (GOP) was launched first in 1999, and, as with the aforementioned "Golden Projects", the purpose is to create a centrally accessible administrative system that collects and transports data to and from users, both the public and the various government departments. The implementation of the GOP is scheduled to take place in three phases, and China is currently mid-way between the second and third phase:

☐ *Phase One* – Enabling Technologies
☐ *Phase Two* – Information Sharing
☐ *Phase Three* – Paperless Government

Launched in June 2000, the Enterprise Online Project is intended to get all enterprises online to spur e-commerce growth. At the end of 2001, the State Economic and Trade Commission (SETC) issued the following statistics on the success of the Project, revealing that the project is still in its initial stages of development: 86.7% of enterprises have connected to the Internet, 69.1% of enterprises have their own websites, and 21.6% of enterprises have engaged in e-commerce. There is still a need for proper online promotion, meaning the development of e-commerce instead of mere website presence.

The Family Online Project was launched in 2001 and is aimed at getting all citizens Internet access. Beyond the official announcement that it has been launched, little development has yet occurred.

Source: MFC Insight

Growth and Control

In 1997, Internet adoption rates first started to "explode" in China, and growth in terms of the number of online subscribers and content providers has been high ever since (*see figure*). This growth rate has created a huge interest, both domestically and internationally, in China's Internet development. The interest can be attributed primarily to two major areas: China's untapped market potential and the available opportunities for content distribution.

With 33.7 million Internet users at the end of 2001, China is already one of the world's largest Internet markets. Despite this large number, however, Internet penetration on a nationwide scale is still low at 2.6 percent revealing that there is significant room yet for subscriber growth – some 97.4 percent of 1.3 billion people are not yet online.

Because there is a direct relationship between the amount of available infrastructure for Internet access (including the emerging telecom,

Internet Growth in China

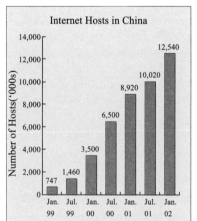
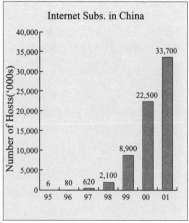

Source: China National Network Information Center (CNNIC)

Internet and other communication networks) in a given area and the number of subscribers, this penetration percentage increases in the more economically developed areas since these areas enjoy a more developed infrastructure. These areas are identifiably the major cities along the east coast corridor. The penetration rate in these leading cities can be as high as 20-25 percent, but falls away rapidly after that (*see table, next page*). Given the populations of these cities – often comparable to small European states or middle-sized countries such as Australia – they make quite attractive target markets already. In addition to these major urban hubs, the east coast provinces of Jiangsu and Zhejiang all boast penetration rates in excess of 3.5 percent province-wide, as does the southern province of Guangdong, again making for significant early Internet populations.

Due to China's landmass, building an Internet network that encompasses the entire nation is an expensive task. Admirably, the majority of the country already now has access to the basic telecom network, however, and the entire country (effectively) has access to the cable TV network, since China's cable television, radio, and media markets are already the largest in the world. This has created bureaucratic rivalry, but again significant potential. The exponential growth of China's Internet off the back of the world's largest communication infrastructure brings together some of the biggest potential markets in the world in a range of opportunities. The most visibly excited and talked about market right now is China's media market and its emergence in the form of online distribution.

Internet Access

How one accesses the Internet is determined first by the available underlying infrastructure and second by the access equipment used to enter the network. Internet access to the underlying infrastructure is

China After WTO

User Penetration Rates

	2000		2001	
	No. of Subs.	Penetration (%)	No. of Subs	Penetration (%)
Beijing	2,787,750	22.08	3,302,600	24.65
Shanghai	2,018,500	13.64	3,100,400	20.44
Tianjin	569,250	5.92	909,900	9.29
Guangdong	2,180,250	2.97	3,504,800	4.69
Zhejiang	1,489,500	3.32	2,224,200	4.89
Shandong	1,199,250	1.35	1,449,100	1.62
Jiangsu	1,221,750	1.69	2,696,000	3.68
Liaoning	1,048,500	2.51	1,280,600	3.03
Hubei	893,250	1.36	1,145,800	2.38
Shaanxi	330,750	0.91	505,500	1.37
Chongqing	456,750	1.48	539,200	1.74
Fujian	807,750	2.43	1,213,200	3.57
Jilin	542,250	2.03	606,600	2.25
Heilongjiang	553,500	1.45	943,600	2.45
Sichuan	1,131,750	1.32	1,752,400	2.02
Xinjiang	339,750	1.89	438,100	2.4
Hainan	69,750	0.91	168,500	2.14
Ningxia	108,000	1.97	101,100	1.8
Hunan	893,250	1.36	1,145,800	1.73
Shanxi	301,500	0.93	404,400	1.24
Henan	524,250	0.56	1,044,700	1.09
Gansu	254,250	0.99	438,100	1.67
Jiangxi	465,750	1.09	606,600	1.4
Guangxi	454,500	0.96	876,200	1.82
Inner Mongolia	272,250	1.15	404,400	1.67
Anhui	546,750	0.87	842,500	1.32
Yunnan	328,500	0.78	505,500	1.18
Qinghai	69,750	1.36	67,400	1.29
Tibet	6,750	0.26	33,700	1.28
Guizhou	180,000	0.48	202,200	0.58
Hebei	555,750	0.81	943,600	1.4
Total	**22,500,000**	**1.78**	**33,700,000**	**2.59**

Source: CNNIC

mediated through Internet service providers. The amount and quality of infrastructure is what determines a user's ability to get online, and the Chinese government has been actively promoting infrastructure growth. This active promotion is often overlooked by outside observers who instead focus on the government's harsh restrictions on content control. Many assume that the government's strict regulations arise from a desire to prevent widespread access to information. Internet growth has without a doubt been and continues to be the government's primary objective when it comes to determining Internet policy, and so far the government has been successful – host computers connected to the Internet have been growing steadily at a CAGR of more than 60 percent.*

The most widely used method of access in China for the individual user is still to dial-up through a PC's modem and then to access the Internet through a browser. Dedicated lines, ISDN, frame relay services, and VPN (Virtual Private Networks) are also available, but until recently only corporate and large institutions are likely to use such services due to their high access fees. As of late 2001, the number of dial-up users was estimated at 21.3 million and the number of leased line users at 6.7 million. In addition, 5.7 million users connect Internet via both leased lines and dial up method. While dial-up access is still the primary way most users access the Internet, China has been keenly developing its broadband market. China had such a myriad of broadband access providers emerging for a while that it seemed that broadband access was being classified as a value-added service. In fact, it is a basic service but has been managed like a value-added service while various reform elements in the government have sought to promote competition in this area.

---

* This is not to say that the issue of content control is trivial in China – it is in fact very important – but controlling it does not have the priority among government agencies that many (outside or Western) observers stress.

Internet Service Providers (ISPs)

There are three different classifications of Internet Service Providers (ISPs). "Tier 1" ISPs are the large backbone networks which provide the fundamental underlying infrastructure from which wholesalers, "Tier 2" ISPs, and smaller retailers, "Tier 3" ISPs, rent access to network lines. China has nine "Tier 1" ISPs: ChinaNet, ChinaGBN, UniNet, CNCNet, CMNet, CERNet, CSTNet, CGWNet and CIETNet (*see table*). Out of these nine ISPs, only the first six ChinaNet, ChinaGBN, Uninet, CNCNet, CMNet and CERNet can sell commercial access to wholesale and retail ISPs. The other three are not commercially viable because CSTNet is used for educational purposes, CGWNet is the army's personal network, and CIETNet is exclusively for the export/import industry. The total number of ISPs in China has grown to approximately 600, the majority of which are retail "Tier 3" ISPs located primarily in urban areas, with the highest concentration being around Beijing, Shanghai and Guangzhou.

Eight of the nine "Tier 1" backbones have international access: ChinaNet, CNCNet, Uninet, ChinaGBN, CSTNet, CMNet, CERNet and CIETNet. Before the year 2000, the only ISPs licensed to provide international access were ChinaNet and ChinaGBN. Up until very recently, therefore, ISPs were forced to shape their international access services around ChinaNet's basic physical network. ChinaNet, which is the Internet arm of China Telecom, exercises a significant amount of influence over the ISP market due to China Telecom's control over the telecommunications infrastructure and its dominance of bandwidth. When Uninet and CNCNet were established in 2000 with licenses to conduct international traffic, however, the market opened up extensively and ChinaNet's control over ISPs was weakened. Regarding domestic services, many of the smaller ISPs' domestic platforms still draw support from China Telecom's public telephone platform. Therefore, due to ChinaNet's (and China Telecom's) role in

Major Backbone Providers

ChinaNet	China Public Computer Network-China Telecom	ChinaNet is still the dominant Internet access provider; often referred to as the 163 network after the number users dial to gain access.
Uninet	China Unicom	In 1999, the State Council authorized Unicom to establish Uninet as a new competitive access provider.
ChinaGBN	China Golden Bridge Network-Jitong	Jitong is a state-owned telecom company formerly linked with (now abolished) MEI. GBNet focuses primarily on the corporate market.
CNCNet	China Network Corp.-China Netcom	Netcom is building a state-of-the-art fiber-optic network in China that runs IP over DWDM. CNCNet leases lines to the other major backbone providers in this table as well as to ISPs, ICPs and enterprises.
CERNet	China Education & Research Network	CERNet is China's principle academic network. CERNet is technically distinct from the main public network (never connected with the ChinaNet system). Therefore, content distributed over CERNet is less restricted than over commercial ISPs. Not available on a commercial level to the public.
CMNet	China Mobile	In January 2000, the MII authorized China Mobile to establish CMNet, the seventh IP backbone network in China.
CSTNet	China Science & Technology Network	Like CERNet, CSTNet is an academic network, but significantly smaller in scale. It connects subsidiaries of the Chinese Academy of Sciences (CAS).

Source: MFC Insight

the ISP market, China's Internet can still be characterized as an incumbent-dominated model.

There are currently roughly 600 small "Tier 2" and "Tier 3" retail ISPs in China with 150 of these located in the major cities, particularly in Beijing, Shanghai, and Guangzhou. The largest obstacle to an ISP's success is China Telecom. For one, China Telecom has shown no compunction to date in squeezing as much money from retail ISPs as possible. A small ISP will spend 50 percent of its total expenditure on line rentals. Although this percentage has dropped from 80 percent in 1999, this percentage is still enormously high. To give a point of comparison, ISPs in the United States only use five percent of cost expenditure for line rental. Even more restrictive is China Telecom's practice of linking line rental fees to the amount of revenue per line. Consequently, instead of rental declining with volume, it rises, making an ISP less profitable the more it increases its user base or usage. Given a playing field tilted so steeply against them, most independent ISPs have found it impossible to stay in business without receiving some degree of assistance or lenience from China Telecom. As a result, although China saw a small blossoming of ISPs in 1997 and 1998 (many being small bulletin board service operations which decided to go commercial), many of the companies that were granted ISP licenses during that time have subsequently stopped offering ISP services or have been incorporated into the ChinaNet framework.

As a consequence, the majority of Internet subscribers, whether companies, organizations or individuals, are connected with ChinaNet and China Telecom either directly or indirectly. To be fair, the ChinaNet 163 access network is available to anyone with a computer and a fixed-line phone. Users can connect and log on without an account and access fees are relatively cheap. Educational users are exempt from this necessity in that they will, of course, access the Internet via CERNet, and those in the Chinese Academy of Sciences via CSTNet.

Internet Content Providers (ICPs)

At inception, Chinese dotcom startups all followed a similar generic path. Many startups mimicked Yahoo! and offered a Chinese search engine, free mailbox services, news, stock quotes, and a chat room. The portals quickly became identical in design, concept and content – making it impossible for the majority of them to survive. As the market began to mature a two-pronged path to ICP development emerged: on the one hand, the government began to push large state-owned enterprises (SOEs) to go online as a means of becoming more competitive and more efficient and, from the other direction, small startups eager to gain from the Internet buzz began to offer more specialized ICP sites. The largest obstacle facing this latter category has been a lack of available capital and/or content.

China's Internet market is still relatively immature in that it has only experienced the first wave of netizen uptake and the majority of content sites have yet to develop their own sustainable and unique business models. As such, by 2002, the websites still going strong online were those either riding off of money raised in 2000 or those providing useful services such as human resource and online education sites.

As of 2002, with 33.7 million Internet users and 145 million mobile subscribers, the size of the mobile market makes services application to both the Internet and mobile phone sectors very appealing indeed. At the same time, the telecom industry's falling average revenue per user (ARPU) is forcing the mobile players to turn to data services to boost revenue. The looming presence of next generation networks is therefore forcing both mobile operators and online content providers to think about how to best prepare for the arrival of this form of convergence. What type of content will be transmitted and, more importantly, who is going to be providing it?

Portals

Sina, Sohu and Netease are the three biggest and most well-known chortals (Chinese portals) because all three listed during the heyday of the Internet market, and their respective leaders have created an international name for themselves. In 2001, as with the rest of the Internet market, these three sites took a financial nosedive. In response, they have all attempted to change significant aspects of their business model and market strategy but, to date, they remain relatively similar in the content offered.

Until recently, when the portals began to provide paid content (including email), services had been predominantly free, with the only significant source of revenue being online advertisements. After the spring 2000 tech stock slump, the summer bore witness to an emerging number of mergers and acquisitions. By the end of 2000, with competition between sites increasingly fierce due to a relatively small Internet population and limited available capital, a new trend emerged: "mutual help agreements" with traditional service companies, enabling websites to provide more value-added services to their users and providing the offline companies with access to the website's online user population.

Despite the differences in content, the ICP sites are still all, of necessity, targeting the same audience – the initial user base. The first Internet user to go online in China was a young male student, and while this population still comprises a large portion of the Internet population, there are different demographics emerging as well as a large *potential* middle class base coming online that could be targeted with different and more creative services.*

---

* For an in-depth look at China's Internet environment, please see: <www.mfcinsight.com>.

Future of Online Content

As the Internet market continues to grow and become more diversified, and as websites continue to seek out their niche and find sources of revenue, a myriad of online services and content will continue to proliferate. This content and these services, will also, more often than not, not necessarily be free. Already some Chinese websites are learning about the advantages of online or VIP cards that help users stick to their site, or about bundling several services together in order to attract a larger user base. As access is improved and convergence starts to happen on a wide-scale, content will likewise adapt and become both more exciting and useful. The personal touch that ICPs need can be found in the integration of mobile and online services. News sites that offer daily headlines via SMS, or music sites that send a subscriber their favorite artist's song to their phone before it hits the radiowaves, will be the type of services that benefit the ICP, the operator and the user.

Today, online content in China is still feeling out its market and testing its capabilities. But the improvement ICPs have undergone in less than three years from a dozen bland chortals to a range of more diverse sites suggests that the continued adaptation of new trends, services and ideas will only continue. The most recent trend is bundling content with access, a move that requires cooperation between the ICP and the operator. As these types of agreements increase, it will become more and more natural for the two media to continually overlap in service offerings.

The Regulatory Environment

Regulatory Bodies

Three ministries have significant responsibilities for China's Internet sector:

☐ **Ministry of Information Industry (MII):** The MII drafts and promulgates plans, policies, laws and regulations relevant to technology, telecommunications, and electronic media.

☐ **Ministry of Culture (MOC):** The MOC is responsible for implementing plans, policies, laws, and regulations pertinent to art and culture. The ministry formulates development plans for the culture industry, and directs reform of the cultural system. It also manages the cultural market, and maintains responsibility for "cultural communication" with other countries, including the formulation of the plans, regulations, and policies.

☐ **Ministry of Public Security (MPS):** The MPS administers the various provincial and municipal Public Security Bureaus (PSBs). The Computer Regulation and Supervision Department (CRSD) of the Ministry of Public Security is responsible for the security, protection and management of computer information networks and the Internet. The CSRD monitors information accessed on-line by users, either "work units" (*danwei*) or individuals, who according to the January 1996 notification MPS#7 are supposed to register with their local PSB. CSRD is charged with coordinating efforts to counter computer hackers and preserve network security.

Not officially related to the government but still extremely important to China's Internet development is the **China Internet Network Information Center (CNNIC)**, a nonprofit management and service organization established in 1997 and managed by the Chinese Academy of Science's (CAS) Computer Network Information Center. The CNNIC reports to the MII and the Chinese Academy of Sciences (CAS), and its responsibilities include domain name registration, IT information collection, and the monitoring of website traffic.

Internet Regulations

In January 1996, China Telecom constructed its national backbone network ChinaNet and began to provide Internet access to the public. The Ministry of Public Security was the first to publish regulations monitoring the security of the Internet. From 1996 until the government was restructured in 1998 and the MII was formed, the State Council was responsible for the issuing of all Internet regulations. From 1998 on, the MII has been responsible for Internet regulations concerning networks, domain names, and other administrative functions. But when it comes to content, security, and business operations, the MII's responsibilities still overlap with other ministries. For example, regulations concerning online education are the responsibility of the Ministry of Education and regulations concerning online business operations also fall under the domain of the State Administration of Industry and Commerce (SAIC). A good example of how government bodies can overlap in the administration of one regulation is the April 2001 Internet Café regulations (*see next page*).

Measures for the Administration of Internet Information Services

Issued in September 2000, the *IIS Measures* were China's first set of regulations specifically aimed at regulating the Internet. In the regulations, "Internet information services" are defined as the activity of providing information services to online users through the Internet. Internet information services are classified into those services of a "business nature" and those not of a "business nature." The *Measures* require all IIS sites that have a business nature to apply for a license. Those not of a business nature must be recorded, but do not need a license. (There have, of course, been a series of disputes resulting from the interpretation of these definitions.)

Then again, should the Internet be regulated? There is a requirement

Places of Business that Provide Online Internet Services

On April 3, 2001, the MII, Ministry of Security, Ministry of Culture, and the State Administration of Industry and Commerce issued the *Measures for the Administration of Places of Business that Provide On-line Internet Services*. On April 10, 2001, to show its support for the new *Measures*, the State Council General Office issued a notice demanding tighter control over Internet cafés. (A Measure does not have the same status as a Regulation. Regulations can only be issued by the State Council. So although these Measures are not on the same level of importance as a Regulation, the State Council's support gives the Measures added weight).

The new regulations divided responsibility between four separate government organizations, with all responsible parties being at the local level. This is significant because it switches control from the national to the regional level, and because it forces coordination between four different government departments. Because the approval of Internet cafés now involves four government departments, the State Council demands café owners to acquire licenses from all four departments. The Business License is from the PTA (as representative of the MII), a Safety Examination Proposal from the local Public Security Bureau, a Network Culture License from the local Bureau of Culture, and an Industry & Commerce License from the local Administration of Industry and Commerce.

Statistics show that at the end of 2000, there were 22.5 million Internet users in China, 20.5 percent of whom accessed the Internet at Internet cafés or other similar businesses. Some large cities have approximately 1,000 businesses providing access to the Internet. The new regulations follow the government's policy of licensing, and therefore charging, any business operation. The new regulations are also a response to the increasing number of Internet cafés that allow or ignore access to sites that contain pornography, gambling, violence, and other content that the state finds harmful.

Source: MFC Insight

when commerce is involved, but for the general transmission of free

Outlawed Content

Article 15 of the *IIS Regs* state that an Internet information service provider is not allowed to make, copy, publish or spread information regarding the following contents:

1. Information that runs opposite to the basic principles fixed by the Constitution

2. Information that jeopardizes national security, leaks the country's secrets, overthrows the government and/or hurts national unification

3. Information that harms the reputation and benefits of China

4. Information that agitates ethnic hatred, discrimination and harms national unity

5. Information that harms the government's religious policy and/or advocates cults and feudal superstition

6. Information that spreads rumors, disturbs public order and social stability

7. Information that spreads pornography, gambling, violence, killing, terror or instigates crime

8. Information that insults or slanders others and thus infringes the legitimate rights of others

9. Any other contents that are forbidden by laws and regulations

Of course, the very nature of the Internet makes it impossible to regulate completely. And the government's desire to promote Internet uptake and growth as an economic tool creates a paradoxical approach to containing the Internet's reach. Internet penetration in China is only 2.6 percent, meaning it is a small, elite part of society (students, intellectuals and business people) has access to online content. As such, the government does not fear the Internet to the extent that outsiders tend to believe. However, its approach to censoring online content is effective and will continue to be so for the time being whilst not hampering the Internet's growth as a tool for economic development.

Source: MFC Insight

content, should the government play the role of watchdog? The government takes a two-pronged approach to the Internet – it both promotes its growth and uptake, while censoring "sensitive" content (*see box*).

Online Content Regulations

What kind of information is allowed to be disseminated via the Internet? For example, who is allowed to issue the news or information about medicine? How does one protect the copyright of audio and video products when they are transmitted online? The answer is predominantly through licensing. Most regulations monitoring content quite simply state that ICPs delivering content in a given area must be properly licensed. As such, the regulation will outline who is qualified to apply, who to apply to, and what responsibilities the ICP has. Content

Internet Content Regulations

Regulations	Key player	Date of Issue
Notice of the Ministry of Culture on Relevant Issues in Regulating Online Dealing in Audio and Video Products	Ministry of Culture	March 2000
Regulations on the Management of Internet Electronic Bulletin Boards Service	MII	November 2000
Provisional Regulations for the Administration of Engagement by Internet Sites in the Business of News Publication	Press Office of the State Council and MII	November 2000
Interim Regulations on the Management of Online Drug Information Services	State Drug Administration	January 2001
Regulations on the Administration of the Human Resources Market	SAIC	September 2001

Source: MFC Insight

regulations are relatively new since China's Internet environment did not previously require them. Table provides a list of China's Internet content regulations.

One year after public Internet access became available, the first Internet security regulation was issued by the State Council.

China's WTO Commitments

The number of government bodies regulating the different aspects of Internet developments is numerous. To date, however, there has been no comment on any type of regulatory restructuring either pre- or post-WTO. One area that will remain gray and cause disputes is content and foreign portals' presence on the mainland. Under the accession agreement, foreign investors will be allowed a 50 percent stake in most types of Internet ventures immediately upon or shortly after accession. The US-China WTO deal ultimately allows 50 percent foreign ownership in ICPs and 49 percent in ISPs. Today, there is already plenty of foreign investment in China's Internet market in the form of direct investment funds and private groups. This financing was accepted by the Chinese government because the start-ups were run by Chinese entrepreneurs who emphasized the Chinese qualities of the websites and the business.

Moving beyond an online presence, China has been reforming the mainland's Internet measurement agencies. Up until 2001, China's official (and only) Internet measurement agency was the China Internet Network Information Center (CNNIC). Since 1998, the CNNIC has issued an Internet Survey every six months depicting China's Internet growth and its netizens' user habits.* Outside measurement agencies,

---

* For detailed bi-annual information on China's Internet growth, China's Internet users' behavior and characteristics, past and present, please go to: <www.mfcinsight.com>. MFC Insight analyzes CNNIC's surveys to sketch a clear portrait on China's Internet development environment.

such as iamasia and NetValue, have been critiqued by CNNIC for their "inaccurate data." However, in October, NetValue received a license from the MII and the State Statistical Bureau to research China's Internet from the mainland. This opening up of the research sector indicates that China's government is becoming supportive of an information sector that is not controlled or influenced by the government.

E-commerce

E-commerce in China was ushered in originally with much the same irrational exuberance as took hold in the US – albeit some three years later. The results have been much the same – albeit over a much shortened time cycle: disillusionment; stock market deflation; market consolidation; and the realization that the so-called New Economy was going to take a while to create, particularly in countries such as China where there are gaps in even the basic infrastructure.

Nevertheless, there is an apparent real commitment on the part of the government to build and promote the development of e-commerce in China, and many of the initiatives that have been launched are taking hold and doing so quite rapidly. Moreover, in many cases China stands to benefit in the transition from traditional commerce to e-commerce by being unencumbered by old – or legacy – structures.

From B2C to B2B

While there exist a variety of business-to-consumer (B2C) models, all of the Chinese B2C enterprises can be seen to be facing a similar set of market barriers. Perhaps not surprisingly, the more successful of the B2C start-ups can also be seen to be dealing with these barriers in a similar fashion. As such, it is possible to outline factors that appear necessary preconditions for success in the market:

☐ Provide quality products at reasonable prices;

☐ Integrate online and offline payment systems and offer secure online payment options;

☐ Provide effective product distribution networks (including services for fast-delivery within 24 hours); and

☐ Provide adequate customer services to better to respond to consumers' needs.

In line with changing market expectations, many e-commerce initiatives have redefined themselves into business-to-business (B2B) initiatives, migrating away from B2C models that, by early 2000, were becoming increasingly unpopular with the financial market. However, as more and more people come online, mass consumer usage of the Internet will continue to increase and e-commerce is widely expected to become integrated with traditional businesses – best summed up in the widely-used expression: "clicks and mortar." How this will play out in China is yet to be seen.

Online Payment Options

The online consumer in China currently has two options for paying for online goods:

☐ Payment by cash-on-delivery (COD) and

☐ Payment by debit or credit card.

However, online payments in China still face several barriers:

☐ There is not a complete inter-bank, inter-regional payment clearance process, and

☐ Credit/debit card use is currently not widespread.

A report in the *Asian Wall Street Journal* in late 2000 indicated that over 16 percent of China's growing Internet community had shopped online, with 94 percent of those shoppers using China-based retailers. The low usage is because it is virtually impossible for Chinese consumers to purchase goods from overseas retailers direct and because of complex banking regulations. At present, credit cards issued by banks can only be used within China. Chinese retailers have primarily relied upon bank transfers, postal remittances, cash on delivery and credit cards to secure payments. Coupled with low credit card penetration, this has meant that both foreign and domestic retailers must develop workable alternatives, and strategic alliances. Of consumers who have not purchased online, 36 percent indicated the lack of credit cards, and 31 percent noted they did not yet trust Internet shopping. These statistics are high indictors of the relative infancy of e-commerce in China.

At present, the *Renminbi* is not a fully convertible currency, and the purchase and sale of foreign currencies is heavily regulated, thus restricting individuals from remitting foreign exchange abroad. Current foreign exchange regulations therefore manage to frustrate commercial objectives of e-commerce until such time as the *Renminbi* becomes a fully convertible currency and payment mechanisms are more certain.

For e-commerce to be viable in any jurisdiction, payment mechanisms must be secure, convenient and reliable. Consumers must also have confidence in the confidentiality of information transmitted online, such as credit card and other financial or personal information. Consumers and business people need to be confident about the identity of the person they deal with and that the messages they send are not tampered with. While encryption technology is available to ensure the confidentiality of such information, users must have confidence in the companies using encryption technologies or providing encryption services. There is also a need to ensure the legal recognition and enforcement of electronic contacts and electronic signatures.

In China what we see therefore, is that the growth of e-commerce will depend upon the availability, reliability and flexibility of payment options. E-commerce will only have access to the broadest base of consumers if payment options are available to all, and are available reliably.

Cash on Delivery

CNNIC reported in January 2002, that 42.8 percent of China's Internet users prefer using cash on delivery (COD) for payment. The widespread use of COD as a form of payment may have contributed to two prevalent misconceptions among foreign analysts about the prospects for online consumer commerce in China:

☐ Credit and debit card use is too low in China for e-commerce to be successful; and

☐ Chinese consumer culture is inherently inclined towards cash-based and face-to-face transactions.

Several practical reasons account for the prevalence of cash payments:

☐ Cash is a familiar financial instrument. This does not suggest that other financial instruments (e.g., smart cards, credit cards, debit cards) will not become popular as well.

☐ Most online consumers currently have few, if any, other options. With the lack of inter-bank and inter-regional payment clearance systems, consumers may be shopping at websites that only accept cards issued by banks other than their own.

☐ Cash payment avoids concerns about online security. Using cash to pay for goods ordered online obviates the need for divulging personal information, which online consumers may fear would be used for other purposes by the vendor or others.

Debit and Credit Cards

The use of debit and credit cards in China has increased considerably

The Golden Card Project

The Golden Card Project was designed in three phases spanning a ten year period.

Pilot Period (1994-1996):
☐ Formulate a bankcard development plan and set up a bankcard management system in which financial entities are the major players. Establish a bankcard information exchange center and network and carry out experiments in each of the 12 trial provinces and municipalities including Beijing, Tianjin, Shanghai, Jiangsu, Hainan, Liaoning, Dalian, Shandong, Qingdao, Hangzhou, Guangdong, and Xiamen, etc.
☐ The goal for the number of bankcards to be issued is 30 million, and coverage will also reach 30 million people.

Expansion Period (1997-1999):
☐ To extend the application of the cards to reach 30-50 trial medium-sized cities, covering 60 million people with 60 million cards in total.
☐ To establish a state-authorized switching center and to set up a switching center in each node city. This will link the municipal and regional bankcard information exchange centers in the trial cities together.

During this period, the Information Exchange Centers of these twelve areas were established.

The National Information Exchange Center was in operation by the end of 1998, and the number of bank cards issued by Chinese banks had exceeded 140 million. By 1999 China had fulfilled the first two phases.

Popularization Period (2000-2003):
To popularize the application and link up 400 cities, covering 300 million people, and to issue 200 million cards throughout the country.

Source: MFC Insight

during the past several years. This is largely because of the Golden Card Project (*see next page*). Golden Card's creation is linked with President Jiang Zemin's June 1993 call to accelerate the development of banking and credit card systems in China's major cities. *The project aims to set up a credit card verification scheme and an inter-bank inter-region clearing system to create a modern, electronic, and cashless payment system.* The back end of the Golden Card Project links and unifies the banking system, and the front end distributes credit and debit cards to the public. The front-end goal of the Golden Card Project when it was set out was to issue 200 million cards amongst 300 million people across 400 cities in about ten years – by the year 2003.

Third Party Payment Services

Online payment solutions currently offered by banks still do not solve the inter-bank payment clearance problem. To solve this problem, a small but growing number of third party intermediate payment providers are developing one-stop solutions that will allow online merchants to accept cards from a wide range of banks.

Three of the major payment intermediaries are Beijing-based Cyber Beijing, Shanghai-based ChinaPay, and Guangdong-based Guangdong Network Service Center. Using the national Golden Card Project, the latter two companies are offering online payment solutions that overcome the inter-bank and inter-regional payment clearance barrier. But until these nationwide services become more prevalent, online merchants in China will either have to depend on services provided locally by individual banks or payment solutions of their own.

Delivery: B2C's Achilles Heel in China

Getting goods to the customer's door in a reliable and timely manner ranks among the top challenges currently facing China's B2C companies. Until very recently most customers receiving anything other

than mail through China's postal service had to pick up parcels at the
local post office. Foreign delivery companies, such as Federal Express
and United Parcel Service, have for several years been providing delivery
service in many of China's major cities, but the cost of these services
remains prohibitively high for Chinese consumers, and by extension
Chinese B2C ventures.

Within individual cities, online merchants have been able to employ
existing private delivery networks – which use every manner of transport from bicycles to trucks – for delivery. These distribution systems,
however, do not readily allow effective oversight of the quality and
timeliness of delivery services. Some Chinese B2C companies have
consequently created their own delivery networks (*see box*).

But these city-centered delivery networks do not extend beyond the
respective city's confines, and often do not even reach beyond individual districts. B2C companies wanting to deliver goods to consumers across large geographic areas currently have economically feasible
options, with the following problems hampering the development of
nationwide delivery systems:

☐ Inter-regional of goods often requires the involvement of several carriers, often operating under greatly varying administrative
standards;
☐ The country's transportation infrastructure (e.g., roads, highways,
and railways), while improving is not always dependable;
☐ Transportation regulations prohibit the operation of distribution
companies across regions.

Despite the growing number of privately provided delivery options
available to Chinese B2C companies, China's Postal Authority provides the only moderately reliable national delivery service for consumer goods ordered online. Several private companies, the Jiuchuan

---

Delivering the Goods

eGuo.com (www.eguo.com) ambitiously launched a one-hour delivery beginning in April 2000, emulating services provided by Internet retailers Kozmo (www.kozmo.com) and Urban Fetch (www.urbanfetch.com) in New York City. The Beijing-based company delivers groceries, software, and personal convenience products to customers within one hour, and will soon add CDs, VCDs, consumer electronics, and books to the one-hour delivery list. Other products sold through eGuo.com website are delivered within eight hours. Ordered goods often arrive at the customer's door on either tri-wheel pedal carts commonly used for deliveries in Beijing or bicycle; at night the deliveries are made by one of the company's small fleet of automobiles.

Although providing one-hour delivery free of charge greatly adds to eGuo.com's costs, the company hopes that rapid delivery will encourage more Chinese to order goods online. A substantial increase in sales since the advent of the delivery service may bear out the companyís optimism. Sales revenues barely reached RMB100 thousand (US$ 10,000) in May 2000, but by June had increased to RMB 1 million (US$ 120 thousand). Mr. Zhang Yongqing, CEO of eGuo.com, predicts that annual revenues will total RMB100 million (US$ 12.1 million) for 2000, and will increase enough in 2001 to cover delivery costs. More daunting for eGuo.com, profits still lie two or three more years down the road.

Logistics Company for example, purport to offer nationwide delivery, but to date their efforts cannot yet match the barely adequate services provided by the Postal Authority.

Although relatively slow and expensive, the government's postal service does extend throughout the country, thus allowing B2C companies to reach customers in China's smaller cities and towns. The Postal Authority operates 236 distribution centers covering more than 2,300 large and medium-sized cities above the county level. In July 2000, the postal service launched door-to-door delivery service in most large cities, later expanding this service to all cities above the county level in October 2000.

E-commerce Regulation

To date, there has been no E-commerce Law, although 2001 has witnessed several developments in this area (*see box*).

In September 2001, the Ministry of Foreign Trade and Economic Cooperation (MOFTEC) set up the Department of International E-commerce Administration (DIECA) to strengthen the overall planning and guidance of China's e-commerce developments. Key responsibilities of the new administration include researching and administering the

---

E-commerce Regulation Developments

China has not yet issued an E-commerce Law. In March 2001, the NPC said that it was not yet time to draft an e-commerce law and China would wait until after its online commerce environment had matured before concentrating on this law.

Despite this announcement, in June 2001, it was announced that the E-commerce Exemplary Law was being drafted as a guideline for e-business. Described as a "game rule" for e-business, it was drafted to help the e-business industry be more open, creative, and forward-looking. There was no indication as to who was drafting it, and there has been no more news on this subject. At the same time, both Guangdong and Shanghai announced that they were drafting e-commerce laws, which would be used as trial laws for drafting the final national version.

Then in August 2001, the initial draft of China's first E-Commerce Law was jointly completed by People's University, Jinan University, and the Beijing Post & Telecommunications University. As with all laws and regulations, after the draft of a law has been completed, it is submitted to the State Council for feedback and advice. During this stage the State Council will ask the relevant ministries and departments for their suggestions. The draft will then be returned to the bodies that wrote it, where it will be revised and then resubmitted to the State Council where the process will continue until everyone is satisfied with the draft. Because this Law has been drafted by Universities with no cooperation with any Ministries – such as the SDPC, SAIC, MOFTEC, or the MII – it can be presumed that this E-commerce Law draft is a very rough draft. It is also not usual for NPC policy statements to be ignored or overthrown. As such, it appears safe to assume there will be no E-commerce Law before late 2002.

Also related to online e-commerce, in August 2001 the central People's Bank of China (PBoC) issued *The Interim Procedures for the Administration of Online Banking Services*. The *Interim Procedures* define "online banking" to be financial services provided by banks via the Internet. They state that banking institutions, whether domestic or overseas, must apply to the PBoC and pass the PBOC's examination before providing online banking services in China. Policy-oriented banks, domestic commercial banks, joint-venture banks, foreign-funded banks and branches of foreign banks must apply to the PBOC's headquarters before opening online banking businesses, but city commercial banks only need be approved by local branches of the PBoC.

Source: MFC Insight

general plan and development strategy for digitizing foreign trade, carrying out the Government's Golden Customs Project, and negotiating foreign e-commerce standards and creating standards and regulations for China's international e-commerce arena.

Growth Prospects

There is still plenty of room for growth in all aspects of China's Internet developments. Penetration among users is still low and utilization of resources offered by the Internet have not reached the level required by China's current state of industrialization. While there are obstacles to free unlimited growth – such as content restrictions and limits on foreign investment – the Chinese government has been pushing infrastructure growth and access at an extraordinary rate. Where else in the world does government-subsidized Internet access exist to the extent that it exists in China? That is, where else in the world can an individual with a computer and a phone line at any time and from any place access the Internet at an affordable price?

China's Internet is on the verge of undergoing its second round of massive uptake and content development. These are two halves of the same circle meaning that the user and content will both spur each other's growth. Due to forthcoming convergence, 2002 could be an extraordinary year as portals renegotiate their business models and users gain more developed means of Internet access. For more insight and consultation on how you can participate in China's Internet growth, please visit <www.mfcinsight.com>.

Chapter 17

The New Media Universe

*By Peter Lovelock, Director of Insight
and Tara Tranguch, Buzz Director, MSC Insight*

Messages via New Media

The past five years have seen China embrace a range of technologies at a speed many in the West would never have believed possible. In the mid-90s, cellular phones, email, and the Internet were technologies many Chinese people had heard of, but never used. As of January 2002, over 150 million people use cell phones and over 30 million use the Internet, with over 80 percent of these users having registered an email account of their own. Factor in that the number of Internet users is growing at more than 1 million per month and the number of cell phone users at more than five million per month, and it becomes apparent that the computer/mobile phone interface is rapidly becoming of enormous importance for advertisers in China.

This "revolution of access" has been both a boon and a headache to marketers looking to target the Mainland Chinese population. On the one hand, the sudden direct access to consumers is amazing – China has long been a place where it is very difficult to segment and target specific demographic groups among the general population; cell phone and Internet technologies suddenly make this possible. The headache, however, is just as perplexing – now that a means exists to reach these consumers, what, exactly, should be delivered to them such that they will respond?

A recent answer has been to employ "2 Way Marketing", a means to not just propel one's brand out into the marketplace, but to also get valuable consumer feedback in return. This has meant, for example, Siemens running SMS campaigns designed to register consumers for sports events, IBM running opt-in email campaigns to create a list of high-end server purchasers, and Xi'an Janssen running registration modules to create a proprietary database of people interested in their latest hair care products.

Since the mid-1990s, a great deal of emphasis has been placed on "interactive marketing." Most people, when asked to define what interactive marketing means, usually equate it to the use of banner ads on web sites. While banner ads are certainly a form of interactive marketing, they form only one part of an integrated whole. Moreover, because banner ads have been given so much coverage over these last few years, this chapter will instead focus on other means of contacting and developing a 2-way relationship with a consumer base.

This chapter will first attempt to provide insight into the legal and regulatory obstacles that impede the rapid growth of the New Media industry. In addition, it will explore New Media agencies, the services they provide, and the tactics professional advertisers in China are adopting to harness the value of New Media.

Included are New Media campaign case studies from professional marketers throughout the PRC, including permission email campaigns conducted by Li Ning, China's leading sports apparel company, IBM, and President Noodles, as well as SMS campaigns run by Heineken and Siemens respectively.

Regulatory Environment

General Advertising Regulations

China's advertising law was originally drafted in 1995, and is still in effect. This law essentially empowers the State Administration of Industry and Commerce (SAIC) to subjectively enforce the rules as they deem necessary. The language in the Advertising Regulations is very specific in some areas and very vague in others. For example, messages which are seen as "hindering the public or violating....social customs" are off limits.

This presents a maddening environment for most foreign advertising firms to work in. They have to comply with laws that hamper their ability to effectively promote their product. Moreover, some of the laws on the books are so vague that any one company can be in violation at any time if the SAIC happens to deem it so. Accordingly, advertising companies spend considerable resources on ensuring that their content is considered acceptable by the SAIC. This is even more difficult because SAIC officials are often quite subjective in their judgments.

Online Advertising Regulations

The Chinese government has long focused on regulation of the online advertising industry because online ads are economical, fast, and have extensive reach. Moreover, the industry draws additional attention because it has received significant investment from overseas. This gave the Chinese government cause for concern, as there was money pouring into a unregulated sector (up to that point) that was capable of reaching millions of people.

The SAIC had reason to be concerned – there were over 15,000 registered websites in China at the end of 1999, generating widespread concern within the government that false advertisements might appear and improper (i.e., unlicensed) business activities could occur. In part to address these very issues, the SAIC decided to require Internet companies to acquire a license prior to publishing advertisements online. Soon after the license requirements became known, the "Big 3" portals (Sina, Sohu, and Netease) passed the qualification examination, and were officially granted permission to run online advertisements. Since that time, a great many companies with an online focus have followed suit.

This license process does not give these companies any special lock on the online advertising market. They are still required to comply with all relevant advertising laws and still have to pass across all questionable content to the appropriate bureau for review prior to publication online. Aside from this very basic licensing requirement, no laws exist on the books for online marketing. This makes entry into the market a risky proposition for foreign players who do not feel comfortable doing business in a space that has little regulatory certainty.

SMS and Email Marketing Regulations

At present, there are very few clear laws specifically pertaining to SMS and Email marketing. That said, this does not mean that companies can advertise as they wish; they are still bound by the basic advertising law regardless of the medium they use.

WTO Implications for Advertising Agencies

At present, foreign advertising companies are required to either set up a representative office on the Chinese Mainland or to create a joint venture in which they hold a minority stake. Both of these approaches are problematic.

An overseas advertising company that chooses to open a representative office in China cannot accept payments in Chinese currency, and must be paid offshore. Most such multinational clients are reluctant to pay overseas, as their accounting systems are largely geared to process payment locally. Conversely, should an ad agency choose to open up a joint venture, they are forced to take a minority stake in it, even if they are responsible for running all aspects of the business.

Following accession to WTO, however, China has pledged to allow majority foreign ownership of joint venture advertising companies within two years, as well as full foreign ownership of subsidiaries within four years. There have been verbal indications from the relevant ministries that this schedule may be increased considerably, but this is by no means a certainty. In any case, these guarantees are encouraging signs to many international advertising firms looking to either beef up their Mainland presence, or open a new office in China.

WTO is almost certain to stimulate increased investment in the Chinese advertising industry. The kind of strong, clear rights and improved market access for foreign investors that are supposed to follow China's entry into the WTO will spur investment in the advertising sector. In addition, the increased transparency the marketplace will gain is of huge value to potential investors.

Advertising in China

China has quickly emerged as one of the largest advertising markets in the world, currently ranked fifth globally, second only to Japan in the Asian market. Advertising spend has increased from US$ 3.6 billion in 1997, to US$ 6.1 billion in 1999, to US$ 11.2 billion in 2001.

In spite of a current global recession, the Chinese ad market has proved itself remarkably resilient. That said, competition for advertising budgets continues to be fierce. Advertising agencies that have consistently stuck with traditional media are being forced to branch out and take on New Media projects. Because of this, portals and interactive agencies are increasingly pushed to compete with these agencies for a piece of the corporate advertising budget.

This is a far cry from the mid-nineties, when "4A" advertising agencies* stuck largely with traditional media and the "Interactive Agencies" (like 24/7, Doubleclick, and Organic) dealt exclusively with the then mysterious interactive media. At the time, interactive marketing promotions were just starting to gain momentum due to the fact that the Internet was rapidly beginning to acquire a substantial user base.

The Portals – Sohu, Sina, and Netease

No discussion of New Media would be complete without mentioning the "Big 3" portals in the Chinese Internet space. By virtue of being the first of the online China plays to list on NASDAQ, Sina, Sohu, and Netease have been able to lead the pack of Chinese portals, or "chortals".

All of these companies are under significant pressure to diversify their revenue stream, reducing their overwhelming reliance on banner ad revenue. Accordingly, they have all started to allow users to send mobile phone text messages via the Internet. Their subscription

---

* Refers to a company that belongs to the American Association of Advertising Agencies, and has come to mean an advertising agency with a global client base and impeccable reputation.

services offer weather reports, news summaries, stock updates, as well as mobile phone ringtones and greeting card services for holidays such as Lunar New Year and Valentine's Day. Material can be downloaded to a mobile phone by forwarding an inquiry to a SMS center or by using the Internet. Box provides a short list of information products currently available.

SMS Information Services, 2001

- ☐ Sports scores
- ☐ Entertainment gossip
- ☐ Mail
- ☐ Mall sales
- ☐ Horoscopes
- ☐ News – world, financial, technology
- ☐ Lottery results
- ☐ Weather
- ☐ Health information
- ☐ Downloadable graphics and ring tones

Source: MFC Insight

All three chortals have put forward ambitious plans for monetizing services in the wireless space. Sina's proposed new direction is to develop a multi-media platform capable of transmitting both cable and Internet content. Its current wireless data content includes a very extensive logo and ringtone download section. Sohu is working on its mobile data services via the "4 E's". Netease has declared that in 2001, its main sources of revenue will come from paid wireless services and online entertainment. All three chortals have signed cooperative agreements offering content with both China Mobile and China Unicom for their respective wireless data services.

Top 10 Portals, July 1998 – July 2000

July 1998

1. www.yahoo.com
2. www.netease.com[a]
3. www.ihw.com.cn
4. www.online.sh.cn
5. www.sohu.com.cn
6. www.east.cn.net
7. www.microsoft.com
8. www.netchina.com.cn
9. www.download.com.cn
10. www.cpcw.com

January 1999

1. www.yahoo.com
2. www.netease.com[a]
3. www.sohu.com.cn
4. www.163.net
5. www.263.net
6. gbchinese.yahoo.com[b]
7. www.sina.com.cn
8. www.online.sh.cn
9. www.microsoft.com
10. www.yeah.net

July 1999

1. www. sina.com.cn
2. www.sohu.com
3. www.263.net
4. www.yahoo.com
5. www.netease.com
6. www.163.net
7. gbchinese.yahoo.com[b]
8. www.cpcw.com
9. www.online.sh.cn
10. www.21cn.com

January 2000

1. www.sina.com.cn
2. www.163.com
3. www.sohu.com.cn
4. www.163.net
5. www.yahoo.com
6. www.263.net
7. cn.yahoo.com
8. www.china.com
9. www.21cn.com
10. www.eastnet.cn

July 2000

1. www.sina.com.cn
2. www.sohu.com
3. www.163.com
4. www.263.net
5. cn.yahoo.com
6. www.163.net
7. www.21cn.com
8. www.china.com
9. www.chinaren.com
10. www.yesky.com

Source: CNNIC

[a]*also 163.com;* [b]*former spelling for cn.yahoo.com*

The Big 3 Portals: Sina, Sohu and Netease

	Sina	Sohu	Netease
Description	Sina.com is an Internet media company for Chinese communities worldwide offering a range of Chinese-language news, entertainment, e-commerce platforms, financial information, and lifestyle tips. With separate websites in Mainland China, Hong Kong, Taiwan, and North America, Sina provides global content and services to each region's audience.	Sohu is an Internet communications, media and commerce company. Sohu offers a directory, keyword search, email, message board, the first Java-based chat room, and virtual communities. Sohu's sixteen branded channels cover news, sports, business and finance, real estate, IT, education, career, fashion and women, entertainment and shopping, music, games, travel, pets and health. Sohu has received ICP, BBS, and news provider licenses.	Netease is a China-based Internet technology company that has developed applications, services, and other technologies for the Internet in China. Their mission is to deliver "Power to the People" by using Internet technologies to enhance information sharing and exchange. Netease websites offer Chinese Internet users Chinese language-based online content, community and electronic commerce services. Netease websites organize and provide access to 16 separate channels of online content through distribution arrangements with over 100 international and domestic content providers.
2001 Strategy	Provide a series of paid and subscription services including paid	Sohu is focusing on providing the "4 E's":	In 2001, its strategy is to have paid wireless services and online

continued

	Sina	Sohu	Netease
2001 Strategy	email services, SMS, and online classified ad services. Sina hopes to make a profit before 2003. Its new focus is on becoming a broadband content provider. After buying controlling stakes in the Hong Kong-based Sun TV Cybernetworks in September 2001, Sina hopes to launch its broadband service in October and become China's largest broadband content provider.	☐ E-marketing solutions, ☐ E-Technology solutions, ☐ E-subscriptions, such as SMS and WAP, and ☐ E-commerce. In addition, Sohu provides a paid, value-added search engine service. Sohu formed a partnership with the Malaysian domain name registration service company DotCC to launch a registration service for the domain name ".cc". Sohu is the first portal in mainland China entitled to offer this service for ".cc".	entertainment become the two major sources of revenues. Now Netease provides IPDA (Internet Personal Digital Assistant) services, enabling NetEase registered users to manage their work and daily lives using Internet-based tools. It also offers SMS, online education, WAP email, and an online mall. In June 2001, Netease cooperated with Gosun to provide Internet access service for RMB 40 monthly fee.
History	Created in March 1999, Sina is a merger between two websites: SINANET.com of Sunnyvale, California and Stone Rich Sight Information Technology Company (SRS) of Beijing. SINANET was	Sohu.com's founder is Charles Zhang, who returned to China in 1995 after obtaining his Ph.D. from the Massachusetts Institute of Technology (MIT). In July 2000, Sohu. com successfully completed an	William Ding established Netease in 1997. Previously, Ding worked as a technical engineer for China Telecom and a technical support engineer in mainland China for the US-based database software

continued

	Sina	Sohu	Netease
History	founded in 1995 by three Stanford University graduate students, while SRS was founded in 1993 by Sina's former CEO and President Wang Zhidong. In June 2001, Wang Zhidong resigned from his posts as CEO and President. The new CEO is Sina's former COO Daniel Mao, and Wang Yan is Sina's new President. Sina has received ICP, BBS, and news provider licenses.	initial public offering (IPO) on the Nasdaq. In September 2000, Sohu. com acquired ChinaRen.com, a separate, smaller, but still sizable, Chinese portal.	company Sybase. William Ding has resigned his post as acting CEO and CFO, but will remain a board member and adviser. Ding was replaced as CEO by board member Ted Sun.
Financial Indicators	On April 13, 2000 Sina became one of the first Chinese Internet companies to list on the Nasdaq stock market. The fiscal year ending June 30, 2001 stated: □ Net revenues of US$ 26.7 million, an increase of 88.3 percent over net revenues of US$ 14.2	Charles Zhang initially acquired financial backing to establish his company from Professor Edward Roberts (MIT) and Nicholas Negroponte, co-founder of the MIT Media Lab. Currently, Sohu.com's investors include Intel, Dow Jones, IDG, Morningside, PCCW, Legend, Hikari and Goldman Sachs.	Netease listed on the NASDAQ in July 2000. Former CEO Ding holds a majority share in the company of 58.5%. In July 2001, Netease managed to defer getting kicked off the NASDAQ board by requesting a hearing, which was successful in keeping them listed. The threat of being delisted was a

contitued

	Sina	Sohu	Netease
Financial Indicators	million for the fiscal year 2000. □ Net loss for the year totaled US$ 36.4 million, or US$ 0.91 loss per share, compared to a net loss of US$ 51.0 million or US$ 3.44 loss per share for the fiscal year 2000. □ Pro forma net loss was US$ 20.9 million or US$ 0.52 loss per share for the year, compared to US$ 25.1 million or US$ 0.78 loss per share for fiscal the year 2000. According to the research company WiseCast, Sina led the Chinese online advertisement market in the first half of 2001 with a 54% market share. Sina still relies heavily on advertising revenue, which comprised more than 85% of total revenue in Q2 2001.	By the end of June 30, 2001, Sohu reported: □ Total revenues of US$ 2.9 million for its second fiscal quarter. Gross margins exceeded Company Guidance by almost double, from 12 percent in the first quarter 2001 to 22 percent in Q2. □ Pro forma net loss was US$ 3.3 million or US$ 0.09 per share for the second quarter 2001, a 22 percent improvement form the previous quarter. □ Advertisement revenue is US$ 2.2 million. □ Non-advertisement revenue is US$ 0.651 million, 23 percent of total revenue. Non-advertisement businesses include short message services, enterprise gateway solutions and e-commerce services.	result of its incorrect 2000 annual financial report. In August, Netease issued its new 2000 annual financial report: □ The total net revenue is US$ 3.7 million instead of US$ 7.9 million; □ The total net loss is US$ 20.4 million instead of US$ 17.3 million.

The 4A Advertising Agencies

Virtually every major global 4A advertising agency has offices in China. Some of these companies have moved strongly into the interactive space, while others have chosen to stay largely in traditional media. Regardless of their present stance, all of these companies are going to need to make a powerful move into two-way marketing communications over the next two years. The reasons for this are twofold: 4A agencies are under significant pressure with regards to revenue in 2002's economic climate, and, their clients are starting to demand that they are competent in using and creating technology driven media programs.

The Chinese advertising market has changed dramatically from where it was in 1995. To date, the advertising companies have made a large part of their revenue from media placement. Design and strategy have essentially been used as a loss leader, to put together the advertisements that could then command substantial fees when placed on billboards, television, in magazines, and on the radio.

The Chinese Advertising Agencies

Much like the United States, there are a number of local advertising agencies doing business on the Mainland. These companies range from startups with one person who does all the design and sales, to companies that have hundreds of employees and millions of US dollars in revenue.

Chinese advertisers have some significant advantages, and equally large disadvantages. On the one hand, unlike the overseas advertising agencies, Chinese advertising agencies do not have to concern themselves with a joint venture partner who owns at least 51 percent of the company. At the same time, the Chinese advertising agencies do not have the global relationships with major multinational corporations that make up the bulk of the 4A advertising companies' revenue stream. In addition, they have difficulty developing a top tier multinational client base, as these companies have usually tied themselves up with a 4A advertising agency before setting up an office in China.

Accordingly, these Chinese agencies have tended to acquire local Chinese companies as clients. While this may have not been particularly lucrative ten years ago, the phenomenal rise of Mainland companies like Legend (a computer manufacturer), Li Ning (a sports apparel company), and Haier (which makes refrigerators, air conditioners, and related products) have allowed Chinese advertising companies to build a client base with significant marketing budgets.

Many of the larger Chinese advertising companies are now actively embracing email and SMS advertising, much like their large 4A brethren, and, they are doing this for exactly the same reasons: the high margins that have traditionally existed in placing media are shrinking quickly, and, clients are demanding a much deeper understanding of the consumer from their advertising agencies.

The New Media Agencies

New Media agencies are advertising companies that primarily deal with advertising projects in which technology is an integral part of the campaign. Most of these companies are quite young, having been started up in the mid-nineties as stand alone entities (like Doubleclick), or, as offshoots of existing traditional advertising companies (like Ogilvy Interactive).

The leading China based interactive agencies are listed as follows:

- ☐ Adexplorer
- ☐ Allyes
- ☐ Madeforchina

- ☐ Ogilvy Interactive
- ☐ China Interactive
- ☐ Groove Street
- ☐ Doubleclick
- ☐ Mezzo Marketing
- ☐ Ion Global

Expect these New Media agencies to continue to produce China's leading edge campaigns, as the traditional agencies will continue to spend the bulk of their resources running out campaigns in the traditional media space and outsourcing technology driven projects to the New Media agencies.

New Media Advertising Techniques

The first sentence in this chapter stated that up to 10% of China's consumers can currently receive advertisements transmitted by email or SMS. This naturally begs the question, "If so many consumers can be reached so easily, why is it that New Media advertising has not taken off much faster than it has?"

The reason this industry was not discovered earlier was that advertisers had not really considered the way consumers were viewing this New Media. For the most part, they were still applying traditional ad space techniques that were bringing ever decreasing results (trackable, normally measured in clicks). Many ad companies decided to place irrelevant banner ads, pop up windows, junk email, or SMS ads in as prominent a position as possible. The results were negative on the two most important fronts; they understandably upset their viewers and got only poor results in return.

Early pioneers of this media such as Charley Kan, Director of The

Media Edge in Beijing, noticed that unlike the TV screen, people surfing the Internet were actively searching for information and news, and, that these inappropriately placed ads were not only cluttering up websites, but also slowing down the download of information. Such problems are especially noticeable on the types of dial-up modem connections prevalent in China.

A new approach being adopted in China by visionary New Media agencies and brand owners such as Mindshare, IBM, Li Ning, and Audi is "permission based advertising, " which is the practice of getting the consumer to first register to receive ads that match their interests and then transmitting the relevant commercial information to them via SMS or email. Think of this as "on demand advertisement."

This technique addresses the issue of advertising space inherent in marketing in a country such as China, where portals are cluttered with advertisements that do little save confuse the end user.

Interactive Marketing in China – Not Just Banners

There are enormous benefits to using email and cellular phones to market to the Chinese masses. There are also significant obstacles to be dealt with. The most significant hurdles to be overcome involve both getting content to a given device and making the user respond. This is no easy task. With regards to the Internet, most people in China are still using a dial-up modem to log on. As for SMS, they are using a mobile phone that can only send or receive a maximum of 160 Latin or 80 Chinese characters.

That said, there are amazing benefits to be gained by using technology to create a two-way relationship with an audience. A brief review of some of the ways technology has been used to conduct large-scale marketing programs in China, along with the amazing results they have produced, is below.

Email has proved itself an incredibly effective tool when the marketing objective is to target a very specific audience, and to drive them to act upon the offer given to them. Many people think of email promotions and immediately picture "spam" or a mass email broadcast to a group of people who have not given permission to be contacted. While spam is widely used in China (as it is in the rest of the world), we are starting to see an increasing trend towards permission email marketing.

Permission email means that the recipients have specifically requested that they receive certain, specific content. Moreover, these users can change their preferences or revoke their permission at any time. There are four levels of permission that email marketers traditionally work with, as follows:

☐ **Single Opt-in:** an approach in which a user who desires to be added to a List must request, actively, such as by checking a box on a web page, to be added to the List.

☐ **Verified Opt-in:** an approach in which after a subscription has been received, a process verifies the E-mail address of the user before mailings commence.

☐ **Incentivized Opt-in:** a direct incentive is offered to the subscriber to join the list

☐ **Opt-out:** a user is offered a prominently placed pre-checked box or other pre-filled permission indicator at the point of Personal Information collection giving permission to be added to a list, unless they actively indicate otherwise.

Below is an example of a cutting edge permission email promotion, conducted in China by IBM. In this case, IBM used a "single opt-in" list of recipients for its campaign.

Email Case Study 1: Single Female Looking for Locally Made PC

Marketing Director 1.1   December 2001

The "Hardware Buyer" Campaign

In the "now" economy, fast return on investment is everything. Marketers are feeling the pressure to perform more than ever before... especially those marketing products such as "computer hardware," items simply not purchased with the frequency of consumer goods.

This month we bring you a inside look at how an email campaign led by IBM has opened up direct channels of communication to consumers across the nation planning to buy hardware products.

The solution was a simple, but ingenious idea to reverse the normal mass marketing campaign process. It began by sending a "sense and respond" email message to over 3 million mainland consumers, each of whom had previously requested Computer Hardware and Internet related promotions.

Which One Do You Want?

The email was designed to be appealing and simple, so that consumers would instantly respond without having to wade through a complicated survey. In order to generate a list of consumers that could be used for further marketing, each consumer was emailed an image rich selection of 5 types of computer products (Desktop PC's, Laptop Computers, PDA's, Printers, and Scanners) and given simple, one-click choices allowing them to indicate which product they plan to purchase.

The Consumers Respond: I Want That One!

Marketers asked, consumers answered. Of the over 56,000 consumers who requested Desktop Computer promotions, over 36,000 (64%) of them chose local brands (Congratulations to Founder and Legend).

However, consumers' preferences were just the opposite when considering Laptop Computers-an amazing 75% of consumers (over

42,000) selected international brands over their local competitors.

Among those planning to purchase a PDA, the split was a bit more even. Although 57% of consumers (over 32,000) chose local brands, 43% of consumers (over 24,000) indicated they plan to purchase an international brand of Personal Digital Assistant. As for Scanners, there existed a similar split; with 58% of consumers (over 32,000) planning to buy an international brand.

When buying a Printer however, consumers again showed strong preferences; over two thirds (37,000+ consumers) plan to buy an international brand of Printer.

Finding the Niche Decision Makers: Marketing Enterprise Servers

As a key partner in the effort to further profile mainland hardware consumers, IBM took advantage of the reach of this email campaign by asking its own, additional question...this time hoping for very little response.

At the upper right hand corner of each email, IBM included a link to a questionnaire designed specifically to target those interested in purchasing Enterprise Servers. Asking questions regarding both consumer budgets, timetables for buying, and personal contact information, IBM designed their survey not to generate a mass response from general hardware consumers, but rather to generate a qualified short list of serious prospects who plan to purchase an Enterprise Server.

Congratulations to the team of innovators at IBM for leading this initiative.

---

*The above campaign was conducted, in its entirety, using the **madeforchina** permission email marketing system.*

Email Case Study 2: Coming Live to a PC Near You

Welcome to this, the eighth edition of Marketing Director 1.1, the newsletter that reveals the latest permission messaging techniques that are successfully generating response from targeted mainland consumers.

For many, the multi-sensory experience a television commercial creates is still the measure by which all other media is judged. While allowances are made for other formats, television raises the bar...it's glitzy, attention grabbing, high power advertising.

But it's not every marketing professional that has a television commercial sized budget at their disposal. For all the buzz it creates, television is not cheap. Production is hardly ever simple. Moreover, as with many types of media, the information flows in only one direction.

However, Television is no longer the only broadcast medium available...

This month we bring you a Spring Festival promotion run by FMCG powerhouse President that was broadcast directly via email to 1 Million consumers throughout PRC. For a fraction of the cost of even a short TV spot during the nationwide New Year Holiday, President brought its Instant Noodles to the homes of hungry families across the mainland, while at the same time associating its brand with the traditional cultural values and themes that mark the all-important Holiday.

The Year of the Horse: An Opportune Time

With the Year of the Horse fast approaching and consumers gearing up for another food filled holiday, President seized the opportunity to reach its audience during a time of year in which they would be particularly receptive to promotional offers.

President knew their product had mass appeal, and chose to market it on that level. Wanting to entertain its audience, express its best wishes for the New Year, and at the same time promote its brand of instant noodles, President decided on a "Year of the Horse" email broadcast to 1 million consumers throughout the mainland, including age groups likely to be students, working professionals, parents, and retirees.

The Right Title at the Right Time

The email's subject header was specifically created with the Holiday in mind. Invoking an ancient Chinese proverb while at the same time playing upon the fact that 2002 is the Year of the Horse, the title "Good luck in the Year of the Horse as the Horse takes the lead," attracted over 297,000 recipients to open President's email.

As each consumer opened their Flash enhanced promotional email, the broadcast began just as a television ad would, with a traditional commercial product shot and Spring Festival greeting from President.

The Broadcast Became Interactive

A real time horse race followed, dynamically displayed above an image of President's instant noodles. Consumers were then presented with a choice of three horses (each horse representing what kind of luck they'd like to receive in the New Year: luck in their Professional Life, Love, or Money). Those who selected the winning horse earned a chance to win an IP phone card. After selecting their personal birth sign, the race began... right within each consumer's email.

In order to extend the reach of their promotion and allow consumers to share their New Year's fortune with others, President included a 'forward to a friend' option within each email. Over 11,500 consumers forwarded President's 'E-Horse' game to a friend or loved one.

In addition, consumers were provided an option to indicate their desire to receive future promotional messages on President's products (29,000 consumers did so).

Conclusion

The success of President's E-Horse email broadcast can be attributed to the use of a clever, culturally sensitive subject header, as well as a strategically timed, entertaining promotion. Moreover, the use of Flash technology to present both a product shot, as in a TV ad, in addition to an interactive game, served to reinforce President's brand recognition.

We thank the team at President for giving us permission to bring you this case study and wish them the best of luck in this, the Year of the Horse.

SMS

SMS (Short Message Service) allows mobile users to send a text message of less than 160 letters (including spaces), or 80 Chinese characters, from one mobile phone to another. Marketers have just begun to effectively use SMS as a marketing tool in China. It is reasonable to expect that SMS marketing will increase in popularity over the next year.

The SMS market has already taken off in Europe, with an estimated 7. 5 billion short messages sent in December, 2000, alone. SMS was first launched in China in mid 2000, so the technology has yet to take off with Chinese mobile subscribers to the extent that it has in Japan, England, the Philippines, and elsewhere. The Chinese language is very precise, involving less ambiguity in interpretation than English. Thus, it readily lends itself to device messaging. Since PC penetration is low and few people have access to PC's at home, there appears to be a pent-up demand in China for simple two-way text messaging.*

SMS Case Study 1

Tel-co giant Siemens, with a market share estimated at 10% of the PRC's total mobile phone market, sought a low cost way to promote a new line of headphones they had launched as an accessory for their mobile phones. These proprietary earphones were specifically engineered to be used for both making and receiving phone calls and for listening to digital music files (MP3 format).

In an effort to target consumers already known to be mobile phone owners in a cost-effective manner, Siemens decided to partner with Tecom Asia, the only authorized SMS Wireless Advertiser in mainland China at that time. Tecom possesses direct access to the user databases of both China Mobile (GSM) and China Unicom (CDMA) in all areas where the service is operational (BJ, SH, GZ, CD).

Preceding this year's Chinese New Year Holiday (1/30/02-2/1/02), Siemens then moved forward in conducting what would be the first-ever legal SMS advertising campaign on the mainland conducted

---

* The stark contrast in SMS adoption between mainland China and Hong Kong can be largely explained by the relative difference in pricing between voice services and SMS. In mainland China, one SMS text message is priced at a rate equaling a quarter of a one minute phone (voice) call, whereas in Hong Kong, one text message is priced at the equivalent of a one minute voice call.

directly from an enterprise to the end user (not on an opt-in basis).

Out of a potential user base of millions of users (as of May 2001 the total number of subscribers for the 4 cities exceeded 12 million), Siemens selected consumers residing in Beijing, Shanghai, and Guangzhou, 20-28 years of age.

To maximize efficiency, they also requested that Tecom exclude those subscribers with pre-paid cards, users thought to be more likely to be inactive (an estimated 1.9 million users nationwide). Taking a random selection of 28.3% of the consumers specified above, Siemens had isolated a total of 501,000 potential recipients across the 3 metropolitan cities.

Scheduling dispatch evenly over three days (Wednesday through Friday), during the peak hours of the day (4 PM to 7 PM), Siemens sent a 69 Chinese character New Year's Greeting to each user providing them with a sales hotline to call for more information (the hotline being local to each city). In addition, they included an option to reply to the SMS (i.e., opt-in) with the letter 'A' indicating their request for more information (to be supplied in a follow up SMS).

First Message (translated):

"Happy New Year! Hope you have a Happy Year of the Horse, wish you lots of fun and lots of music! You are invited to purchase a pair of Siemens multi-function MP3 earphones, designed as an accessory for use with your mobile phone. For more information, we welcome you to call 021-51005100 or reply to this message with the letter 'A'."

Second Message (translated):

"This pair of headphones is designed as an accessory for Siemens' mobile phones. Not only can they pick up phones calls, they can also play MP3 music, produce high-quality sound, and come equipped with 32MB of internal memory. We welcome your call at 51005100, otherwise please visit your authorized reseller."

According to a monitoring report published on Feb 4, 2002, Tecom, via their proprietary monitoring system, registered the successful delivery of 147,039 SMS messages in Beijing alone. 3,013 consumers out of that group opted-in for further information, a response rate of 2.05%

Response was marginally higher in Shanghai (successful delivery of 173,904 SMS messages), with a response rate of 2.15% (3,734 consumer opt-ins). However, the best results were achieved in Guangzhou, where 4,275 consumers requested further information (180,468 SMS messages were registered as being successfully delivered [a response rate of 2.36%]).

Summary:
Total Successful Delivery (1st message) 501,411
Total Opt-in requested for 2nd message 11,022
Average response rate 2.18%

SMS Case Study 2

Having conducted wireless marketing campaigns in January of 2001 at the Australian Open, Heineken is regarded as a pioneer in the use of wireless and permission based marketing to bolster its brand, create customer loyalty, and encourage participation in the various sporting and music related events it sponsors. As the primary sponsor of two separate dance parties being held on consecutive nights in Guangzhou and Shenzhen, the company needed an effective way to drive consumers to its website, generate awareness of the event held under Heineken's "Super Club" moniker, and ultimately bolster ticket sales.

However, the China market, as it does for most marketers, presented the beer giant with a unique challenge. In previous such efforts, the Dutch beer company had used WAP (Wireless Application Protocol) to achieve similar goals. However, due to the slow development of WAP services in China, significant issues existed at the time with regards to availability. To overcome this obstacle, Heineken teamed up with Groove Street, a Shanghai-based marketing company that specializes in integrating offline, Internet, and Mobile marketing technologies.

The Heineken campaign was structured to go wireless quickly by gaining consumers' permission to contact them via SMS. Consumers already online were offered a Heineken screensaver for their mobile phones (sent via SMS) to encourage them to register for Heineken's loyalty program and provide profiling information. In addition, they also received an SMS reminder (which they could forward to friends), encouraging them to purchase tickets to the dance events. Finally, Heineken dispatched branded email messages promoting the event to consumers in its proprietary email database, utilizing demographic data to target the email dispatch to reach only consumers it thought would be interested in the promotion. Within each email, an additional effort was made to emphasize the wireless component of the campaign, as each message included a field allowing consumers to provide their mobile phone number if they wished to be contacted by Heineken in the future.

Each consumer who then purchased tickets to one of the events was given branded, coded promotional material that provided instructions on how to enter Heineken's Lucky Draw via SMS (winners were announced via SMS during the party). Upon verification of the ID number, accomplished through Groove Street's partnership with Linktone, a Shanghai based mobile content and application provider, a reply was sent to each individual consumer, thanking them for registering and participating in the event.

It this combination of wireless, viral, permission based technologies put together by Groove Street that allowed the Heineken events to succeed as they did. Not only did both events sell out, over 20,000 profiled consumers were added to Heineken's consumer database.

New Media is sweeping China at unprecedented rates of speed. Expect this pace to only increase, as traditional agencies, both Chinese and foreign enter the fray in ever increasing numbers. In addition, expect government regulation to begin to keep pace with this New Media development, as China hustles to keep pace with its recent WTO commitments, and in preparation for the 2008 Olympic Games in Beijing.

PART VI

FINANCE

There is no sector of the Chinese economy which will be so fundamentally effected by WTO entry as the field of finance. The doors will open to foreign firms to participate in China's capital markets, banking and insurance areas, fields once closely protected. This will open the doors of opportunity while creating a new competitive environment. The end effect will not only be enhanced services for the customer but the more efficient utilization of Chinese capital in the productive forces which an efficient banking and insurance system will create through institutional investment and management of capital in China's fast emerging and dynamic securities markets.

Chapter 18

China's Securities Markets

By Jonathan Li, CEO, Fayhoo Southwest Securities Company Limited

Introduction to China's Securities Market

Along with the booming domestic economy, the fledgling China's stock markets have been growing at an accelerating pace during the past ten years. China's stock markets mainly fall into A share market and B share market. A-shares are limited to domestic investors. B-shares are traded among foreign investors and Chinese residents. Other securities products available in China include funds, debt, and some commodities futures. There are also many Chinese securities listed overseas including Hong Kong "H" Shares, and depositary receipts listed on the NASDAQ in New York, in Tokyo, and in Singapore.

In the early 1990s, Shanghai Stock Exchange (SHSE) and Shenzhen Stock Exchange (SZSE) were established. The A-share market has been growing from 13 listed firms to over 1,000 firms. The market value has exceeded RMB 4,600 billion, accounting for 50% of China's Gross Domestic Product in 2000. Currently, there have been 101 local security houses with more than 2,600 branches. More than 56 million residents invest in the markets. Institutional investors such as the investment funds have also played important roles.

Number of Listed Companies and Investment Accounts

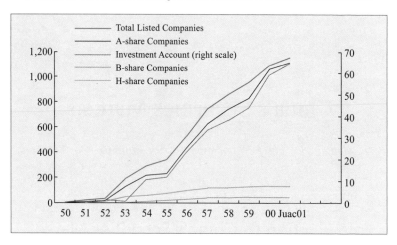

The performance of China's stock markets has topped the global markets during the last decade. For example, from the end of 1999 to March 22, 2001, the Shanghai A-share index increased by 53.8%, and the Shanghai B-share index increased by 296.9%. Despite the global slowdown in 2001, China will avoid a major economic downturn, benefiting from revival in domestic consumption and investment and its growing role in world trade. As the cornerstone of economic restructuring, the China's stock markets will sustain valuation and growth, with potential outweighing risks.

With China having entered the WTO, the country is continuing its efforts preparing for the opening-up of capital market to foreign investors. One example is the qualified foreign institutional investor (QFII) scheme, which allows qualified foreign institutions to invest directly in the domestic stock markets through a special account. Another example is to allow foreign companies to set up Sino-foreign joint venture fund management firms and brokerages.

In the absence of aggressive legislation, the emerging markets have been dogged by speculation and irregularities in recent years. The CSRC, watchdog of China's securities markets, has vowed to crack down on irregularities to build completely fair, impartial and transparent markets. Moves are afoot in the CSRC to hold market manipulators liable for their Security Act violations. It has issued a series of new regulations, and appointed talented professionals abroad as senior supervisors and consultants.

The Shanghai Stock Exchange

The Shanghai Stock Exchange (SSE) was inaugurated in November 1990, and is wholly state-owned. It started operations in December 1990. In 1991, the Municipal Government in Shanghai introduced regulations to allow listed companies in Shanghai to issue B shares to attract foreign investments. The first B share issue was launched by Shanghai Vacuum in February 1992.

At present, the SSE has tradable equities, including A and B shares, funds, closed-end funds, treasury bonds, financing bonds and corporate bonds. All these instruments are operated in a scripless environment. Both individual and institutional investors can invest in the Shanghai market, however, with the exception of B shares, all other instruments are available to domestic investors only.

The Shenzhen Stock Exchange

The Shenzhen Stock Exchange (SSE) was officially established on April 11, 1991, and is wholly state-owned. Similar to its counterpart in

Shanghai, the exchange deals in both A and B shares. China Southern Glass launched the first B-share issue in March 1992.

The Shenzhen Stock Exchange offers tradable equities, including A and B shares, funds, closed-end funds, treasury bonds, and financing and corporate bonds. All these instruments operate in a scripless environment. Both individual and institutional investors can invest in Shenzhen market. However, except for B shares, other instruments are only available to domestic investors.

Stock Exchange Membership

Only Chinese financial institutions can become members of the SSE. Exchange members must:

☐ Be the financial institution authorised by the relevant authorities to deal with securities related business

☐ Have a registered capitalisation of no less than RMB 5 million;

☐ Enjoy good reputation in the industry and outstanding performance;

☐ Comply with the requirements set by relevant securities authorities and stock exchanges;

☐ Acknowledge SSEs' Articles of Association and business regulations, and pay various membership fees as requested;

☐ Submit an application to the SSE with all necessary documentation.

A Shares: A Shares are all listed and traded in *renminbi* (RMB), may only be purchased by domestic investors in the PRC.

B Shares: B Shares were restricted to foreign investors only. In February 2001, B Shares were opened up for local investors to trade, although the original system where all B-share transactions were processed under a book-entry system whereby the holdings of shares of the

Listed Companies on the Chinese Stock Exchanges

Year	1990	1991	1992	1993	1994	1995	1996	1997	1998	1999	2000
National	10	14	53	183	291	323	530	745	851	949	1088
Shanghai Stock Exchange	8	8	29	106	171	188	293	383	438	484	572
Shenzhen Stock Exchange	2	6	24	77	120	135	237	362	413	465	516

Source: Shanghai Shenzhen Stock Exchange 2001

Share Structure (end –1999)

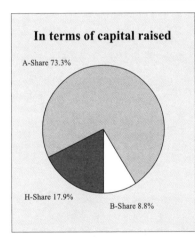

In terms of capital raised

A-Share 73.3%
H-Share 17.9%
B-Share 8.8%

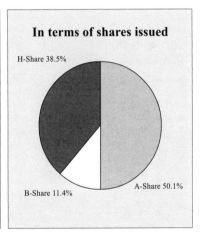

In terms of shares issued

H-Share 38.5%
B-Share 11.4%
A-Share 50.1%

participants (brokers, custodian banks, etc) are updated electronically by the Stock Exchanges on a trade-by-trade basis. The cash transactions are settled on net cash basis, with corresponding debit or credit of the participants' cash accounts maintained with the respective stock exchange. All B shares are still traded with foreign currency, with the Shanghai B Share traded in US Dollars and Shenzhen B Share traded in Hong Kong Dollars.

H Shares: H Shares are Chinese companies that have listed on the Hong Kong Stock Exchange. H Shares are not tradable by Mainland Chinese Nationals.

Issuing Summary for H Shares

Issuer	Issued Vol.	Issuing Price (Mil. Shares)	Level of over (HK$)	Raised Capital Subscription	Issuing Date (Mil. HK$)	Place Listed
Beijing Capital International Airport Co.	13.46	1.87	1.3	27.39	2000.02.01	HK
Petro China Co., Ltd	175.8	1.28	1.29	225.024	2000.04.07	HK US
Beijing Beida Jade Universal Sci-Tech Co.,Ltd.	0.264	11	4.28	2.9	2000.07.27	HK
Shanghai Fudan Microelectronics Co., Ltd.	1.25	0.8		1.05	2000.08.04	HK
China Petroleum & Chemical Corporation	167.8	1.61	2.92	268.287	2000.10.19	HK Lon. NYC
Beijing Tongrentang Co., Ltd	0.72	3.28		2.36	2000.10.31	HK

They are open to trading by foreigners only. Chinese enterprises being listed overseas have produced multiple effects:

☐ First, a number of important enterprises have entered the international capital market, learning and drawing on experience from the management method, accounting system, laws and regulations, regulatory measures and experience of well-established markets, which shall benefit from the improvement and development of domestic securities markets.

☐ Secondly, capital has been raised for the construction and growth of Chinese economy.

☐ Thirdly, the transition of the operation mechanism of SOEs and segregation of SOEs from government control has been promoted.

☐ Fourthly, the Hong Kong listing of Chinese enterprises has also strengthened Hong Kong position as an international financial centre.

☐ Fifthly, China opening up has strengthened the contact and exchanges between China and the international securities community.

Debt Market

In China, corporate bonds, financing bonds and government bonds (treasury bonds) are traded in the debt market, which is not open to foreign investors. Although many Chinese companies do offer debt products in the London, New York, Tokyo, and Singapore markets.

The government is planning to open up the local debt market and allow more local and foreign participation. The government recently released over RMB 60 billion worth of treasury bonds and will continue to aggressively develop the Chinese debt market as an alternative investment option to stock in order to improve market stability.

Bond market in China is weak relative to stock market, with the bond issuance being only 1/2 of stock issuance in 1999, as compared to 12 times for international capital markets. The weakness is attributed to the tiny corporate bond market. Corporate bonds account for only 5% of total bond issuance, and their issuance was actually shrinking in most times of the 1990s. The secondary market for corporate bonds is even smaller, with listed bonds being only 2% of their issuance.

All the three parties involved are responsible for the weakness of

Annual Issuance of Securities (Shares vs Bonds)

	1992	1996	1999
In China Market (RMB bn)			
Shares	94.1	425.1	945.0
Bonds	332.9	149.0	421.5
In International Market (RMB bn)			
Shares	23.5	57.7	-
Bonds	333.7	710.6	-

corporate bonds – the government, whose approvals are too strict for risk concerns, the corporate which see bond issues as liabilities while not being willing to pay interests, and the investors who prefer short-term investment to long-term investment. But this trend is beginning to change as investors become more aware of the benefits of having a good investment mix and as the government seeks greater stability for the markets.

Money Market

Currently, the money market in China is not open to foreign investors.

Securities Companies

There are currently 101 securities houses, with about 2500 securities retail branches, 203 Itics, and 1 JV investment bank, which are engaged in securities dealing business. The number of employees employed in securities companies is estimated at about 100,000.

Number of Securities Companies (end June 2000)

Securities Houses	101
Itics	203
JV Investment Bank	1

According to the financial business segregation principle stipulated in the Securities Law and Commercial Bank Law, Itics, for which

Securities Market Summary

	1996	1997	1998	1999	2000
# of Listed Co's (A, B share)	530	745	851	949	1088
# of Listed Co's (B share)	85	101	106	108	114
# of Listed Co's (H share)	25	42	43	46	52
Total Issued Capital (million)	12.20	19.43	25.27	30.89	37.92
Negotiable Shares (million)	4.30	6.71	8.62	10.80	13.54
Total Market (million RMB) Negotiable Market	9842.38	17529.24	19505.64	26471.17	48090.94
Capitalization (million RMB)	28.67	52.04	57.46	82.14	160.88
Trading Volume (billion RMB)	253.31	256.08	215.41	293238.88	475.84
Total Turnover (million RMB)	213.32	307.22	235.44	313.20	608.27
Shanghai Stock Exchange Composite Index	917.01	1194.10	1146.70	1366.58	2073.48
Shenzhen Stock Exchange Composite Index	327.45	381.29	343.85	402.18	635.73
PE Ratio					
Shanghai	31.32	39.86	34.38	38.13	58.22
Shenzhen	35.42	41.24	32.31	37.56	56.03
Turnover Ratio					
Shanghai	913.43	701.81	453.63	471.46	492.87
Shenzhen	1350.35	817.43	406.56	424.52	509.10
Number of Investors (million)	23.07	33.33	39.11	44.81	58.01
Number of Securities Investment Funds			6	22	34
Amount Issued of Securities Investment Funds(100,000,000)			120	510	562
Turnover of Securities Investment Funds (1,000,000,000)			555.33	1623.12	2465.79
Futures Transaction Volume(10,000)	34256.77	15876.32	10445.57	7363.91	5461.07
Futures Turnover (100,000,000)	84119.16	61170.66	36967.24	22343.01	16082.29

Source: Shanghai and Shenzhen Stock Exchanges

securities dealing has been part of business for a long time, should stop the business. But this would take some more time to materialize.

Before China's accession to the WTO, there was only one JV investment bank in China – China International Capital Corporation Limited, is granted the right to engage in securities underwriting, but not trading. CICC is a joint venture between the China Construction Bank and Morgan Stanley Dean Witter.

It was BNP Peregrine Paribas that won approval to establish the first joint venture investment bank in China since Beijing joined the World Trade Organisation, signalling a milestone for the industry. BNP's chosen partner is Changjiang Securities, a regional company based in the central city of Wuhan and linked to Qingdao Haier, one of China's most successful consumer electronics companies

Foreign Brokers

Foreign B-share brokers are prohibited from becoming members of the SSE, but are allowed to obtain special seats with the Shanghai Stock Exchange for dealing in B shares.

If a foreign broker wishes to participate in B-share trading, it is required to submit documentation including the application, the company's articles of association, the company's audited financial reports for the last two years, and the financial business dealing licence granted by the Chinese authorities to the China Securities Regulatory Commission (CSRC) for approval.

After obtaining approval, the foreign broker should then sign an agency agreement with a local approved broker, and pay several fees, i.e. risk fund contribution of US$ 50,000 and an annual fee of US$ 2,500 to the stock exchange.

The foreign broker can then be regarded as an indirect foreign broker able to place buy/sell orders through its local broker. If the foreign broker wants to place its orders directly on the market, it needs to pay a seat fee of US$ 75,000 in order to obtain special seats. At present, there are 87 B-share brokers in the SSE, comprising 49 local brokers and 38 foreign brokers.

The stock exchange uses stamp duty, transfer fees, annual fees and seat fees collected from its members to fund its operation. Foreign banks can not become members of the exchange.

Foreign Shareholding

In China, foreign investors are restricted to B-share investments only. If any investors hold more than 5% of the total issued share capital of a particular company, they are required to report the details to the China Securities Regulatory Commission (CSRC), the relevant Stock Exchange and the issuing company within three days of the acquisition in writing and make a public announcement.

While there are no specific requirements for the format of such a report, it should include the investor code, stock name, holdings and the reason for exceeding the limit, stating whether there is any intention of acquisition. Additional announcements are required whenever such a holding increases or decreases by 2% or more of the company's total issued shares. The investor should not make any purchase or sale of the company's shares before reporting.

Foreign Companies Listing in China

Foreign-funded companies will be permitted to list in China's Shanghai and Shenzhen stock markets in three stages-first the Sino-foreign joint ventures in China's inland, then foreign-funded enterprises, and finally trans-nationals. But the detailed timetable for the list and for the issuance of China-Depositary-Receipt (CDR) of foreign companies is still under consideration. In addition, departments in charge are still considering the plans of qualified foreign institutional investors (QFII)* and of qualified domestic institutional investors (QDII)**.

China has begun seriously considering allowing foreign funded companies to list on the Chinese stock markets after gaining WTO membership. Although this process may take a long period of time to come about. The government's first priority is to make sure that the state owned enterprises are able to compete for capital. If the markets were to open up too quickly, state enterprises may not have access to capital and this could lead to serious social problems. The convertibility of the Chinese *Yuan* might be a slight technical problem incurred for the listing of foreign companies.

Qualified Domestic Institutional Investor (QDII) & Qualified Foreign Institutional Investor (QFII) in the Pipeline

The CSRC is currently studying a proposal by the HKSAR government to establish Qualified Domestic Institutional Investors (QDIIs) in China. Under the proposal, QDIIs from the mainland will be allowed to invest in offshore capital markets including Hong Kong. The CSRC is also planning to set up a QFII (Qualified Foreign Institutional Investor) system through which investors from Hong Kong may invest in the mainland stock markets.

The central government is supportive of the QDII issue because its establishment will create an outlet for the excessive forex savings and idle capital in the mainland and will help boost Hong Kong's role as an international financial centre, providing a stimulus for its economic

---

* QFII: Qualified foreign institutions to invest directly in the domestic stock markets through a special account.
** QDII: Qualified Mainland Chinese Investment Managers that are allowed to trade on foreign markets via specially designed accounts.

recovery. It is understood that QDIIs will be allowed to invest in red chip, SOE (state-owned enterprise) and blue chip stocks listed in Hong Kong.

Under the proposal, certain domestic institutional investors will be allowed to establish closed investment funds denominated in foreign currencies for investing in Hong Kong stocks. The investment cap and duration of each institutional investor will be restricted so as to facilitate supervision by the State Administration of Foreign Exchange (SAFE) on the flow of capital.

According to latest PBOC statistics, as of end-September 2001, the total forex savings at mainland-funded financial institutions in China amounted to US\$ 134.79 billion (HK\$ 1,050 billion), up 11.9% from the previous year, while the outstanding balance of forex loans dropped by US\$ 2.48 billion (HK\$ 19.24 billion) since the beginning of the year to US\$ 82.45 billion. The widening gap between savings and borrowings has created a big pressure on domestic banks.

Also, China is studying a proposal on the listing of China Depository Receipts (CDRs) in the mainland market by overseas companies. However, the proposal is still at the discussion stage without any timetable for implementation.

The Fund Management Industry

In China, the rapid expansion of domestic stock markets has led to the introduction of the globally popular investment vehicle. The Tentative Regulation of Securities Investment Funds was promulgated in November 1997. In the following months, China Southern Fund Management Co. Ltd., Guo Tai Fund Management Co. Ltd., and China Asset Management Co. Ltd. were given permission to operate. Presently, China has 14 fund management companies, which have launched 45 listed closed-end investment funds and 2 open-end funds. As of

China After WTO

October 27, 2001, the total asset under management have exceeded RMB 60 billion, accounting for more than 4.6% of the market capitalization of A shares in China.

The introduction of investment funds is regarded as a mark of crucial changes for China's financial structure. Funds investment serves as a reliable investment instrument for the public. They provide an ideal investment channel for pension funds. Also, they greatly buoy the stock market and reduce the market volatility. As the end of 2000, the cumulative dividend of the first 33 investment funds is US$ 8 billion. Four

Investment Mix by 33 Securities Investment Funds (end-Sept 2000)

Rank	Industry	Valuation (RMB bn)	Number of Funds involved	Share in total fund valuation (%)
1	Electronics & communications	18.45	30	37.81
2	Others	4.37	30	8.96
3	Transportation	3.71	26	7.60
4	Commercial & trade tourism	3.22	29	6.59
5	Petrochemicals	3.04	29	6.23
6	Energy & power	2.85	30	5.83
7	Phamcrocutions	2.13	29	4.37
8	Machinery	2.00	30	4.11
9	Montorgy	1.89	29	3.88
10	Textile & garments	1.84	29	3.76
11	Finance	1.38	26	2.82
12	Agricultural	1.17	29	2.39
13	Building materials	0.93	28	1.91
14	Home electronics	0.88	23	1.81
15	Auto & parts	0.58	23	1.19
16	Food & wine	0.37	21	0.75
	Total	**48.79**	**-**	**100.00**

of the five three-year old investment funds have rewarded investors' dividend return of over 80%.

The unveiling of guidelines for open-end funds by the China Securities

Regulatory Commission has set the standard for the industry. Many fund management companies have kept pressing ahead with preparations for the launch of open-end funds. The draft of investment fund law has been tabled for readings by the National People's Congress last year (2001). People have pinned great hopes on open-end funds to take root in China.

According to the contracts signed by China and its trade partners for its WTO entry, the authority will permit foreign companies to hold a 33% share in mutual fund management companies after it joins the WTO. The share can be raised to 49% three years after the WTO entry. Presently, joint ventures are not allowed. The CSRC suggests that local fund managers and their foreign counterparts should begin with technical cooperation and then proceed to joint ventures.

With a history of only three years, the fledgling fund management companies have not had enough time to mature in such fields as investment, operation, risk management, and corporate governance. Through cooperation with foreign companies, China's fund management companies will improve their expertise and be well-prepared for tremendous growth as China embarks on life post-accession to the WTO.

The following are Sino-Foreign alliances fund management companies that have been established recently:

- ☐ BNP Paribas – *Shen Wan*
- ☐ Dredsner – *Guo Tai*
- ☐ HSBC – *Nan Fang*
- ☐ INVESCO – *Peng Hua*
- ☐ JP Morgan Fleming – *Hua An*
- ☐ Montgomery – *Fu Guo*
- ☐ Schroders – *Yin He*
- ☐ ABN-AMRO, Barings and Credit Lyonais are negotiating with potential partners.

A New Phase of Stock Market Reform with WTO Opening-up

China has committed on JV securities houses and fund managers in the WTO deal. More than this, a key step will be the opening of A-shares for foreign investors, with a variant of QFII system at the initial stage

The opening-up will have both negative and positive impacts. Negative impact would be short-term pains for securities houses and increased volatility for stock market, while positive impact would be long-term benefit on the modernization of China's stock market.

The CSRC is therefore set to pay a balancing act, to press ahead with stock market reform on the one hand, and to control the pace of the reform on the other. A restructuring of China's stock market is expected over next 5 years, with an unification of the two A-share markets, a merger of the A shares and B shares, an establishment of a second board market, a rapid growth of open-ended funds, and a wave of M & As of listed companies, etc.

Meanwhile in the securities service sector, a upgrading of securities houses, an emergence of more fund managers, an expansion of securities intermediary institutions, and a more rapid and diversified business development with a relaxation of the "segregation principle" for the sector as a whole, are to be observed.

A New Development Stage of Securities Markets

Latest correction in China's stock market is a joint result of government's reform efforts and cyclical adjustments. The correction is actually intended by the government. While the correction is near the end, the stock market is likely to continue to adjust in the months ahead.

But a collapse of China's stock market is not anticipated, and on the contrary there should be still large room for the market to grow, given expected continuing robust economic growth, sustainable high domestic liquidity, and accelerating capital inflows as well as the government's capability to control the market.

China's stock market is therefore expected to nearly quadruple over the next 10 years, in terms of market capitalization, with the number of listed companies to double and stock market prices to nearly triple.

The Impact of WTO Entry on China's Securities Industry

It important to note that over the next decade, many forces will be at work in shaping the Chinese securities market and putting pressure on local securities houses. On one side, one has the foreign firms and

Major Terms of Sino-US WTO Agreement on China's Securities Industry

☐ Foreign securities firms will be allowed to establish JVs with ownership < 30% to engage in underwriting A-shares and in underwriting and trading B-shares and H-shares as well as goverment and corporate debt no later than 2003.

☐ Foreign as set managment firms will be allowed to establish JVs with ownership < 30% to engage in domestic securities investment fund management business upon WTO entry, and the ownership ceiling will rise to 49% no later than 2003.

their involvement as stipulated by the WTO agreement. On the other side there are the domestic forces that will come into play, indirectly as a result of the WTO agreement. These domestic forces come in the shape of local banks and the Internet. The government is currently making provisions to allow local banks to trade securities with the Bank of China International most likely as the first candidate to be allowed to trade.

The Internet is coming in to the picture more and more. With several online trading licenses being allocated to securities firms last year and licenses to be released for pure-play online brokerages, like Fayhoo Southwest Securities (www.fayhoo.com) this year, the online trading industry is looking to boom.

Positive Impact

☐ On local securities houses, positive impact will be a long term one, that is, foreign investors' penetration in JV securities houses and JV fund management companies will undoubtedly accelerate the pace of their reforms by bringing in international competition. It would also enable the reforms to target on international practices by forcing and also facilitating a learning process of the practices.

☐ On stock market, the A-share market opening will provide a new way of attracting foreign investment, which should help sustain the expansion of the stock market with large capital inflows to the country. This is important, not only because the SOEs reform requires more capital, especially quality capital, to facilitate the listing of more SOEs, but also because foreign investors would be a more effective supervisor over the performance of listed companies and market irregularities.

Negative Impact

☐ On securities houses, given poor competitiveness of Chinese securities houses as compared to international securities houses as shown above, the emergence of JV securities firms is set to have an adverse impact on local securities houses. Given the nature of the securities business, which is basically a business of personal relationships, the impact would be that the JV houses take away both customers and talent staff from the local houses.

☐ On stock market, the negative impact would be an increased volatility of the market as a result of foreign investors' speculations with the help of JV securities houses. This is also set to bring about difficulties for the country's FX control.

Overall Impact

☐ Overall, the impact should be negative in short term, and positive in long term.

☐ The severity of short-term pain depends on the pace of opening-up. A too fast pace would be destructive leading to a collapse of domestic securities houses as well as the stock market. This will very much hinge on the approach and strategies as well as skills the government adopts to deal with the reforms and opening-up.

☐ How much of the positive long-term effect can be gleaned will also count on how the reforms and opening-up are carried out. Well-managed reforms and opening-up would enable China to maximize the long-term benefits, which will be incomparably more significant than the short-term pain.

Expected Domestic Market Reforms

Stock Market Restructuring

A main board stock market is expected to be established in Shanghai, by consolidating the existing two A-share markets in Shanghai and Shenzhen, while a second board market is set to be launched in Shenzhen. The launch of the second board is likely to be followed by the introduction of a modern venture capital system, and thereafter the formation of an integrated capital market comprising main board, second board and venture capital system in China.

Now it seems that the realization of such a restructuring would come later than expected. The launch of the second board, which has been postponed for several times, is expected to be further put off to later this year. The consolidation of the two A-share markets would be even later, as the Shenzhen city government would not likely let its A-share market to move to Shanghai until the second board market has developed into a decent scale. But it should not be later than 2005.

The state shares and legal persons shares in listed companies are expected to sold out gradually, being reduced from current 65% to below 50% of total shares in the next 3 years, and being phased out in the next 5-8 years. A large scale of M & As among listed companies is expected to take place over the next 5 years, and longer term there will be a new structure of listed companies by ownership, industry and region.

The A/B share merger expected for next 3 years will then result in a unified share product in China's stock market, in terms of investors and currency, available to everyone including both domestic investors and overseas investors and denominated in one currency.

The first open-ended securities investment funds launched during the end of last year, which will be followed by more such launches as well as the migrations of many existing close-ended funds to open-ended ones in the years ahead. As a result, institutional investors are set to witness a rapid expansion, while individual investors continuing to grow fast. Meanwhile corporate bond market is likely to pick up, while more products of government bonds are expected to be developed

The Restructuring of Securities Service Sector

A wave of M & As is also expected for the securities service sector, given expected challenges from JV securities firms. As a result, a number of large-sized securities houses by international standards are likely to emerge in the coming years. Meanwhile, modern investment banking businesses other than brokerage such as derivatives, M&A, fund sales, asset management, consulting, and so on, are set to be introduced and develop rapidly. So that some securities houses will become modern investment banks.

Before opening up to foreign securities firms, domestic opening-up is likely to go first, which means more local securities houses will emerge. While the 203 ITIC's are to be consolidated and restructured into 40 in the next two years, their securities business will gradually spin off to form independent securities houses.

Being more in demand, other intermediary institutions of accounting, law, asset appraisal and securities rating are also expected to emerge strongly, in terms of both firm number and firm size. The restructuring of the two securities clearing & settlement companies into the branch companies of the CSDCC is likely to take place during the early part of year. Technically, a central system is expected to establish, while its location as well as its link with the existing two systems are still under consideration. In the meantime, the development of on-line securities business is set to gather pace, and as a result the existing over 2,500 securities retail branches are expected to consolidate.

Stock market in China is expected to nearly quadruple over next decade, in terms of market capitalization:

Outlook for 2001~2010 China's Stock Market Development

	2000	2005 (f)	2010 (f)	2010/2000 (%) (f)
Number of Listed Companies	1088	1,665	2170	200
Stock Market Price Index				
Shanghai A Share	2074	3,680	5800	280
Shenzhen A Share	636	1,080	1700	270
Market Capitalization (RMB bn)	4809	10000	19000	395
Number of Securities Investment Accounts (million)	57.9	107	174	300
Number of Investors (million)	20.0*	40.7	70.0	350
Valuation of Securities Investment Funds (RMB bn)	85	230	510	600
Number of Securities Housess	90	140	200	222

* *Estimate*

In light of the above, China's stock market is expected to witness a more rapid and exciting development over next decade, driven by both demand and supply. It is expected that, over the next 10 years:

☐ Market capitalization will nearly quadruple,
☐ number of listed companies will double,
☐ number of investment accounts,
☐ as well as number of investors, will triple, and number of securities houses increase by 1.2 times.

Chapter 19

Banking And Finance

By William Stancer, Director of Intcgrated Marketing Asia, Accenture

Financial Restructuring

The restructuring of China's financial and banking system continues to underpin the nation's whole program of economic reform. Premier Zhu Rongji – once acting Governor of the People's Bank of China (1993-1995) and credited as the architect of restructuring – has long recognized that without fundamental reform of the financial system, tools of macro-control would be unavailable for regulating economic growth. And without a restructured banking sector, there would be no solid base for either expanding foreign investment, or for his planned re-engineering of the ailing State-owned enterprise sector.

Regulatory reform has been spearheaded by four key laws adopted in 1995: "The Law of the People's Republic of China on the People's Bank of China", "The Commercial Banking Law of the People's

Republic of China", "The Commercial Bills Law of the People's Republic of China" and "The Financial Guarantees Law of the People's Republic of China".

This legislation has set the scene for a fundamental restructuring of the banking sector – unquestionably one of the pillars of China's future economic growth – providing increasingly efficient credit supply to reforming State-owned enterprises, foreign-invested enterprises as well as private Chinese enterprises.

At the head of this reforming banking sector stands the People's Bank of China (PBoC), already well on the way of becoming a true central bank, along the lines of the Federal Reserve in the United States. The PBOC has increasing independence from the State Council in its role as both formulator and implementer of monetary policy.

Three Policy Banks – newly established in 1994 – have assumed responsibility for all 'policy lending' activity (such as financing macro-investment and State development projects). This has freed the Commercial Banks – particularly the Bank of China, the Industrial and Commercial Bank of China, the Agricultural Bank of China and the China Construction Bank, collectively known as the "Big Four" – to expand banking services and develop systems of commercial credit supply.

Also due for restructure are the Non-Banking Financial Institutions, specifically international trust and investment corporations (ITICs), finance companies and leasing companies. Foreign Financial Institutions – particularly foreign banks – play an important and expanding role, both as providers of services to foreign-invested enterprises and as mentors to the Chinese banks.

This chapter will describe the role that each of these performs in the financial and banking system, look at specific reforms to the foreign exchange system and finally consider likely future developments.

People's Bank of China (PBoC) 中央银行
人民银行

The People's Bank of China (PBoC) is fast reforming as a true central bank, overseeing a powerful regulatory and control mechanism essential for financial stability and continuing growth. Integral to the bank's restructuring is a streamlining of operations that will see the number of branches and staff continue to gradually fall. The final intention is to retain about a dozen regional offices in the whole country.

The PBOC's primary mandate in respect of monetary policy is to maintain stability of the Renminbi and, through such stability, promote economic growth. Macro control policy tools at the bank's disposal include deposit reserve rates, central bank credit interest rates and central bank discount rates for foreign exchange operations/bills of acceptance.

Specifically, the PBoC is responsible for:

- ☐ ensuring the correct formulation and implementation of State monetary policy;
- ☐ instituting and perfecting a macro-control system through the central bank;
- ☐ strengthening supervision and administration of the banking industry;
- ☐ formulating and implementing monetary policies in accordance with the law;
- ☐ issuing Renminbi (RMB) and controlling its circulation;
- ☐ examining, approving, supervising and administering banking and insurance institutions in accordance with regulations;
- ☐ supervising and controlling the financial market in accordance with regulations;
- ☐ promulgating ordinances and rules concerning financial administration and business;

□ holding, administering and managing the State foreign exchange reserve, bullion reserve and silver reserve;

□ managing the State Treasury;

□ maintaining the normal operation of the systems for making payments and settling accounts;

□ being responsible for statistics, investigation, analysis and forecasting for the banking industry; and

□ engaging in relevant international banking operations in its capacity as the central bank of the State.

The PBoC is required to report its decisions concerning:

□ the annual supply of banknotes;

□ interest rates;

□ foreign exchange rates; and

□ other major issues

to the State Council for approval before implementation. The PBoC's decisions on matters concerning other monetary policies must be reported to the State Council, but do not require its approval.

The more China opened up and reformed its economy, the more financial risks were beginning to appear. So after China's accession to WTO, the tighter regulation has been put on the top priority by the PBoC as part of regulatory body.

Policy Banks

Three "Policy Banks" – The State Development Bank (SPD), The Agricultural Development Bank of China (ADBC) and The Export-Import Bank of China (Eximbank) – were established in 1994. These banks were created to take over policy lending activities from the "Big Four", to allow these to develop into true commercial banks.

The State Development Bank (SDB) provides long term loans for major State construction projects with policy considerations (such as the Three Gorges Dam), including capital construction and technical transformation projects. Recently the SDB also started to provide long term Renminbi financing to foreign-invested enterprises in key industrial sectors.

The Agricultural Development Bank of China (ADBC) administers loans for the State contracted purchase of grain, cotton, edible oil and other agricultural products. It also provides finance to agricultural development projects, and acts as the State's agent by allocating funds earmarked as agricultural aid and further supervising the use of such aid.

The Export-Import Bank of China (Eximbank) provides loans to facilitate the import and export of complete plants of machinery and electrical equipment. It is currently also the main borrower of concessionary credits provided by foreign countries to China.

Commercial Banks 商业银行

Freed from their policy lending role in 1994, China's "Big Four" were nevertheless overstaffed and lacking the management systems necessary to fulfill a commercial banking role. Their capital bases were also seriously eroded by a history of non-performing policy loans.

Determined to transform the "Big Four" into true commercial banks - able to compete amongst themselves, with non-banking institutions and with foreign financial institutions both in and outside China – the Government required them to consolidate their branch networks, reduce total head counts and improve their management and risk assessment systems.

The "Big Four" responded by implementing risk classification systems of credit control, improving their accounting and reporting systems and increasing transparency. They were rewarded at the beginning of 1998, when the PBoC abolished the credit quota system, which had previously been used to keep close central control over lending. Henceforth, China's banks' lending decisions will be based on sound credit evaluation and maintenance of certain ratios, such as asset/liabilities or deposit/loans. In the summer of 1998, this increased autonomy was backed by a RMB 270 billion re-capitalisation of the "Big Four", restoring their capital adequacy ratios to an internationally acceptable 8%.

The commercial banks in China include:

State-owned commercial banks, or the "Big Four", previously known as the "Four Specialised", which in total account for more than 90% of the banking market:

- ☐ Bank of China (BOC)
- ☐ Industrial and Commercial Bank of China (ICBC)
- ☐ Agricultural Bank of China (ABC)
- ☐ China Construction Bank (CCB)

Commercial Banks:

- ☐ Bank of Communications
- ☐ CITIC Industrial Bank
- ☐ Everbright Bank of China
- ☐ Huaxia Bank
- ☐ China Merchants Bank
- ☐ China Minsheng Bank (China's first "private" bank, owned by Chinese private enterprises)
- ☐ Fujian Industrial Bank
- ☐ Guangdong Development Bank

☐ Shenzhen Development Bank
☐ Shanghai Pudong Development Bank

Rural and City Credit Co-operative Banks (now being redefined as commercial banks). In China there are about 90 City Shareholding Commercial Banks with over 3,000 branch offices such as:

☐ Beijing Commercial Bank
☐ Bank of Shanghai (formerly known as Shanghai City United Bank)
☐ Shenzhen Commercial Bank

China's domestic banking sector will be put under heavy pressure brought by foreign rivals after the WTO accession, in areas such as competition for high-quality customers and high-profile personnel, because of their superior management systems, supervision mechanisms and capabilities.

The WTO time schedule for China's banking sector is pushing them into a race for competition and eventual success in the huge China market. The regulator and the commercial banks have launched some strategic initiatives, in order to establish the modern corporate governance and implement the internationally accepted, cautious accounting standard that will help them ward off risks. The State-owned commercial banks will be transformed into State-owned companies; some will even be converted into shareholding companies. The PBoC will increase the capital assets of these banks through various methods including listing on the capital market and the introduction of shareholders. They will also be required to lower their non-performing assets ratio through stringent internal controls and business innovation.

Non-Banking Financial Institutions

On the fringe of the banking sector in China sit three categories of non-banking financial institutions, namely International Trust and Investment Corporations (ITICs), Finance Companies and Leasing Companies. Some of the services offered by these are similar or compete indirectly with those offered by the banks: the ITICs are even nominally subject to PBoC regulation.

International Trust and Investment Corporations (ITICs) were originally established as financing vehicles by local governments in the early years of reform and opening. The PBoC now treats them as quasi-banks, though some of the restrictions it imposes – notably those on their raising of funds – are different. The closure of the Guangdong Trust & Investment Corporation, China's largest ITIC at that time in October 1998, marked the starting point of China's attempts to restructure this part of financing sector. PBoC declared a reshuffle of the industry and combined its 240-odd ITICs into around 50. In January 2001, PBoC launched related rules governing the management and operation of ITICs.

Finance Companies are typically attached to major Chinese Group Enterprises, mainly providing in-house finance service, cash pooling for enterprise group companies and sometimes end-user leasing/financing service. There are now 69 major Chinese Group Enterprises that have established their own finance companies.

Leasing Companies exist in two forms: Chinese Leasing Companies (approved by PBoC) and Joint Venture Leasing Companies (approved by the Ministry of Foreign Trade and Economic Co-operation). The former provide vendor leasing and financial leasing services mainly to Chinese companies, whereas the later typically provide leasing facilities for the import of capital goods.

The Leasing industry in China has been hampered in recent years by a number of problems, including significant rent arrears, the absence of a leasing law, unclear accounting standards, a lack of appropriate tax incentives and impaired funding. The Central Government of China has however taken steps to regularize the leasing industry and it is expected that a Leasing Law will be promulgated in the near future.

Foreign Financial Institutions

With the exception of the Shanghai branches of the Bank of East Asia, Hongkong & Shanghai Banking Corporation, the Overseas Chinese Banking Corporation and the Standard Chartered Bank (which remained open after China's Liberation in 1949), foreign banks only re-entered the People's Republic of China in the late 1970's. Initially they established representative offices, only opening foreign bank branches, wholly foreign-owned banks or joint venture banks when this had been sanctioned by the PBoC.

By the end of 2001, foreign financial institutions had set up 214 representative offices and 190 business institutions in China, with combined asset of US$45.2 billion. A total of 31 foreign banks have been ratified to deal in Renminbi.

Representative offices of foreign banks can only operate within a scope of non-profit making activities. A foreign bank having a representative office in China for at least two years, assets of not less than US$ 20 billion and sound financial supervisory and administrative systems in its own country, may apply to the PBoC to open a branch in China. The application must be for establishment in one of major cities designed by the PBoC as open to foreign financial institutions. Similar prerequisites exist for an application to establish a wholly foreign-owned bank/ financial institution or a joint venture bank/financial institution.

The business scope of a foreign bank branch, joint venture bank or wholly foreign-owned bank will typically include:

☐ foreign exchange transactions for Foreign Investment Enterprises

☐ trade finance, loan guarantees and bill discounting

☐ foreign trade accounts, remittances and foreign shares and bonds

☐ advisory services on doing business in China and introductions

☐ project finance advisory for both Chinese and foreign sponsors

☐ hard-currency credit card transactions agent

☐ certain share underwriting, stock custody, and share flotation assistance for foreign purchasers

☐ syndicated hard-currency loans

☐ foreign currency loan and foreign exchange exposure hedging

☐ target Chinese clients who need foreign exchange

☐ safety deposit boxes

☐ credit investigation and consultancy

However, the situation is changing significantly after China's accession to WTO. Foreign banks are allowed to perform foreign currency business with local enterprises and Chinese citizens, right after the accession to WTO; and China will expand the geographical coverage of RMB business license. Within the 1st to 5th year after becoming the member of WTO, China will perform the scheduled opening up of the wholesale banking market; China will allow foreign banks to conduct Renminbi business with local enterprises two years after its WTO entry; and it will open 4 cities each year to foreign banks, with a total of 24 cities by the end of 5th year.

Five years after China's joining WTO, China will abolish all the existing non-prudent measures to limit the ownership, operation and way of establishment, including restriction on branches and issuing licenses. At that time, China will allow foreign non-banking financial institutions to provide auto consumption loans just like their Chinese counterparts; and will allow foreign banks to provide auto loans to Chinese citizens and allow foreign capital financial leasing companies to provide leasing services at the same time as that of Chinese companies.

Foreign Exchange System Reform

During the years following Liberation in 1949, China embarked on a policy of economic centralization, concentrating on domestic economic issues except where international support for brother socialist countries was required. Because China's external relations were rather limited prior to 1979, foreign exchange inflow and outflow was also very limited. Consequently, prior to 1979, there was no great need for legislation governing foreign exchange.

In 1979, China opened relations with the west and began to promote foreign investment. One immediate impact of the resulting sudden influx of foreign investment was to create a need for foreign exchange legislation. In 1980, the first legislation concerning foreign exchange – "Provisional Regulations for Exchange Control of the People's Republic of China" – was promulgated by the State Council.

This legislation was meant to address fundamental issues concerning foreign exchange in the country, implementing Central Government policy decisions that included:

☐ establishing the State Administration of Exchange Control (SAEC), which in 1996 was renamed the State Administration of Foreign Exchange (SAFE). Under the People's Bank of China (PBoC), SAFE is the body in China responsible for handling and implementing all matters relating to foreign exchange control;

☐ permitting only financial institutions and banks which had received proper government authorization to engage in foreign exchange activities (at the time only Bank of China was permitted, though permission would eventually be granted to a wider range of institutions); and

☐ establishing the foreign exchange retention system for all enterprises in China, under which domestic enterprise were able to retain a certain percentage of foreign exchange from their domestic exchange earning.

Between 1986 and 1994, China witnessed the establishment of over 100 foreign exchange "Swap Centres" throughout the country. Eighteen of these became "open markets," where daily membership trading took place based on a computerized offer-price system. The situation was sometimes confusing, as different Swap Centres quoted different conversion rates between the USD and *Renminbi*.

In the last four years a series of reforms have been implemented in order to gradually reach the goal of convertibility under the Current Account, as well as prepare the ground for convertibility under Capital Account.

On January 1, 1994, the Chinese Government merged Foreign Exchange Certificates (FEC) – a currency that had been used by foreign enterprises and individuals – with the Renminbi. At the same time, the official State peg on the Renminbi was removed, replaced by a "market value," determined by a national average of the Swap Centre rates.

On March 28, 1994, the China Foreign Exchange Trading System (CFETS), China's first inter-bank market, was established in Shanghai. Instituting a membership system, the CFETS's main role was to administer and supervise trading at its branches established in 25 cities in China.

In the spring of 1996, China moved one step closer to full convertibility on the current account with the promulgation of the "Regulations of the People's Republic of China for the Control of Foreign Exchange." These set forth the framework for China's foreign exchange controls and provided for a greater degree of Renminbi convertibility.

In March 1996, a pilot scheme for conducting currency conversions on foreign-invested enterprises' current accounts by means of over-the-counter bank transactions was introduced on a trial basis in the cities of Shenzhen, Shanghai, Dalian as well as Jiangsu Province. In July 1996, this scheme was extended with the promulgation of the "Regulation on Foreign Exchange Sale, Purchase and Payment," allowing current account conversion at designed foreign exchange banks throughout the country.

In December 1996, Dai Xianglong, the Governor of the PBoC, announcing that China had put the finishing touches to convertibility on the current account, enabling China to comply with the definition of current account convertibility contained in the article VIII of the International Monetary Fund's charter. The old State Administration of Exchange Control (SAEC) was renamed as the State Administration of Foreign Exchange (SAFE) to mark the change. China has stated repeatedly that it is intent on eventually making the currency fully convertible, i.e., also under the Capital Account, when conditions are ripe. This issue is considered in more detail under Future Developments (*page 317*).

Exchange Rates and Interest Rates

Exchange Rates are published daily by the PBoC, which uses the middle rate of the Renminbi against the US dollar, according to the transaction price prevailing in the inter-bank foreign exchange market on the previous day. With reference to the exchange rate of other major foreign currencies against the US dollar on the international foreign exchange market, the PBoC also publishes the Renminbi rates against these currencies.

Based on the foreign exchange rates published by PBoC, commercial banks will then list their own exchange rates within a floating range (also defined by the PBoC), and purchase or sell foreign exchange to their customers at these listed rates. With the prerequisites of maintaining a stable domestic currency, the PBoC will intervene when necessary, also buying and selling foreign exchange in the foreign exchange market in regulates.

Interest Rates in RMB are also set by the PBoC. Changes are not made on set dates, rather as and when required by macro-economic policy, typically only two or three times a year. Chinese Commercial Banks are allowed to increase or reduce the Base Interest Rate set by the PBoC by a maximum 10%. The most recent interest rate change made by the PBoC was a cut in rates made on February 21 2002. The following deposit and lending rates were introduced:

Current Account   -   0.72%

Fixed Deposits Accounts:

3 months	-	1.71%
6 months	-	1.89%
1 year	-	1.98%
2 years	-	2.25%
3 years	-	2.52%
5 years	-	2.79%

Short Term Working Capital Loans:

Up to 6 months   -   5.04%

Up to 12 months   -   5.31%

Medium and Long Term Loans - Working Capital Loans up to 3 years and Fixed Asset Loans:

1-3 years   -   5.49%
3-5 years   -   5.58%
Over 5 years   -   5.76%

Interest rates for Foreign Exchange Loans are fixed in accordance with comprehensive interest rates set by the central office of the Bank of China or fixed through consultation by both parties in accordance with interest rates on the international market.

PBoC has set up the general principles that would govern the liberalizing of interest rates over the next several years: the foreign currency rate should be liberalized before the Renminbi rate; rural before urban areas; loans before deposits; and flotation of the rate before total liberalization.

Future Developments

Full *Renminbi* convertibility is consistent with China's policy goals of increasing inward foreign investment and expanding international trade: that it will happen is a question of "when" rather than "if."

WTO accession requires neither the convertibility of *Renminbi* under the capital account nor the total convertibility of *Renminbi*. China needs greater overall national strength, a stable and sound financial system, and better government ability for macro control. Therefore, China will proceed in an orderly and gradual way and refrain from acting too hastily. After WTO accession, however, following the expansion of China's capital market, trade, and direct foreign investment, the free trading of *Renminbi* will be steadily promoted.

Full convertibility – when it occurs – will have a positive impact, reducing bilateral trading conflicts, further leveraging full membership of the World Trade Organization (WTO) and poising China to become one of the world's foremost economies.

Membership of the WTO will also – according to many analysts – trigger the full opening of China's banking sector to foreign banks. The presence of foreign banks in China has already stimulated healthy competition, requiring Chinese banks to understand and adopt new systems and services. Foreign banks are of course also providers of capital at a time when this is much needed – and sometimes their very presence can encourage their international customers to invest and transfer technology to China.

This said, the financial sector is likely to be one of the last to open fully to foreign participation, with the Chinese Government making concessions on a gradual basis. It correctly sees a secure, well-regulated financial and banking system for domestic entities as a prerequisite to allowing large scale foreign participation.

In the coming years we can expect to see new concepts and products introduced into the banking system in China, and an improved degree of transparency as international accounting standards become more widely adopted, both by Chinese financial institutions and by enterprises in general. This will certainly further enhance China's position as an attractive destination for direct foreign investment.

Chapter 20

Insurance

*By Tony Cheung, Deputy General Manager
eBusiness / Contact Center, China Pacific Insurance*

Foreign Companies
are Waiting at the Gate

T he insurance industry will be one of the first industries to become open to foreign companies, as a result of China's entrance to the WTO.

Foreigners are waiting at the gate leading into the Middle Kingdom. After the 9-11 event, a downward economic environment in the developed world has led to strains on insurance companies' profitability, balance sheet and capital strength. Please keep in mind that many aspects of the insurance industry are already very well developed (which is a better way to state that they are already saturated or oversaturated). One of the very few options left for them, is to expand into emerging markets.

Let me name a few of these factors, which many of you who are in the insurance/finance industry probably already knew:

- ☐ An improving economy
- ☐ An ever increasing middle class population
- ☐ Businesses become more responsible
- ☐ People are living longer
- ☐ A rising customer sophistication and expectation, which leads to their interest in foreign insurance companies
- ☐ Reform in welfare systems and social security systems, etc....
- ☐ Others.

All these, seem to lead to a major and consistent increase in demand, which, according to basic economic theory, lead to an increase in quantity and increase in price.

There are many foreign insurance companies are waiting for their licenses, into a partially open Chinese insurance market, which will eventually become a very open market in a few years.

Local Companies Are Getting Ready

Many local insurance companies, especially the largest players like China Pacific and Ping An, are busy getting themselves ready, to improve themselves and to get ready for the competitive environment after the foreign companies become active throughout the nation and across many industries. By introducing world class foreign partners, adopting modern practices, re-engineering the operation and employing foreign and return-to-homeland executives, more and more aspects of the Chinese insurance industries, are getting better on a daily basis.

Many local non-insurance companies, such as energy companies, manufacturing companies and service companies, are busy working with foreign companies. The formula works like this, they provide the capital, and market accessibility, and the foreign insurance company provides the capital, the management and professional skills.

As a result of these improvements, even after the Chinese insurance industry becomes more or less completely opened, there will be a number of local insurance companies who will be strong and professional enough to work with players from all over the world, to enhance and share the Chinese market, and to enhance and share the world market.

Even for some local insurance companies who may not have the resources to change themselves, many of them will still be able to maintain some share of their market because of their remaining leading edge over foreign companies:

Distribution Channel and Local Connection

Traditionally speaking, people and businesses brought from other people and other businesses that they can trust and have a connection with. In a mature market, there are many well established businesses around and therefore, customers put their money on these well established businesses. In China, insurance is not yet as mature as in the developed world. Therefore, customers often put their money on people whom they think they can trust and have a connection with, as a result of their long term relationship. That also means, local Chinese companies will always maintain a significant advantage over foreign companies in terms of distribution and connection.

As of the most important channel, agencies and brokers, only local Chinese companies will have enough in-depth knowledge of the strength and weakness of these individuals and companies. Therefore, They could probably maintain a significant advantage in the area of channel management as well.

Compliance

The China government and management authorities are now busy setting up and implementing the rule of law throughout China. This includes but not limited to the insurance industries. Like everything else that is new to China, it is still full of areas, which need to be further defined, changed and enhanced. Local companies will always maintain a competitive edge over foreign companies in this area. In order not to leave behind too much, a foreign company has to find, trust and work with people and companies that understand both the international and mainland Chinese environment.

Advantages Foreign Insurance Companies Have, over Chinese Companies

There are many aspects which, foreign insurance companies will maintain an advantage over local Chinese insurance companies who are not able to transform themselves into a world class insurance company.

These aspects include, but not limited to the following:

- ☐ Investment / capital utilization
- ☐ International connection
- ☐ Product research and development / actuary
- ☐ And others

Two aspects which many foreign companies have a significant advantage over Chinese companies are the areas of eBusiness – which in many companies are part of IT, and contact center – which in many companies, are part of customer service.

The two aspects, which foreign companies have, over Chinese companies are human resources and management systems.

The Chinese people are one of the most hardworking people in history, and hopefully in the future, too. And, many of China's youth are busy educating themselves after work, by attending training classes, by self studying, and by taking examinations. Local and foreign companies are also busy operating training courses for their local staff. All these, are very useful for the development of China.

However, in the world of business, it takes more than a good student, to become a professional executive. The business environment here, especially in the finance industries, are simply not as well developed as places like New York, Hartford, London, Hong Kong, California, Tokyo, Geneva, Singapore, Paris and Frankfurt. It will simply take many years for China to produce a mature business environment, which will then be able to produce enough experienced business executives.

Although Chinese insurance companies can overcome some of these shortages by employing expatriate staff such as me and many others, it will not be as easy as the foreign insurance companies. Foreign insurance companies come with a well-tested integrated management system and an army of executives who are already very familiar with the way this system works back home. All they need to do is to integrate it with the local environment and implement it. Chinese insurance companies have to do a lot more than that. They will need to integrate all these expatriate staff who come from different parts of the world. Then, we need to integrate all these expatriate staff with the local management. Then, we need to develop the entire management system by integrating many aspects of these multinational and local skills, culture, background, personality and management style. Then, we need to test run it. Finally, after everything starts to come into place, we can then implement these international practices and upgrade ourselves into a world class insurance company.

A Few More Thoughts

To summarize, in my personal opinion, there are too many opportunities there in China, for foreign companies and for local Chinese companies. And no one, should miss the opportunity of, at least come over, talk to someone and take a careful look at China. Actual, if you wish to miss the opportunity, you will not be reading up to there, right?!

Let me assure you, if you are willing to put in the effort, find and work with the Chinese whom you can and you have to trust, you will become successful. However, it takes a lot of commitment from a foreign company, in terms of capital, time, etc.... So, think and investigate carefully before any decision is made.

Advices to foreign insurance companies setting up in China are the following:

☐ You need to understand the way insurance works here and change some of the ways you think and do business elsewhere.

☐ In addition to recruiting local talents and bringing in overseas professionals, you have to find, trust and work with people and companies that understand both the international and mainland Chinese environment.

☐ However, you have to maintain your unique global competitive edge and in most cases, I will not recommend you to lose your foreign company identity. That means, you have to bring in and implement your best management practices into China, localize some, but not all of it. In that way, you will raise the standard of the entire Chinese insurance industry.

If I were a typical Chinese customer looking at a foreign insurance company, I will think, "If you look, act and think the same as a local company. Why I even need to work with you?" On the other hand, I will also think, "if you look, act and think as a completely foreign company. I don't think I can work with you, well, I may as well give up."

The entrance of foreign companies is useful to China. To a Chinese customer, these foreigners are bringing in more options, and in some cases, better options. To the local Chinese companies, these foreign businesses can bring in serious competition. But, don't worry, before these foreigners enter the Middle Kingdom, some Chinese companies will be ready.

Appendix I

Sample Joint Venture Contract

THIS CONTRACT is entered into on_____ , 2002, between _____(hereinafter referred to as "Party A") and _____(hereinafter referred to as "Party B").

Chapter 1 General Principles

After friendly consultations conducted in accordance with the principles of equality and mutual benefit, the Parties have agreed to establish a Sino-foreign equity joint venture enterprise in _____ , People's Republic of China, in accordance with the Law of the People's Republic of China on Sino-Foreign Equity Joint Ventures, the implementing regulations issued thereunder, other relevant laws and regulations of the People's Republic of China and the provisions of this Contract.

Chapter 2 Parties to the Joint Venture

Party A: _____ , an enterprise legal person of China with its legal address at _____ , People's Republic of China.

Legal Representative of Party A:

Name:

Position:

Citizenship:

Party B: _____ , a company incorporated in_____ , with its legal address at_____.

Authorized Representative of Party B:

Name:

Position:

Citizenship:

Chapter 3 **Definitions**

Definitions

Unless otherwise provided herein, the following words and terms used in this Contract shall have the meanings set forth below:

"Affiliate" means, in relation to a Party, any company which, directly or indirectly, is controlled by, under common control with, or in control of, such Party; the term "control" meaning ownership of fifty percent or more of the voting stock or registered capital, or the power to appoint or elect a majority of the directors, of a company.

"Articles of Association" means the Articles of Association of the Joint Venture Company signed by the Parties and approved by the Examination and Approval Authority simultaneously with this Contract.

"Board of Directors" means the board of directors of the Joint Venture Company.

"Business License" means the business license of the Joint Venture Company issued by the State Administration for Industry and Commerce or its authorized local administration for industry and commerce.

"Contract Term" means the term of this Contract as set forth in Chapter 17.

"Effective Date" means the effective date of this Contract, which shall be the date on which this Contract has been approved by the Examination and Approval Authority.

"Examination and Approval Authority" means the government department authorized under the State Council rules regarding the examination and approval of foreign investment projects to examine and approve this Contract and the Articles of Association.

"Joint Venture Company" means the Sino-foreign equity joint venture enterprise jointly invested in and established by Party A and Party B pursuant to the relevant laws and regulations of China and this

Contract.

"Management Personnel" means the Joint Venture Company's General Manager, Deputy General Manager, Chief Accountant and other management personnel who report directly to the General Manager.

"Third Party" means any natural person, legal person or other organization or entity other than the Parties to this Contract.

"Three Funds" means the Joint Venture Company's reserve fund, expansion fund and employee bonus and welfare fund as required to be established in accordance with applicable laws and regulations of China.

Chapter 4 Establishment of the Joint Venture

4.1 Establishment of the Joint Venture Company

1) The Parties hereby agree to establish the Joint Venture Company in accordance with the relevant laws and regulations of China and the provisions of this Contract. Promptly following the formal signature of this Contract by the Parties, Party A will handle application procedures for the approval of this Contract and the Articles of Association, and procedures for enterprise registration. Party B will cooperate with Party A in providing documents and information required from Party B in connection therewith.

2) The Joint Venture Company's term of operations shall be ___ years, commencing upon the issuance of its Business License, and may be extended together with the Contract Term pursuant to Article 16.2.

4.2 Name and Address of the Joint Venture Company

1) The name of the Joint Venture Company shall be _____in Chinese and _____ in English.

2) The legal address of the Joint Venture Company shall be _____ People's Republic of China.

4.3 Laws and Decrees

The Joint Venture Company shall be an enterprise legal person under the laws of China. The activities of the Joint Venture Company shall comply with the laws and regulations of China, and its lawful rights and interests shall be protected by the law of China.

4.4 Limited Liability Company

The Joint Venture Company shall be a limited liability company. The Joint Venture Company shall undertake liability for its debts with all of its assets. The liability of each Party to the Joint Venture Company shall be limited to its subscribed registered capital. Subject to the foregoing, the Parties shall share the Joint Venture Company's profits, and bear the losses and risks arising from their investments in the Joint Venture Company, in proportion to their respective contributions to the Joint Venture Company's registered capital.

Chapter 5 **Purpose and Scope of Business**

5.1 Purpose of the Joint Venture Company

The purpose of the Joint Venture Company is to use advanced technology and scientific management methods to research, develop and produce _____ , to further open the market for _____ , and to obtain satisfactory economic benefits for the Parties.

5.2 Scope of Business of the Joint Venture Company

The Joint Venture Company's scope of business: _____.

5.3 Scale of Production

[*specify based on anticipated production volumes*]

Chapter 6 **Total Investment and Registered Capital**

6.1 Amounts of Total Investment and Registered Capital

The Joint Venture Company's total amount of investment shall be United States Dollars (US$_____) and its registered capital shall be United States Dollars (US$_____).

6.2 Contributions to Capital

1) The registered capital of the Joint Venture Company subscribed by Party A is _____ United States Dollars (US$_____), representing a _____ percent share of the Joint Venture Company's registered capital. Party A shall make its contribution to the registered capital of the Joint Venture Company in the following forms: [*specify cash, land use rights, buildings, equipment, intangible assets, etc., and corresponding amounts or values*]

2) The registered capital of the Joint Venture Company subscribed by Party B is _____ United States Dollars (US$_____), representing a _____ percent share of the Joint Venture Company's registered capital. Party B shall make its contribution to the registered capital of the Joint Venture Company in the follows forms: [*specify cash, equipment, intangible assets, etc., and corresponding amounts or values*]

6.3 Payment of Registered Capital

Each Party shall pay to the Joint Venture Company fifteen percent (15%) of its share of the Joint Venture Company's registered capital within three (3) months from the date of issuance of the Business License. The timing for contribution of the balance of the registered capital shall be decided by the Board of Directors based on the Joint Venture Company's operational requirements, provided that all of the registered capital must be contributed in full within _____ years from the date of issuance of the Business License. If either party fails to make any capital contribution when due, such Party shall pay simple interest to the Joint Venture on the unpaid amount (or the value of the in-kind contribution) from the date due until the date such contribution is made at [*specify interest rate*].

6.4 Capital Verification

The Parties' contributions to the Joint Venture Company's registered capital shall be verified by a Chinese registered accounting firm engaged by the Board of Directors and the accounting firm shall issue a capital verification report to the Joint Venture Company within sixty (60) days from the date of the contribution. Within thirty (30) days from receipt of the capital verification report, the Joint Venture Company shall issue an investment certificate to such Party in the form prescribed by the applicable regulations of China, and a copy shall be submitted to the Examination and Approval Authority for the record. The Joint Venture Company shall maintain a file of all capital verification reports and copies of all investment certificates that have been issued to the Parties.

6.5 Increase or Reduction of Registered Capital

An increase or reduction of the registered capital of the Joint Venture Company shall require the written consent of both Parties, the unanimous affirmative vote of the Board of Directors, and the approval of the Examination and Approval Authority. Upon receipt of such approval, the Joint Venture Company shall register the change in registered capital with the competent administration for industry and commerce.

6.6 Assignment of Ownership Interest

The stipulations set forth in this Article 6.6 shall apply to transfers of the registered capital of the Joint Venture Company.

1) The Parties agree that, subject to compliance with the relevant laws and regulations of China, each Party may transfer all or part of its interest in the registered capital of the Joint Venture Company to any Affiliate at any time during the Contract Term without the further consent of the other Party. Each Party hereby waives its preemptive right of purchase with respect to such transfers of interest.

2) Except as provided in clause (1) above, each Party shall have a preemptive right of purchase with respect to the transfer of all or a part of the other Party's interest in the registered capital of the Joint Venture Company to a Third Party. [*specify procedures for exercise of preemptive rights*]

3) A Party transferring an interest in the registered capital of the Joint Venture Company must ensure that its transferee signs a legally binding document making it a party to this Contract and bound by the terms and conditions of this Contract to the same extent as was the transferor.

4) The Parties hereby consent to any transfer of registered capital that meets the requirements of this Article 6.6. Each Party agrees promptly to take all actions and to sign all documents, and to cause its appointees on the Board of Directors promptly to take all actions and sign all documents, that are legally required to effect the transfer of registered capital. The transfer of registered capital shall be submitted to the Examination and Approval Authority for approval and, following receipt of such approval, the Joint Venture Company shall carry out procedures for the amendment of registration with the competent administration for industry and commerce.

6.7 Loan Financing

The Joint Venture Company may obtain loans in China or abroad to fund the difference between the total amount of investment and the registered capital.

6.8 Encumbrances of Interest in Registered Capital

No Party shall mortgage, pledge or otherwise encumber all or any part of its share of the Joint Venture Company's registered capital without the prior written consent of the other Party.

Chapter 7 **Responsibilities of the Parties**

7.1 Responsibilities of Party A

In addition to its other obligations under this Contract, Party A shall undertake the following responsibilities:

1) assist the Joint Venture Company in obtaining other approvals, licenses and authority required for the Joint Venture Company to undertake activities within its scope of business during its term of operations;

2) assist the Joint Venture Company in purchasing, leasing or otherwise procuring equipment and machinery, tools, raw materials, office furniture and equipment, vehicles and other materials required for the Joint Venture Company's operations from sources in China;

3) assist the Joint Venture Company in applying for licenses for the import of equipment and machinery, tools, raw materials, office furniture and equipment, vehicles and other materials required for the Joint Venture Company's operations, and in carrying out all import and customs formalities in respect thereto;

4) assist the Joint Venture Company in recruiting skilled managers and technical personnel;

5) assist the Joint Venture Company in opening *Renminbi* and foreign currency bank accounts and in obtaining loans from local banks;

6) handle other matters entrusted by the Board of Directors.

7.2 Responsibilities of Party B

In addition to its other obligations under this Contract, Party B shall undertake the following responsibilities:

1) assist the Joint Venture Company in purchasing, leasing or otherwise procuring equipment and machinery, tools, raw materials, office furniture and equipment, vehicles and other materials required for the Joint Venture Company's operation from sources outside of China;

2) assist Chinese employees of the Joint Venture Company and members of the Board of Directors who travel outside China for Joint Venture Company business in obtaining foreign country visas and invitation letters and certifications required for processing other necessary travel documents;

3) assist the Joint Venture Company in recruiting skilled managers and technical personnel;

4) assist the Joint Venture Company in obtaining loans from foreign lenders;

5) handle other matters entrusted by the Board of Directors.

Chapter 8 **Board of Directors**

8.1 Formation of the Board of Directors

1) The Board of Directors shall be the highest authority of the Joint Venture Company and shall decide all matters of major importance to the Joint Venture Company. The date of issuance of the Business License shall be the date of establishment of the Board of Directors.

2) The Board of Directors shall comprise _____ directors, _____ of whom shall be appointed by Party A and _____ of whom shall be appointed by Party B.

3) Each director shall be appointed for a term of _____ years, provided that the Party that has appointed a director may remove that director and appoint a replacement at any time. A director may serve consecutive terms if reappointed by the Party that originally appointed him. If a seat on the Board of Directors is vacated by the retirement, resignation, removal, disability or death of a director, the Party that originally appointed such director shall appoint a successor to serve out such director's term.

4) Party _____ shall designate a director to serve as the Chairman of the Board and Party _____ shall designate another director to serve as the Vice-Chairman of the Board. The Chairman of the Board is the legal representative of the Joint Venture Company, but shall not contractually or otherwise bind the Joint Venture Company without the prior written authorization of the Board of Directors. Whenever the Chairman of the Board is unable to perform his responsibilities for any reason, the Chairman shall appoint a director to perform such responsibilities.

8.2 Meetings

1) The first meeting of the Board of Directors shall be held within _____ days from the date of issuance of the Business License. Thereafter, the Board of Directors shall hold at least _____ regular meeting in each calendar year. Upon the written request of one-third or more of the directors of the Joint Venture Company specifying the matters to be discussed, the Chairman of the Board shall within _____ days of receipt thereof convene an interim meeting of the Board of Directors. The Chairman of the Board also may himself convene an interim meeting.

2) The Chairman of the Board shall give written notice, including the time and place of the meeting and the agenda, to each of the directors at least _____ days prior to any meeting of the Board. A Board meeting held without proper notice having been given to any director shall be invalid unless such director, either before or after the meeting, delivers a written waiver of notice to the Chairman and Vice-Chairman. Meetings shall be held at the registered address of the Joint Venture Company or such other address in China or abroad as may be determined by the Chairman of the Board. The Chairman of the Board shall set the agenda for Board meetings and shall be responsible for convening and presiding over such meetings.

3) Each Party has the obligation to ensure that its appointees to the Board of Directors attend all meetings either in person or by proxy. Two-thirds of all of the directors shall constitute a quorum for all meetings of the Board of Directors (such directors may be present in person or by proxy).

4) If a director is unable to attend Board of Directors meetings or to carry out his other duties as director, he may issue a proxy and entrust a representative to attend meetings or carry out his other duties on his behalf.

5) The Board of Directors will cause complete and accurate minutes (in both Chinese and English) to be kept of all Board meetings. Draft minutes of Board meetings shall be distributed to all the directors within _____ days after the date of the meeting. Any director who wishes to propose an amendment or addition shall submit the same in writing to the Chairman and the Vice-Chairman within _____ days after receipt of the draft minutes. The Chairman shall complete the final minutes and distribute them to each director and each Party not later than _____ days after the meeting. The Joint Venture Company shall maintain a file of all Board meeting minutes and make the same freely available to the Parties and their authorized representatives.

8.3 <u>Resolutions</u>

1) Each director shall have one (1) vote.

2) The adoption of resolutions concerning the following matters shall require the unanimous assent of all the directors who are present in person or by proxy at a duly convened meeting of the Board of Directors:

  i) amendments to the Articles of Association;

  ii) increase or reduction of the registered capital of the Joint Venture Company;

  iii) termination of the joint venture and dissolution of the Joint Venture Company;

  iv) merger or division of the Joint Venture Company.

3) The adoption of all other resolutions shall require the assent of a majority of the directors who are present in person or by proxy at a duly convened meeting of the Board of Directors. [*consider need for any supermajority voting requirements*]

4) The Board of Directors may adopt any resolution without a meeting if such resolution is signed by all of the directors then holding office. Such written resolutions shall be filed with the

minutes of Board meetings and shall have the same force and effect as a unanimous resolution adopted at a meeting of the Board.

Chapter 9 Management Organization

9.1 Management Organization

The Joint Venture Company's management organization shall be under the leadership of a General Manager, who shall report directly to the Board of Directors. In addition to the General Manager, the Joint Venture Company shall have a Deputy General Manager, a Chief Accountant and other department managers, each of whom shall report directly to the General Manager.

9.2 Appointment of Management Personnel

The General Manager and the Chief Accountant shall be nominated by Party _____ , the Deputy General Manager shall be nominated by Party , and each of them shall be appointed by the Board of Directors. Other Management Personnel shall be nominated by the General Manager and appointed by the Board of Directors. All replacements for any of the Management Personnel, whether by reason of the retirement, resignation, disability or death of a manager or of the removal of a manager by the Board of Directors, shall be nominated and appointed in the same manner as the original appointee.

9.3 Scope of Management Authority and Performance of Duties

1) The General Manager shall be in charge of the day-to-day operation and management of the Joint Venture Company and shall carry out all matters entrusted by the Board of Directors. The Deputy General Manager shall assist the General Manager in his work and shall report to the General Manager. The Board of Directors shall determine the duties of the Chief Accountant and other Management Personnel.

2) The General Manager and the Deputy General Manager shall not concurrently serve as the general manager or deputy general manager of any other company or enterprise, nor shall they serve as a director of or consultant to, or hold any interest (except for less than _____ percent of the shares of a publicly listed company) in, any company or enterprise that competes with the Joint Ven-

ture Company.

Chapter 10 **Purchase of Materials, Equipment and Services**

The Joint Venture Company may purchase equipment and machinery, tools, raw materials, vehicles, spare parts and supplies, and may obtain technology and services, required for the Joint Venture Company's operations from sources within and outside China.

Chapter 11 **Technology Transfer**

[*specify general provisions governing the licensing or assignment of technology to the Joint Venture Company by one or both Parties - detailed provisions are typically set out in a separate technology contract*]

Chapter 12 **Labor Management**

12.1 Governing Principle

Matters relating to the recruitment, employment, dismissal, resignation, wages and welfare of the staff and workers of the Joint Venture Company shall be handled in accordance with the Labor Law of the People's Republic of China and the Regulations of the People's Republic of China on Labor Management in Foreign Invested Enterprises and related Chinese laws and regulations (hereinafter collectively referred to as the "Labor Laws"). The labor rules and policies of the Joint Venture Company shall be approved by the Board of Directors.

12.2 Employment, Examination and Recruitment

1) The Joint Venture Company's employees, other than the Management Personnel, shall be employed by the Joint Venture Company in accordance with the terms of a standard individual labor contract. Management Personnel shall be employed by the Joint Venture Company in accordance with the terms of individual employment contracts approved by the Board of Directors.

2) Employees will be selected according to their professional qualifications and working experience. [*The specific number and qualifications of the employees shall be determined by the General Manager in accordance with the operating needs of the Joint Venture Company.*]

12.3 Social Insurance and Welfare Benefits

Social insurance and welfare benefits for employees of the Joint Venture Company shall be handled in accordance with the Labor Laws. The Joint Venture Company shall conform to the laws and regulations of China concerning labor protection and shall ensure safe and civilized production and operations.

12.4 Labor Union

The Joint Venture Company's employees shall have the right to establish a labor union and to conduct labor union activities in accordance with the Labor Laws and the Labor Union Law of the People's Republic of China.

Chapter 13 Financial Affairs and Accounting

13.1 Accounting System

1) The Chief Accountant of the Joint Venture Company shall be responsible for the financial management of the Joint Venture Company.

2) The Chief Accountant shall prepare the Joint Venture Company's accounting system and procedures in accordance with the relevant laws and regulations of China, and submit the same to the Board of Directors for adoption. The accounting system and procedures shall be filed with the department in charge of the Joint Venture Company and with the relevant local department of finance and the tax authorities for the record.

3) The Joint Venture Company shall adopt *Renminbi* as its bookkeeping base currency, but may also adopt United States Dollars as a supplementary bookkeeping currency.

4) All accounting records, vouchers, books and statements of the Joint Venture Company must be made and kept in Chinese. All financial statements and reports of the Joint Venture Company shall be made and kept in Chinese and English.

13.2 Fiscal Year

The Joint Venture Company shall adopt the calendar year as its fiscal year. The Joint Venture Company's first fiscal year shall commence on the date that the Joint Venture Company receives a business license and shall end on the immediately succeeding December 31.

13.3 Auditors

1) The Parties shall have full and equal access to the Joint Venture Company's accounts. The Joint Venture Company shall furnish to the Parties unaudited financial reports on a monthly and quarterly basis so that they may continuously be informed about the Joint Venture Company's financial performance. In addition, each Party, at its own expense and upon advance notice to the Joint Venture Company, may appoint an accountant registered in China or abroad to audit the accounts of the Joint Venture Company on behalf of such Party. The Joint Venture Company shall permit such auditor to examine all of its accounting and financial records and other documents, provided that the auditor agrees to maintain the confidentiality of such documents and that the audit does not interfere with the normal operation of the Joint Venture Company.

2) The Joint Venture Company shall engage an accountant independent of any Party and registered in China to audit its accounts and annual financial statements and to prepare an audit report. Drafts of the audited financial statements and audit report shall be provided to each Party and to the Board of Directors for review within _____ months after the end of each fiscal year, and the final audit report shall be issued not later than _____ months after the end of each fiscal year.

13.4 Bank Accounts

The Joint Venture Company shall separately open foreign exchange accounts and *Renminbi* accounts at banks within China authorized to conduct foreign exchange operations. With the approval by the State Administration of Foreign Exchange, the Joint Venture Company may also open foreign exchange bank accounts outside China.

Chapter 14 **Distribution of Profit**

14.1 Distribution of Profit

1) Losses from previous years must be made up before any profits from the current year are distributed to the Parties. Profits retained by the Joint Venture Company in previous years may be distributed together with the profits of the current year.

2) After the Joint Venture Company has paid income taxes and made up any losses incurred in previous years, the Board of Directors shall determine the annual allocations to the Three Funds from the after-tax net profits, subject to the requirements of relevant laws and regulations.

3) Within _____ months after the end of each fiscal year, the Board of Directors, based on the Joint Venture Company's operational needs, shall decide whether or not to retain all or part of the profit of the Joint Venture Company available for distribution. After the Board of Directors makes this decision, the amount of profit not retained shall be distributed to the Parties immediately in accordance with the ratio of their respective actual contributions to capital.

4) Remittances of profits and other payments by the Joint Venture Company to Party B shall be made in United States Dollars to a foreign bank account designated by Party B, subject to compliance with the foreign exchange control regulations of China.

Chapter 15 Taxes and Insurance

15.1 Income and Other Taxes

The Joint Venture Company shall pay taxes in accordance with the laws, administrative regulations and local regulations of China. The Joint Venture Company's Chinese and expatriate personnel shall pay individual income tax in accordance with the Individual Income Tax Law of the People's Republic of China. The Joint Venture Company shall apply for all the preferential tax treatment to which it is entitled under the relevant laws and regulations of China.

15.2 Insurance

Throughout the Contract Term, the Joint Venture Company shall maintain insurance coverage of the types and in the amounts determined by the General Manager and approved by the Board of Directors. The Joint Venture Company may obtain insurance from insurance companies or organizations inside and outside China, subject to compliance with the laws and regulations of China.

Chapter 16 Contract Term

16.1 Contract Term

The Contract Term shall commence upon the Effective Date and shall extend for a period of _____ years from the date of issuance of the Business License.

16.2 Extension of the Contract Term

Upon the agreement of all of the Parties, an application to extend the Contract Term may be made to the Examination and Approval Authority no less than _____ months prior to the expiration of the Contract Term. The Contract Term may be extended only upon approval of the Examination and Approval Authority.

Chapter 17 Termination and Liquidation

17.1 Termination

1) Under any of the following circumstances, either Party shall have the right to terminate this Contract by giving _____ days' prior written notice to the other Party:

i) the Joint Venture ceases to carry on business, or becomes unable to pay its debts as they come due;

ii) the terminating Party has the right to terminate this Contract pursuant to Article 19.1.

2) Under any of the following circumstances, either Party shall have the right to terminate this Contract with immediate effect by written notice to the other Party:

i) the other Party transfers all or any part of its share of the Joint Venture Company's registered capital in violation of the provisions of this Contract;

ii) the other Party otherwise materially breaches this Contract and such breach or violation is not cured within _____ days of written notice to the breaching Party;

iii) in the course of the approval process for this Contract or the Articles of Association, their respective terms and conditions have been altered or additional obligations have been imposed on either Party or on the Joint Venture Company without the prior agreement of both Parties;

iv) there are material discrepancies between the Joint Venture Company's scope of business as stated on the Business License and as set forth in Article 5.2;

v) either Party is declared bankrupt, or is the subject of proceedings for bankruptcy, dissolution or liquidation, or becomes unable to pay its debts as they become due.

3) Upon termination of this Contract in accordance with clause 1) or 2) above, the Joint Venture Company shall forthwith submit to the Examination and Approval Authority an application to terminate this Contract and to dissolve the Joint Venture Company. Each Party agrees to take all actions and to sign all documents, and to cause its appointees on the Board of Directors to take all actions and to sign all documents, that are legally required to effect termination of this Contract and dissolution of the Joint Venture Company.

4) Except as otherwise provided in this Contract, the termination of this Contract by one Party due to breach of contract by the other Party shall not prejudice the non-breaching Party's right to claim damages for breach of contract.

17.2 Liquidation

Upon expiration of the Contract Term or approval of an application to dissolve the Joint Venture Company pursuant to this Chapter 17, liquidation of the Joint Venture Company shall be handled in accordance with the relevant laws and regulations of China and with the provisions set forth in the Articles of Association.

Chapter 18 **Breach of Contract**

If a Party breaches this Contract, it shall bear the liabilities arising from such breach in accordance with the provisions of this Contract and of applicable law. In the event that both Parties breach this Contract, each Party shall bear the liabilities arising from its own breach.

Chapter 19 **Force Majeure**

19.1 Force Majeure

1) "Force Majeure" shall mean all events which were unforeseeable at the time this Contract was signed, the occurrence and consequences of which cannot be avoided or overcome, and which arise after the signature of this Contract and prevent total or partial performance by any Party. Such events shall include earthquakes, typhoons, flood, fire, war, failures of international or domestic transportation, epidemics, strikes and other events which are accepted as force majeure under the law of China. A Party's lack of funds is not an event of Force Majeure.

2) If an event of Force Majeure occurs and affects the performance of a Party's obligations under this Contract, such performance shall be suspended during the period of delay caused by the Force Majeure, and this shall not constitute a breach of contract.

3) The Party claiming Force Majeure shall promptly inform the other Party in writing and shall furnish within _____ days thereafter sufficient evidence of the occurrence and duration of such Force Majeure.

4) In the event of Force Majeure, the Parties shall immediately consult with each other in order to find an equitable solution and shall use all reasonable endeavors to minimize the consequences of such Force Majeure. If the occurrence or consequences of Force Majeure results in a major impairment to the functioning of the Joint Venture Company for a period in excess of _____ months and the Parties have not found an equitable solution, then either Party may commence procedures to terminate this Contract in accordance with the provisions of Chapter 17, provided that the terminating Party has performed its obligations under this Chapter 19.

Chapter 20 Applicable Law

The formation, validity, interpretation and performance of this Contract, and the resolution of any disputes arising under this Contract, shall be governed by the laws of the People's Republic of China.

Chapter 21 Settlement of Disputes

[specify dispute resolution mechanism, such as arbitration in China or abroad]

Chapter 22 **Miscellaneous Provisions**

22.1 Waiver

Failure or delay on the part of any Party hereto to exercise a right under this Contract shall not operate as a waiver thereof; nor shall any single or partial exercise of a right preclude any other future exercise thereof.

22.2 Assignment

Except as otherwise provided herein, neither this Contract nor any rights and obligations hereunder may be assigned in whole or in part by any Party without the prior written consent of the other Party and, where required by law, the approval of the Examination and Approval Authority.

22.3 Amendment

All amendments to this Contract must be agreed to in a document signed by both Parties and, where required by law, approved by the Examination and Approval Authority.

22.4 Severability

The invalidity of any provision of this Contract shall not affect the validity of any other provision of this Contract.

22.5 Language Versions

This Contract is signed in Chinese and English, with _____ originals and _____ duplicates in each language. Each Party will hold one original of each language version. Both language versions shall be equally valid.

22.6 Notices

Unless otherwise provided in this Contract, any notice or written communication provided for in this Contract from one Party to the other Party or to the Joint Venture Company shall be made in writing in Chinese and English and sent by courier service delivered letter or by facsimile with a confirmation copy sent by courier service delivered letter. Notices or communications hereunder shall be deemed to have been received _____ days after the letter is given to the courier service or _____ day after sending in the case of a facsimile, provided that the facsimile transmission is evidenced by a transmission report and the confirmation copy is sent. All notices and communications shall be sent to the appropriate address set forth below, until the same is changed by notice given in writing to the other Party.

Party A:
[address]
Facsimile No:
Attention:

Party B:
[address]
Facsimile No:
Attention:

22.7 Appendices

The Appendices hereto listed below are made an integral part of this Contract and are equally binding with these Chapters 1-22:

22.8 Entire Agreement

This Contract constitutes the entire agreement between the Parties with respect to the subject matter of this Contract and supersedes all prior discussions, negotiations and agreements between them with respect to the subject matter of this Contract. In the event of any conflict between the terms and provisions of this Contract and the Articles of Association, the terms and provisions of this Contract shall prevail.

IN WITNESS WHEREOF, the duly authorized representative of each Party has signed this Contract in _____ , People's Republic of China, on the date first set forth above.

Appendix II

Model Labor Contracts

File: _____

Labour Contract
of
Firm X

Party A: Firm X

Party B:

Date:

Party A:

Party B:

Legal Representative:

Education:
Address:
Sex:
Birth:___ Yr. ___ Mo. ___ Day
Resident Certificate:

Tel:
Fax:
Home Address:

In accordance with the relevant regulation, < The Labour Law of The People's Republic of China >, Party A and Party B, following the principles of equality, free will and mutual consent have concluded this Labour Contract. The two parties agree to comply with the terms and conditions specified in this contract.

Article 1 Employment

Party A has agreed to employ Party B. Party B must terminate or rescind his or her employment contract or employment relationship with his former employer. Party B shall be responsible for any labour disputes arising from their failure to do so.

Article 2 Employment Period

1. The type of this contract is fixed term contract.

2. The effective date of the labour contract is_____(Y/M/D), in which a probation period of _____months is included.

3. This labour contract shall be terminated on _____ (Y/M/D).

4. During the probation period, either of the parties can terminate the contract at any point based on their satisfaction of the employment arrangement.

5. Prior to the expiration of this contract, if either party intends not to renew the contract as of the date of its expiration, the party shall terminate this contract by giving a written notice to the other party 30 days in advance or one-month salary in lieu of the written notice (in the case where Party B holds a Manager's position or above, 3-month prior written notice or 3-month salary is required). Either party shall not have any liability to pay any compensation to the other party.

Article 3 **Job Content**

1. Party B has agreed to, according to the business needs of Party A, work in the _____ Department. Party B shall submit to the management and arrangement of Party A. Party B is obligated to reach certain assignment standard set by Party A with accepted working quantity and quality in required time.

2. Party A is entitled to adjust Party B's post in line with management operation requirement, or capacity and performance of Party B.

Article 4 **Labour Protection and Condition**

1. Party A shall arrange work for Party B under state regulatory working hour system.

2. Under standard working hour system, Party B works normally 8 hours per day, and 40 hours in average per week. Party B works 5 days a week and rests 2 days a week. (Office hour starts at 8:30 am and ends at 5:30 pm There is one-hour break for lunch.)

3. In accordance with Party A's business needs, Party B may be required to work overtime. Under the standard working hour system, Party A shall pay Party B the overtime payment according to the state regulations.

4. Overtime payment for administrative staff of manager level and above, and professional staff of senior level and above have been built in their salary payment. Therefore no extra overtime shall be paid to Party B by Party A. Those staff will be eligible to receive an annual

bonus which will usually be not less than 1 month salary paid at the end of the fiscal year.

5. Party B, within the effective period of the employment contract, is entitled to enjoy statutory holidays and paid leaves such as marriage leave, compassionate leave and maternity leave.

6. Party B is entitled to an annual leave of ___ days.

Article 5 **Remuneration for Party B**

1. Party A shall pay Party B monthly salary and wage in currency of RMB _____ before 30th of each month.

2. Salary and staff grading are determined on 1 July each year based on evaluation of Party B's performance. Party A has rights to change Party B's grading and salary in accordance with Party A's business situation and the appraisal of Party B's performance.

3. Party A has rights to withhold Party B's individual income taxes in line with regulations of State and Local tax bureau.

Article 6 **Insurance & Welfare**

1. Party A and Party B shall respectively pay insurance confirming to the relevant regulations of the State and local governments.

2. Party A and Party B shall respectively pay housing fund confirming to the relevant regulations of the State and local governments.

3. In addition to the paying for Party B's social insurance confirming to the relevant regulations of the State and local governments, Party A shall provide life and disability insurance premiums with maxim amount of RMB 200,000.

4. If on business trips, Party B incurs personal financial loss, Party A shall remunerate Party B maximum amount of RMB 25,000 upon confirmation of the related supporting documents concerned.

5. Party B goes out of office for business requirement, Party B may, with approval of Party A, claim expenses actually incurred. If Party B must work overtime, Party A shall reimburse Party B's meal and travel expenses after verifying the necessity and relevant receipts of Party B. For more detail, please refer to policy & procedures of the firm.

6. Party B shall entitle to receiving annually a thirteenth month's

salary payment if Party B has continuously worked for Party A for 12 months. If Party B joins Party A's firm in middle-year and the period of working with Party A is less than 12 months, the 13th month salary shall be calculated proportionally based on Party B's actual working period with Party A. The 13th month salary is payable in the month of Chinese New Year each year. Party A shall not pay Party B the 13th month salary if Party B leaves Party A's firm before the end of the month in which the payment is made each year.

7. Party B is allowed to take sick leave for more than one day only if Party B goes to see doctors at the assigned hospitals by Party A and provides Party A the doctor's diagnosis documents, then Party B shall enjoy the medical treatment periods set forth by state and Party A firm's regulations.

8. The treatment including salary payment for Party B's having work-related injury will be conforming to state and local government regulations.

Article 7 **Employment Discipline**

1. Party B shall comply with Party A's regulations set forth in accordance with law, strictly follow rules of safety and sanitation, protect the property of Party A, maintain professional ethics, actively participate in training arranged by Party A, develop moral and professional skills.

2. Party B shall participate in the professional training arranged by Party A, profession qualification examinations relevant to their works.

3. Party B shall strictly comply with the policy set forth by Party A regarding independence and avoidance of conflicts of interest. The independence policy of Party A restricts Party B from having interest relationship with Party A's clients; restricts Party B from having any business dealings with other parties that may place them in situation of real or apparent conflict with their professional responsibilities within the firm. Within the employment period, Party B shall not hold any post in other entities or invest in Party A's clients in terms of stocks or other securities. Party B shall not engage in any business operation by stealing the name of Party A. Party B shall not participate with any other entity or business organisation in any competition against Party

A. As such, Party B may not act as officers or directors of any corporation, business enterprise, or other business organisation other than charitable, civic, educational, social or other similar non-profit organisations. Appointment as officers or directors of any civic, educational, social or other similar non-profit organisations requires prior approval from Party A. Party B is requested to sign confirmation letter of independence every year.

4. Party B shall strictly comply with the confidential policy set forth by Party A. Party B is not allowed to disclose client's business information or to use it for illegitimate purpose. Party B is not allowed to disclose Party A's proprietary and confidential information including processes of carrying out business, market plan, sale list, software, hardware, intellectual property, know-how, patent, copy-rights, commercial secret, trademark, service mark, all non-publishable, unopened and confidential information. The above policy is effective in and out of Party B's employment periods with Party A. Party B is requested to sign confidential letter every year.

5. Party B shall follow the management and working arrangement by Party A. Violation may result in written warning, salary deduction to dismissal eventual.

6. Party B shall not leave the firm without approval of Party A. Such action is considered as break of the Contract. Party B shall pay one month salary to Party A as compensation for break of the contract. Party B shall compensate all losses to Party A if such action has aroused economic lose for Party A.

7. While resign from the office, Party B shall transmit work to other staff of Party A and go through the checking-out process by returning all the office's facilities, materials and payment in advance to Party A. Party B shall also repay and indemnify Party A the training expenses if Party B receives training arranged by Party A in outside of the Party A's Firm. Details please refer to the training agreement.

Article 8 Amendment, Rescission, Termination and Renewal of Contract

1. Where the relevant laws and regulations have been changed, the

related terms of the contract will be changed accordingly.

2. Where the objective circumstances, such as change in market, Party A's business situation and organisation structure, etc., which formed the basis of the contract are substantially changed making it impossible to perform the contract, the related section in the contract can be changed accordingly by mutual agreement between Party A and Party B.

3. The contract may be rescinded if Party A and Party B agree by mutual and unanimous agreement.

4. Party A may unilaterally rescind the contract without paying Party B any compensation if Party B has conducted one of the following actions:

1) Has been proved to have failed to satisfy the recruitment condition during the probation period;

2) Has seriously violated the regulations of Party A and caused damages to Party A due to such actions.

3) Has committed severe negligence in his or her duty which results in serious damages to Party A (action leads to dismissal of Party B by professional associations, violate the independence code, disclose client's confidential information and leads to investigation by professional organisations or actions under the table.); or negligence in his or her duties which causes damages to Party A's reputation and interests of Party A's clients.

4) Has committed fraud (writing false statement about professional qualifications in the application form, offering false recommendation letters, illness, identification, timesheet and expenses form.);

5) Has violated other co-worker's rights;

6) Has been immoral or done immoral commitment;

7) Has been incapable to work due to abuse of alcohol or drugs;

8) Has been absent from duty for 2 days in succession without approval, 3 days such absence in accumulation;

9) Has received valuables, money or securities from the clients without Party A's permission;

10) Has been subject to criminal prosecution;

11) Has not properly performed his or her duty after receiving

warning in written form;

12) Has numerously violated the policies of the Party A's firm;

13) Without the firm's permission, Party B copied software of the firm;

14) Has improperly used Party A's facilities and equipment, and has incurred economic loss to Party A for more than RMB5,000.

Except for the situation of term 1, Party A shall have right to claim for indemnity for any economic loss; training expenses previously paid for Party B outside of the firm and overseas training.

5. Under any of the following conditions, Party A may rescind the contract subject to a written notice to the Party B 30 days in advance (for managers or above, three month early notice is required):

1) Party B, who has been down with illness or non-work related injury, at the end of the required medical treatment period, is proved no longer competent for his previous task and for any other job rearranged for him within the Firm;

2) Where the objective circumstances which formed the basis of the contract are substantially changed making it impossible to perform the contract, Party A and Party B failed to reach an agreement on the amendment of the related section in the contract accordingly following consultation and Party A rescinds the contract;.

3) Where position assigned by Party A is adjusted, such as cancelling a position, Party B is incapable to continuously engage in a new assigned work due to his or her personal issues;

4) Party B is approved to be unequal to his or her work, and after having been trained, still found unqualified for the job.

6. Party A may not rescind the contract under any of the following circumstances:

1) Party B has totally or partially lost the ability to work due to occupational disease or injuries suffered at work;

2) Party B is undergoing the required medical treatment for an illness or injury;

3) Party B during pregnancy, confinement or the breast-feeding period;

4) Party B to be a demobilised armyman, or used to be a farmer yet currently a worker due to land command, who takes the job firstly and has been working for less than 3 years.

7. Within the employment period, Party B may rescind the contract with Party A in any of the following circumstances:

1) Within the probation period;

2) Where Party A forces Party B to work by resorting to violence, intimidation or illegal restriction of personal freedom; and

3) Failure of party A to pay remuneration or provide working conditions as agreed on in the contract.

8. If Party B intends to resign, a written notice should be submitted 30 days before leaving the Firm. (a 3 months' notice should be provided by manager level and above) Normally the request of termination of service should be approved. In case the assignment charged by the employee has not been achieved, or the Firm may incur financial losses, the Firm may hold and take time to give the approval.

Article 9 **Financial Compensation in Dispute**

1. Should Party A violate this contract under any of the following situations, financial compensation shall be made to Party B in line with regulations by the State and Local government.

1) Under the payment of wages, delay payment of wages or refusal of overtime wage payment;

2) Should Party A pay lower than the minimum wages of Beijing City;

3) Party A terminates this contract with the agreement of Party B;

4) Party B cannot perform up to the requirement of the job even after additional training thus resulted in Party A terminating this contract;

5) Party B is confirmed by the Labour Identification Committee to be no longer competent for working. Party A determines to terminate the contract;

6) The objective conditions, based on which the contract is worked out, changed significantly, and as a result, the labour contract can

not be fulfilled, and the two parties failed to reach an agreement on the modification of the content of the contract, Party A determined to terminate the contract;

7) When the Party A is on the verge of bankruptcy, during the statutory rectification period, Party A has no alternatives but to cut down the number of employees.

2. On terminating Party B's contract, Party A has to pay compensation regulated as above. If Party A failed to do so, it will be ordered to make not only all the compensation but also an addition of 50%.

3. Party B who has been working with Party A less than one year will be paid one month salary as compensation if Party A terminates Party B's contract.

4. Where Party A violates the stipulations of the contract and terminates it or the contract itself is invalid, and as a result, the rights of Party B have been infringed, Party A will have to bear all the responsibilities.

5. Where Party B violates the stipulations of the contract or disclose Party A's business intelligence, and as a result, Party A has incurred a heavy loss, Party B will have to bear the responsibilities for compensation.

6. Party B, who had been sent out for training courses outside of the firm in China when terminating the contract, has to pay back the training expenses.

7. Party B, after receiving the overseas training sponsored by Party A, shall serve Party A at least 3 years after the training. Party B shall sign the training agreement with Party A before secondment starts. This training agreement is an appendix of the contract. If Party B intends to terminate the service term, Party B shall pay back the training expenses. The whole payment of training expenses amounts to US$ 25,000 plus the cash cost of transport to the overseas location, language training, obtaining visas and initial accommodation overseas. The compensation payment shall be reduced according to the length of service term of Party B for Party A. Party B shall pay back 70% of such amount after his first year service, 40% after the second year.

Article 10 **Labour Disputes Settlement**

When there is dispute aroused in fulfilling the contract or due to dismissal, the two parties may handle this themselves by discussion of the problems, or they can, following lawful procedure, apply for mediation and arbitration. When the dispute occurred, the two parties may negotiate for a settlement within the Firm, if failed, the employer of the Firm may apply for arbitration within 60 days, if one of the two parties refuses to take the outcome of the arbitration as final, he may file a suit with a People's Court.

Article 11 **Other Aspects**

1. Policies and procedures of Party A, Training Agreement, Confidential Agreement and Independent Letter and other regulations of Party A's firm are appendixes of this contract and all have the same legal effectiveness.

2. Within the effective period of this contract, all agreements agreed and signed by both parties in response to special circumstances are deemed as complementary documents of this contract and must be abided by both parties. Should there be conflicts on certain clauses between contract and the agreement, it should be deemed as the amendment of the clause by the firm.

3. Party B will have to bear all the responsibilities if he fails to transfer his personal file to the appointed agency within 15 days; transfer his social insurance to the firm within 30 days from the date he joined Party A.

4. At the signing of this contract, Party B has carefully read the firm's policy and procedures; understands all the details, and has agreed to accept and abide by it.

5. Other agreements concluded and signed by two parties are included in this.

Article 12

Other issues which are not included in this contract should be carried out in accordance with relevant laws. Any policies hereafter found running counter to the regulations of the State or Local Municipal

Government, the regulations of the State and the Beijing Municipal Government should be obeyed.

Article 13

This contract is in duplicate, each of two parties holds one of them.

Party A (Chop)   **Party B** (Signature)

Signing date:_____(Yr.) (Mo.) (Day)

Appendix III

Provisions for Guiding the Direction of Foreign Investment

Order No. 346 of the State Council of the People's Republic of China

The Provisions for Guiding the Direction of Foreign Investment are hereby promulgated for implementation from April 1, 2002.

Premier **Zhu Rongji**

February 11, 2002

Article 1

Based on the provisions of State laws concerning foreign investment and the requirements of State industrial policies, these Provisions are formulated in order to guide the direction of foreign investment, to adapt the direction of foreign investment to China's national economic and social development plans, and to help protect the lawful rights and interests of investors.

Article 2

These Provisions apply to projects for investment in the establishment of Sino-foreign equity joint ventures, Sino-foreign cooperative joint ventures and wholly foreign-owned enterprises ("Foreign Invested Enterprises") and other forms of foreign investment projects in China ("Foreign Investment Projects").

Article 3

The Catalogue for Guiding Foreign Investment in Industry and the Catalogue of Priority Industries for Foreign Investment in the Central and Western Regions shall be drafted and issued by the State Development Planning Commission, State Economic and Trade Commission, and Ministry of Foreign Trade and Economic Cooperation in conjunction with the relevant departments of the State Council following approval by the State Council. When parts of the Catalogue for Guiding Foreign Investment in Industry and the Catalogue of Priority Industries for Foreign Investment in the Central and Western Regions need to be adjusted in line with the actual situation, the State Economic and Trade Commission, State Development Planning Commission, and Ministry of Foreign Trade and Economic Cooperation in conjunction with the relevant departments of the State Council shall make and publish amendments in a timely manner.

The Catalogue for Guiding Foreign Investment in Industry and the Catalogue of Priority Industries for Foreign Investment in the Central and Western Regions shall form the basis for guiding the examination and approval of Foreign Investment Projects and for applying relevant policies to Foreign Invested Enterprises.

Article 4

Foreign Investment Projects shall be divided into four categories: encouraged, permitted, restricted and prohibited.

Encouraged, restricted and prohibited Foreign Investment Projects shall be listed in the Catalogue for Guiding Foreign Investment in Industry. Foreign Investment Projects that do not fall into the encouraged, restricted or prohibited categories shall be in the permitted category of Foreign Investment Projects. Foreign Investment Projects in the permitted category shall not be listed in the Catalogue for Guiding Foreign Investment in Industry.

Article 5

In any one of the following cases, Foreign Investment Projects shall be listed in the encouraged category of Foreign Investment Projects:

(1) Projects for new agricultural technology, overall agricultural development or energy, transportation and key raw materials industries;

(2) Projects for high and new technology, advanced and appropriate technology, and new equipment and materials that can improve product performance or enhance enterprises' technological and economic benefits or for which domestic production capability is insufficient;

(3) Projects that meet market demand and can upgrade products, open up new markets or enhance the international competitiveness of products;

(4) Projects for new technology and/or equipment that can save energy and raw materials, comprehensively utilize resources and renewable resources, and prevent and control environmental pollution;

(5) Projects that can make full use of the advantages of the human and other resources of the central and western regions, and conform with the State's industrial policies;

(6) Other cases stipulated in laws and administrative regulations.

Article 6

In any one of the following cases, Foreign Investment Projects shall be listed in the restricted category of Foreign Investment Projects:

(1) Projects with backward technology;

(2) Projects that do not help to save resources or improve the ecology and environment;

(3) Projects for engaging in the prospecting and mining of specific types of mineral deposits that are subject to protective mining measures as stipulated by the State;

(4) Projects for industries which the State is gradually liberalizing;

(5) Other cases stipulated in laws and administrative regulations.

Article 7

In any one of the following cases, Foreign Investment Projects shall be listed in the prohibited category of Foreign Investment Projects:

(1) Projects that jeopardize State security or harm the public interest;

(2) Projects that cause pollution damage to the environment, destroy natural resources or harm people's health;

(3) Projects that occupy large tracts of arable land and do not benefit the protection and development of land resources;

(4) Projects that jeopardize the security and effectiveness of military installations;

(5) Projects that use techniques or technologies that are specific to China to make products;

(6) Other cases stipulated in laws and administrative regulations.

Article 8

The Catalogue for Guiding Foreign Investment in Industry may stipulate in regard to Foreign Investment Projects: "limited to equity or cooperative joint ventures", "Chinese party to have the controlling interest" or "Chinese party to have the relative controlling interest". "Limited to equity or cooperative joint ventures" means that only Sino-foreign equity joint ventures or Sino-foreign cooperative joint ventures are permitted; "Chinese party to have the controlling interest" means that the aggregate ratio of investment of the Chinese investor(s) in the Foreign Investment Project shall be 51% or more; "Chinese party to have the relative controlling interest" means that the aggregate ratio of investment of the Chinese investor(s) in the Foreign Investment Project shall be greater than the ratio of investment of any single foreign investor.

Article 9

In addition to being entitled to preferential treatment in accordance with the relevant laws and administrative regulations, encouraged Foreign Investment Projects with large amounts of investment and a long payback period for the construction and/or operation of energy, transportation and urban infrastructure (such as coal, oil, natural gas, power, railways, highways, ports, airports, urban roads, waste water treatment and garbage treatment) may, following approval, expand their business scope to related business.

Article 10

A permitted Foreign Investment Project for which all the products are directly exported shall be deemed to be an encouraged Foreign Investment Project. A restricted Foreign Investment Project for which the sales of its exported products account for 70% or more of the total sales of its products may be deemed to be a permitted Foreign Investment Project, following approval from the People's Government at the level of province, autonomous region, municipality directly under the Central Government or municipality with independent development plans or from a competent department of the State Council.

Article 11

The requirements may be appropriately relaxed for permitted or restricted Foreign Investment Projects that are really able to make full use of the advantages of the central and western regions. Of these, projects that are listed in the Catalogue of Priority Industries for Foreign Investment in the Central and Western Regions may enjoy the preferential policies for encouraged Foreign Investment Projects.

Article 12

Based on current approval authority limits, Foreign Investment Projects shall be subject to examination and approval and filing for the record by the development planning departments or economic and trade departments in accordance with the nature of the project. The contract and articles of association of a Foreign Invested Enterprise shall be subject to examination and approval and filing for the record by the foreign economic relations and trade department. Of these, restricted Foreign Investment Projects below the limit shall be subject to examination and approval by the appropriate competent department of the People's Government at the level of province, autonomous region, municipality directly under the Central Government and municipality with independent development plans. At the same time, filing for the record shall be carried out with the higher-level competent department and the department in charge of the industry. Examination and approval authority for these kinds of projects may not be delegated to lower levels. Foreign Investment Projects in the service trade sectors that are gradually being liberalized shall be subject to examination and approval in accordance with relevant State regulations.

Where Foreign Investment Projects involve quotas and/or licenses, an application for quotas and/or licenses must first be made to the foreign economic relations and trade department.

Where laws and administrative regulations contain other provisions concerning examination and approval procedures and methods, such provisions shall be followed.

Article 13

The higher-level examination and approval authority shall cancel Foreign Investment Projects that are examined and approved in violation of these Provisions within 30 working days of receiving filing documents for the project. The contracts and articles of association for such projects shall be void, the enterprise registration authority shall not grant registration, and the Customs shall refuse to carry out import and export procedures.

Article 14

Where an applicant for a Foreign Investment Project fraudulently obtains project approval by improper means such as deception, legal liability shall be pursued according to law, based on the seriousness of the circumstances. The examination and approval authority shall cancel the project approval and the relevant competent departments shall appropriately handle the project in accordance with law.

Article 15

Where examination and approval authority personnel abuse their power or neglect their duties, criminal liability shall be pursued in accordance with the provisions concerning crimes of abuse of power and dereliction of duty in the criminal law. If an offense does not warrant criminal penalties, a special demerit or more serious administrative sanctions shall be imposed according to law.

Article 16

Reference shall be made to these Provisions when handling projects established by Overseas Chinese investors and investors from the Hong Kong Special Administrative Region, Macao Special Administrative Region and Taiwan region.

Article 17

These Provisions shall be implemented from April 1, 2002. The Interim Provisions for Guiding the Direction of Foreign Investment approved by the State Council on June 7, 1995 and issued by the State Planning Commission, State Economic and Trade Commission and Ministry of Foreign Trade and Economic Cooperation on June 20, 1995 shall simultaneously be repealed.

图书在版编目（CIP）数据

入世后的中国 = China After WTO/(美) 龙安志 (Brahm,L.) 编著.—北京：五洲传播出版社，2002.10

ISBN 7–5085–0098–9

Ⅰ. 入...

Ⅱ. 龙...

Ⅲ. 世界贸易组织 – 规则 – 影响 – 经济 – 中国 – 英文

Ⅳ.F125

China After WTO

Published by China Intercontinental Press. For information address China Intercontinental Press, 31 Beisanhuan Zhonglu, Beijing, 100088, China.

入世后的中国

编 著 者 (美)龙安志
责任编辑 邓锦辉
版式制作 北京天人鉴图文设计制作
出版发行 五洲传播出版社 (北京北三环中路 31 号 邮编：100088)
承 印 者 深圳中华商务联合印刷有限公司
开 本 889 × 1194mm 1/32
印 张 12
字 数 210 千
版 次 2002 年 10 月第 1 版
印 次 2002 年 10 月第 1 次印刷
书 号 ISBN 7–5085–0098–9/F·143
定 价 40.00 元

China after WTO

We deeply trust that China's entry into WTO will certainly push forward the development of Chinese foreign economic trade into a new era and push forward economic trade cooperation between China and the world to a new epoch. This will create new opportunities for the world economy, and for stability prosperity in the new century.

Shi Guangsheng
Minister, Ministry of Foreign Trade and Economic Cooperation

China after WTO will be a China of rapid change and dynamic entrepreneurial spirit. WTO will serve as catalyst for further investment and trade liberalizations which will in turn bring China's complicated investment environment closer in line with international standards and in turn encourage foreign investment on a larger and broader scale than anticipated before.

Laurence J. Brahm
CEO, Naga Group Limited

If the changes that are now transforming China's economy are successfully implemented over the next years, a good bit of the great potential of this country can be realized.

Michael Furst
Executive Director, American Chamber of Commerce

ISBN 7-5085-0098-9

9 787508 500980 >

ISBN 7-5085-0098-9/F·143　Price: 40 yuan　(RMB)